"In this important work, Bockm... of the world of the early church .... of modern New Testament scholarship. His diagnosis of the contemporary state of New Testament studies is acute, and his recommendations for future directions are suggestive and important."

Richard Bauckham, professor of New Testament studies, University of St. Andrews

"Markus Bockmuehl's *Seeing the Word* offers fresh possibilities for reading biblical texts in their historic role as the church's Scripture. There is something to be learned on every page of this study, but the book is especially persuasive in arguing the case for an integrated reading of Scripture that overcomes the specious dichotomy between historical and theological issues and in demonstrating that theological exegesis can draw from and contribute to both the church and the academy. Whether one's interests lie primarily with historical questions or with theological ones, readers will find no guide more capable and learned."

Marianne Meye Thompson, professor of New Testament interpretation, Fuller Theological Seminary

"Witty, sure-footed, and erudite, Markus Bockmuehl's *Seeing the Word* is a gift to all who care about the future of New Testament studies. Though severe in his diagnosis of the field's present crisis, Bockmuehl is heartening and enlightening in his account of how scholars today can reconstitute the study of the New Testament in an intellectually coherent and theologically fruitful way, without sacrificing the genuine gains of recent decades. By highlighting the integrative potential of New Testament study from the perspective of its implied readers and *Wirkungsgeschichte*, Bockmuehl models an approach whose historical interest is broad enough to encompass the New Testament's historic identity as Christian Scripture and whose theological concern is confident enough to dare public conversation about truth."

R. Kendall Soulen, professor of systematic theology, Wesley Theological Seminary

STUDIES *in* THEOLOGICAL INTERPRETATION

SEEING THE WORD

Refocusing New Testament Study

MARKUS BOCKMUEHL

Baker Academic
Grand Rapids, Michigan

©2006 by Markus Bockmuehl

Published by Baker Academic
a division of Baker Publishing Group
P.O. Box 6287, Grand Rapids, MI 49516-6287
www.bakeracademic.com

Printed in the United States of America

Library of Congress Cataloging-in-Publication Data
Bockmuehl, Markus N. A.
   Seeing the Word : refocusing New Testament study / Markus Bockmuehl.
      p.   cm. — (Studies in theological interpretation)
   Includes bibliographical references and indexes.
   ISBN 10: 0-8010-2761-6 (pbk.)
   ISBN 978-0-8010-2761-1 (pbk.)
   1. Bible. N.T.—Criticism, interpretation, etc. 2. Theology—Methodology.
I. Title. II. Series.
BS2361.3.B63 2006
225.072—dc22   2006012001

CONTENTS

SERIES PREFACE

As a discipline, formal biblical studies is in a period of reassessment and upheaval. Concern with historical origins and the development of the biblical materials has in many places been replaced by an emphasis on the reader and the meanings supplied by present contexts and communities.

The Studies in Theological Interpretation series will seek to appreciate the constructive theological contribution made by Scripture when it is read in its canonical richness. Of necessity, this includes historical evaluation while remaining open to renewed inquiry into what is meant by history and historical study in relation to Christian Scripture. This also means that the history of the reception of biblical texts—a discipline frequently neglected or rejected altogether—will receive fresh attention and respect. In sum, the series is dedicated to the pursuit of constructive theological interpretation of the church's inheritance of prophets and apostles in a manner that is open to reconnection with the long history of theological reading in the church. The primary emphasis is on the constructive theological contribution of the biblical texts themselves.

New commentary series have sprung up to address these and similar concerns. It is important to complement this development with brief, focused, and closely argued studies that evaluate the hermeneutical, historical, and theological dimensions of scriptural reading and interpretation for our times. In the light of shifting and often divergent methodologies, the series will encourage studies in theological interpretation that model clear and consistent methods in the pursuit of theologically engaging readings.

An earlier day saw the publication of a series of short monographs and compact treatments in the area of biblical theology that went by the name Studies in Biblical Theology. The length and focus of the contributions were salutary features and worthy of emulation. Today, however, we find no consensus regarding the nature of biblical theology, and this is a good reason to explore anew what competent theological reflection on Christian Scripture might look like in our day. To this end, the present series, Studies in Theological Interpretation, is dedicated.

ACKNOWLEDGMENTS

T

he argument of this book has occupied my thinking for more than a decade, and it remains very much a work in progress. Nevertheless, I wish briefly to record my thanks to some of the many friends and institutions who have helped me along the way. Much of this book has repeatedly been "road tested" in lectures, in conference or seminar papers, and in informal talks to students and church groups. I am most grateful to these audiences for their patience with my half-formed thoughts and for their stimulating feedback. These settings have included seminars or symposia at Cambridge; the universities of Aberdeen, Berne, Durham, Oxford, and St. Andrews; as well as Fuller Theological Seminary, College Church in Wheaton, and the Center of Theological Inquiry at Princeton. Other valuable settings included the lunchtime theological discussion group at Little St. Mary's Church, Cambridge. I want to record my indebtedness and affectionate thanks to the "Grantchester Meadows Group" of Ph.D. students meeting fortnightly at my house in Cambridge, who in the Easter and Michaelmas terms of 2004 volunteered to forgo our regular program in order to offer feedback on draft chapters of this book. Members of the group at that time included Charles Anderson,

Wayne Coppins, Justin Hardin, David Rudolph, Joel Willitts, Todd Wilson, Stephen Witmer, and John Yates.

Of equal importance have been the many individuals who have assisted in various ways or from whom I have learned in personal conversation and correspondence. Some may have offered a full critique and others a single incisive suggestion; some were more and others less sympathetic to my views; but all were unfailingly patient and constructive in encouraging me with their praise or criticism. Although there are many others, at least the following may be singled out here: Susanna Avery-Quash, Richard Beaton, Michael Cain, James Carleton Paget, Sarah Coakley, Brian Daley, Mark Elliott, Christopher Evans, Richard Hays, Jane Heath, Martin Hengel, William Horbury, Winrich Löhr, Robert Morgan, Werner Neuer, Aidan Nichols, Gordon Plumb, Kavin Rowe, Michael Scott-Joynes, Kendall Soulen, Graham Stanton, Peter Stuhlmacher, John Sweet, Marianne Meye Thompson, Peter Tomson, Benedict Viviano, Francis Watson, and Rowan Williams.

During research and writing stints away from home, I have repeatedly enjoyed the peace and quiet of Steve and Rachel James's cottage in the lovely Welsh village of Rowen; and I am equally grateful for the generous hospitality offered at Tübingen by the Haizmann family and by the staff of the Theologicum, University Library, and Evangelisches Stift. Among the many providers of small mercies, I would like especially to mention Frau Specht of the document delivery unit at Tübingen's University Library for her swift and generous help in emailing an otherwise elusive journal article. For much of the research underlying chapter 6, the British Academy generously assisted me through one of its Research Readerships (1999–2001).

Parts of the first five chapters have appeared elsewhere, although in its present form all of this material is extensively revised and (I trust) improved. The relevant original publications are listed in the bibliography as Bockmuehl 1998a, 1998b, 2000c, 2003b, 2004b, and all are reused by permission of the respective copyright holders.

The quotations from Eusebius's *Ecclesiastical History*, which appear in chapters 6 and 7, are reprinted by permission of the publishers and the Trustees of the Loeb Classical Library from *Eusebius: Volume I*, Loeb Classical Library® Volume 153, translated by Kirsopp Lake, Cambridge, Mass.: Harvard University Press, Copyright 1926 by the President and Fellows of Harvard College. The Loeb Classical Library® is a registered trademark of the President and Fellows of Harvard College.

Every attempt has been made, too, to secure reproduction rights for the illustrations in this book. The picture on the cover and in the introduction is included by permission of the British Library, while the icon in chapter 5 appears by permission of Mondadori Electa Photoservice, Milan, Italy. The etching in chapter 2 is reproduced from the frontispiece of Thomas Aquinas 1966 by permission of St. Scholastica's Priory, Petersham, Massachusetts.

M.B.
Princeton
Easter, 2006

INTRODUCTION

Watching Luke Paint the Virgin

A Fifteenth-Century Clue

In 2003–4 London's Royal Academy of Arts, in partnership with the British Library and the Getty Museum of Los Angeles, mounted an unprecedented and extraordinarily successful exhibition entitled "Illuminating the Renaissance." It was designed to document the final flourishing of manuscript illumination in the fifteenth century and for the first time ever brought together the greatest works produced by Flemish illuminators during this period. Among the 130 items were works ranging in size from a monumental genealogy to the tiniest of private prayer books and miniature parchment altarpieces. In one corner of the exhibition, easy to miss, was a miniature of *St. Luke Painting the Virgin and Child*, produced in the 1460s at Valenciennes by Simon Marmion or members of his workshop. While touring the exhibition with my family, I thought little of this small page at first and passed it by, but later I returned for a second look. I discovered an arresting image that has continued to occupy me ever since. It is reproduced below and on the front cover of this book, and will provide a useful backdrop for my concern in these pages.[1]

1. See Kren and McKendrick 2003: 103–5, no. 9b (British Library Add. Ms. 71117 leaf B, Valenciennes, late 1460s). The image was cut from a Book of Hours; its size is barely 10.5 cm x 7.9 cm.

The theme as such is well attested, if not perhaps widely familiar today. Beginning in antiquity, and certainly no later than Theodore the Lector (early sixth century), Luke came to be widely regarded as a painter of Mary, and soon as patron saint of icon painters.[2] Both in the East and in Rome, icons of the Virgin Mary

2. *Ecclesiastical History* 1.353. Cf. subsequently the letter of Patriarch Germanus I (ca. 640–733) to Emperor Leo III (ca. 675–741), quoted in Stephen the Deacon's *Life of St. Stephen the Younger* 9.34 (Auzépy 1997). Similar statements around this time

began to be attributed to Luke with surprising frequency; the
prototype of an icon known as the *Hodegetria* ("signpost") was
said to have been painted by the evangelist in Jerusalem. According to widespread medieval belief, the most famous of these icons
saved Rome from the plague when St. Gregory the Great (ca.
540–604) had it paraded through the city of Rome and placed
in the church of S. Maria Maggiore, where a probably different
but equally famous icon known as *Salus Populi Romani* is kept
today in the Cappella Paolina.[3] Unsurprisingly, the idea of Luke as
a painter of the Virgin eventually attracted artists' attention in its
own right. Among the most famous depictions are Netherlandish
examples by Rogier van der Weyden (1400–1464) and Maerten
van Heemskerck (1498–1574), as well as Italian ones by Giorgio
Vasari (1511–74) and Guercino (1591–1666).[4]

Simon Marmion went on to produce other representations of
this subject, including a miniature from the Berlaymont Hours in
the same exhibition, which shows significant family resemblances
with the piece to be discussed here but also suggests greater artistic
refinement (Kren and McKendrick 2003: 108–10, pl. 12a). The
painting here in view is one of four cuttings from a large Book of
Hours whose stripped-down codex is now in Kraków (104). But
this particular miniature offers a strikingly unusual perspective
on its theme and is worth a closer look.

At first sight the scene seems pretty but unremarkable. The
setting is a beautiful, airy room. A tiled floor and decorated ceil-
ing vault recede toward a window with leaded-glass panels at
the top and wooden shutters that have been opened to allow the
sunlight to stream in. Blue skies and a mountain landscape are
visible in the distance. The bearded and partly hooded artist sits

---

are found in St. Andrew of Crete, Michael Syncellus, and others; see the discussion in
Bacci 2000: 79–80 and Bränden 2002: 10.

3. Another supposedly Lukan icon is kept atop the Santa Scala, the marble steps
near St. John Lateran that, according to a medieval legend, Christ had ascended in
Pilate's praetorium and that were later miraculously transported from Jerusalem. On
Gregory, see his life in the *Golden Legend* of Jacobus de Voragine (1230–98). Cf.
further Hornik and Parsons 2003: 14–16.

4. For further discussion and additional references to secondary literature on these
artists and the theme of Luke as painter, see Hornik and Parsons 2003: 17–23.

upright on a backless wooden bench, facing a tall easel that holds a panel portrait nearing completion. Against the background of the embroidered tapestry and green cloth-covered panel or dais sits a youthful Mary with her baby. The richly flowing folds of her characteristically ultramarine and gold-embroidered robe constitute the strongest color impression in the picture—matched only by her equivalent but much smaller garment in St. Luke's portrait itself. Our attention is drawn to that smaller image by the concentrated poise of the evangelist, peering at it with his enlarged, deep-set dark eye, brush and palette at the ready. The two blue-robed figures are in turn framed by the strong greens of the painter's hood and the dais behind the Virgin. The subtle haloes of Mother and Child are represented, in the fifteenth-century Flemish custom, as rays of light emanating from their heads.

So far, so good. But it takes only a moment's reflection to realize that rather more is going on than first meets the eye. The contrast between the life-size figures and Luke's painting is remarkable. The "sitter" is a realistic-looking Northern European girl from the Low Countries. Long, flowing red hair, restrained only by a narrow black hairband, surrounds a distinctive round face with broad cheekbones and a somewhat plain and fatigued appearance. Her head tilts to her left, with drooping eyes watching a lively and somewhat impish-looking baby whose less-than-pristine swaddling cloths are coming unraveled as his elongated right arm reaches up, in playful menace, to tug on his mother's necklace. The appearance is that of a youthful mother somewhat exhausted by the taxing demands of an active infant son.

The portrait, by contrast, is deliberately and strikingly different. The artist's most obvious hint to the viewer is that instead of facing a baby in her left arm, Mary is now looking the other way and holding Jesus in her *right* arm. Her hair is still red, but now for the most part discreetly covered under a hood of her robe or perhaps a headscarf in the same color. This Mary's facial features are generally less pronounced: the cheekbones are less prominent, and the shape of her face has become a little more oval. Her translucent skin tone helps accentuate the impression of a more composed, ethereal beauty. The grasping arm and the mischievous twinkle in the baby's eyes, like the look of wary exhaustion in his mother's, have given way to a more peaceful, contemplative expression. In particular, Jesus's arms are foreshortened and his midriff modestly concealed from us by Luke's palette. All in all, the scene is one of restful contemplation, as would be expected in an icon.

What is the point of all this? The unprepared viewer will need to dispel three possible immediate reactions, each of which is on its own terms perfectly reasonable: first, that Marmion shows his Luke simply having a bit of fun, whether in a bored doodle or in a Monty Pythonesque vein; second, that his artist is presented as slapdash or incompetent; or, third, that he engages in deliberate distortion or deception. None of these is plausible for a sacred subject treated in the devotional context of a fifteenth-century Book of Hours: while illustrations in works like the *Macclesfield Psalter* do indeed include plenty of bawdy jokes and grotesques, their purpose is never to deride or deprecate the biblical subjects themselves.

We must assume, then, that Marmion is both serious and deliberate. What his unusual work demonstrates is at one level a reflection on the work of the evangelist as spiritual artist. In a poise of keenly observant contemplation, Marmion's Luke represents the true depth and fullness of the scene set before him, setting forth as it were the divine glory and beauty that is enfleshed in the human frailty. His spiritual optics permit him to grasp in the seeming familiarity of an all-too-human mother and toddler the Mother of God cradling and presenting her Son to the world. Medieval legend associated the Marian hymn known as "Salve Regina"[5] with the angelic song that accompanied St. Gregory's procession of Luke's icon of the Virgin to the church of S. Maria

5. The "Salve Regina" reads as follows (words in parentheses represent secondary additions):

Hail, queen (mother) of mercy,	Salve Regina (Mater) misericordiae,
Hail, our life, our sweetness, and our hope.	Vita, dulcedo, et spes nostra, salve.
To you we cry as exiled children of Eve,	Ad te clamamus, exsules filii Hevae;
To you we sigh with mourning and weeping in this valley of tears.	Ad te suspiramus gementes et flentes in hac lacrymarum valle.

Maggiore. As in that hymn, so here there is a sense that in the Mother of the Word incarnate the old Eve is both assumed and transformed, manifesting both mercy and hope to Eve's grieving and oppressed children in offering the world (in the language of Luke 1:42) the "blessed fruit of her womb."

In thus distinguishing the empirical subject from its artistic representation, Marmion draws out the exquisite and excruciating dilemma of the religious artist. Before Luke are a mother and child who, in the disarmingly unremarkable humanity of their demeanor, appear at one level like a thousand others, as if arbitrarily invited in from the street to sit for the artist on this particular fine spring morning. And yet Luke's piercing eye perceives the deeper reality of what is barely hinted at in the faint haloes of his models: his gaze and brush reveal the truth that this is none other than the Mother of the divine Word made flesh. The portrait is strikingly different from the appearance of the living model. It presents an image that is two-dimensional, selective, and patently interpretative rather than reproductive. Yet for all that, Luke's icon is shown to us as an act not of fiction or creation, but of keen observation and truthful representation—designed, in the classic conciliar definition, to "lift" its beholder "to the remembrance of the prototypes and longing after them."[6]

The Conundrum of Biblical Interpretation

But how is any of that relevant for a book concerned ostensibly with the scholarly study of the New Testament? Before readers

---

Ah! Turn, then, our advocate, your merciful eyes upon us	Eia ergo advocata nostra, illos tuos misericordes oculos ad nos converte.
And show us Jesus, the fruit of your womb, after this exile:	Et Jesum, benedictum fructum ventris tui, nobis post hoc exsilium ostende.
O compassionate, godly, sweet (Virgin) Mary.	O clemens, O pia, O dulcis (Virgo) Maria.

6. Canon 7 of the Seventh Ecumenical Council (= Second Council of Nicea, 787): οἱ ταύτας θεώμενοι διανίστανται πρὸς τὴν τῶν πρωτοτύπων μνήμην τε καὶ ἐπιπόθησιν (ed. Denzinger, §601). For the notion of the images serving as a memorial of the prototype, see also John of Damascus, *Lectures on the Sacred Imagination* 1.17.

nervously flick back to the title page for reassurance that this volume is what they thought it was, it is indeed time to address that question.

Simon Marmion's miniature allows us to appreciate what Jacques Maritain (1882–1973) characterizes as the nature of visual or poetic representation—namely, the recognition that "things are not only what they are; . . . they give more than they have, because from every side they are pervaded by the creative influx of the first cause" (Maritain 1944: 397). As a result, the evangelist offers not photographic imitation but the exposition of his subject's deeper significance and relational substance. Elsewhere, Maritain develops this thought as follows:

> Art does not draw from itself alone what it gives to things; it spreads over them a secret which it has first seized by surprise in them, in their invisible substance or in their endless exchanges and correspondences. Withdraw our art from "that blessed reality given once and for all, at the center of which we are placed," and it is no longer anything. It transforms, it moves about, it brings together, it transfigures; it does not create. It is by the way in which he transforms the universe passing into his mind, in order to make a form divined in things shine on a matter, that the artist imprints his mark on his work. For each work, he recomposes, *such as into itself at last poetry changes it*, a world more real than the real offered to the sense.[7]

In serious study of the Gospels, of greater importance than any archeological or critical dexterity is an appreciation that a similar correlation frequently pertains between the empirical phenomena and the narrative gospel portraits of Jesus Christ. The student or scholar writing, say, about Jesus of Nazareth will in a sense find herself, like Simon Marmion, painting the biblical author painting Christ.

7. See his essay "The Frontiers of Poetry" in Maritain 1962 (also available online at http://www.2nd.edu/Departments/Maritain/etext/frontier.htm); the clause in quotation marks is from Paul Claudel (1868–1955), and the translator notes that the phrase in italic type borrows from Stéphane Mallarmé (1842–98). Cf. similarly Williams 2005: 26 and passim, to whom my discussion is indebted.

Two images of Virgin and Child appear on Marmion's canvas, plain for all to see. It is significant that there are two and that the implied observer understands both the difference and the relationship between them. The temptation equally of the naïve and the doctrinaire, and one popularly associated with fundamentalism, is to assume that the two images must appear identical, or as nearly so as makes no difference. Another temptation, which more commonly afflicts those prepared to perceive and exploit the differences between the two images, is to declare one of them vitally important and the other largely irrelevant. On the spectrum of faith and unbelief, viewers inclined to skepticism would strip away all but the "real" empirical appearance of Mary of Nazareth, while those of a more ecclesial or fideistic bent may find all that "really" matters is the icon of the Mother of God.

The fact is that, for all their differences, the two images make sense only in relation to each other and only because they both denote the same reality. They perform different functions, but each interprets and validates the other. In a sense, each *is* the other. Exegesis fails to do justice to both if it denies either their difference or their sameness.[8]

What we see here is not, in the end, image versus reality, nor even, in the strict sense, two separate pictures. We have a painting within a painting, and both are the work of Simon Marmion—which brings us back to the conundrum of the New Testament scholar, whose interpretation creates not a photocopy but pictures (of a biblical subject or event) containing other pictures (the biblical authors' diverse interpretations of that same subject).

Whether from a position of faith or of unbelief, how can biblical scholars do justice to historically and culturally contingent human figures like Jesus of Nazareth or his apostle Saul of Tarsus—and yet make sense of the texts' insistence on these same figures as, respectively, "Son of God" or divinely appointed apostolic witness? Each of these pairs of images is finally intelligible only in the light of the other.

8. *Distinguer pour unir* ("distinguishing in order to unite") is another of Maritain's art-critical principles brought eloquently to the fore by Williams 2005: 9, 41.

To put the dilemma more sharply still, for Marmion as for the New Testament scholar: no Lukan icon of the Virgin can ultimately do its job *as icon* if it does not also truthfully signify the person of Mary of Nazareth, just as no true-to-life representation of Mary can ultimately function *as empirical picture* if it does not also truthfully signify the Mother of God. Yet how is it possible to affirm the one without at the same time denying the other? There is still one further twist in the tale of this miniature. Marmion's picture-within-a-picture succeeds only on the daring assumption that there is a communicative coherence connecting the hermeneutical links in the chain. Unlike social-anthropological and other modern approaches that tend to stress the unbridgeable remoteness of the biblical culture from our own, Marmion evidently takes for granted that those who will pray through this Book of Hours in fact share with his subjects an inculturation into a common Christian way of seeing and reading. It is this that makes his painting not merely artistically intelligible but spiritually transparent, inviting the implied viewer to enter and indwell the biblical author's optical space, learning to see as he sees.

After two and a half centuries of modernist exegetical optics, these hard and uncomfortable notions raise a complex cocktail of questions about the place of rationality, ideology, and power relations in the act of interpretation. What is more, our newly pluralist world throws up many unfamiliar challenges in a conversation about Scripture that will increasingly involve those of faith, those of other faiths, and those who claim to have none. Nevertheless, I am convinced that in seeking to come to grips with the New Testament, interpreters of all stripes can derive immense benefit from the rediscovery that adequate—that is, object-appropriate—interpretation of this text is bound to resemble Marmion's task of portraying an evangelist painting Mary of Nazareth as the Mother of God. This book seeks to contribute to that rediscovery and to the hospitable and open-ended conversation about Scripture that such a rediscovery could facilitate.

The Shape of This Book

In what follows, I proceed essentially in three steps. Chapter 1 is an exercise in taking stock. By comparing a "snapshot" assessment of present-day New Testament studies with a similar exercise seventy years ago, it suggests some of the major areas of challenge and difficulty for a discipline that is now widely felt to lack agreed criteria, not just for appropriate methods and results, but in many cases even about the subject to be studied. This first chapter also assesses a number of recent proposals to take the discipline forward. Two in particular, I suggest, emerge as carrying particular promise for a reenergized, common conversation about the New Testament between scholars of diverse methodological and faith approaches. The first is to attend more seriously to the text's assumptions about its implied readership and its implied readings; the second is to discuss the early history of the text's aftermath, its plural and diverse effects, as a resource for renewed reflection on how or what it might communicate. Or in other words, the exegetical question of the implied readers is linked to that of implied readings, but both of these questions are illuminated by the early history of how the apostolic voices were in fact remembered, heard, and heeded—and vice versa.

The twin themes of implied readers and readings, along with that of effective history, are then further developed in the chapters that follow. Does the New Testament itself already carry a presumption of who will read it, and perhaps even how? In that vein, chapter 2 asks about the hermeneutical stance of the exegete implied in the text, especially how that interpreter negotiates the place of reason and of wisdom vis-à-vis revelation. Does the text itself call for a certain kind of interpreter?

Chapter 3 traces an initial movement from implied readers to implied readings. Modern critical biblical scholarship rightly and irreversibly draws our attention to the polyphonous diversity of voices in the Bible. But what is implied in this polyphony? Here we will ask about the extent to which these diverse perspectives nevertheless entail a canonical "impulse," as is suggested by some scholars. Is the frame of the canon, as is often claimed, merely the late and arbitrary imposition of order upon diversity and of conformity upon otherness—or is it to some extent already an implied reading of the two-testament Scripture's constituent parts, indeed an effect of the text?

This issue of the negotiation of convergence and conflict in the implied readings and their aftermath is itself a matter of attending more carefully both to the text and to that which readers bring to the text. Chapter 4 presents a more specific case study of this problem. Here we focus on the famous thesis of a "conservative," more or less observant Petrine Christianity caught up in an irreconcilable conflict against a "radical," law-free Pauline one. That view became a standard paradigm for New Testament scholarship in the nineteenth century and remains surprisingly influential today. We will ask how interpreters might arbitrate between two seemingly irreconcilable facts: on the one hand, the critical assessment of an undeniable, and for many scholars profound and lasting, division between Peter and Paul; and, on the other hand, the virtually unanimous effective history of their relationship as a partnership in the gospel.

Chapter 5 turns to a second, rather different case study on the relationship between implied readings and implied readers. British New Testament scholar Sir Edwyn Hoskyns inspired a generation of students between the two world wars with an approach to the text that saw it as organically linked to, and generative of, the historic faith of the church. He serves as a particularly potent case study in that he held this view, well before the current disputes between "synchronic" and "diachronic" approaches, because of his commitment to both viewpoints—what the text implies and generates as well as what gave rise to it. We will examine his views about the coherence of history and theology and ask what impulses, if any, may usefully serve our task of recovering the subject of New Testament study in the changed circumstances of the twenty-first century.

After taking stock and considering what it might mean to attend to implied readers and readings in the interest of recovering a common focus, I turn in the last two chapters to an exploration of the text's early effective history by a study of apostolic memory in the early church. My suggestion is that, during the first two centuries, living memory of the apostolic generation served as a kind of hermeneutical magnetism with the potential to orient a profusion of centrifugal particularities toward the New Testament's implied readings and readers—and thereby to the identity of the Jesus Christ of whom all its authors speak. By tethering the text's historical impact or effects to the compelling formative events that gave rise to it, that chain of living memory can serve to channel and enrich our historical knowledge, as chapter 6 attempts to show with particular reference to several patristic figures. Chapter 7 offers a case study of how the apostolic authors' memory of Jesus may help facilitate either the confirmation or indeed the correction of subsequent understandings in light of those same formative events. The vivid case in point here is today's gradual but profoundly fecund rediscovery of the *Jewish identity* not just of the "historical" Jesus of Nazareth, but vitally also of the risen Christ of faith.

Three stages, then, govern the argument of this book: (1) taking stock of the current predicaments of New Testament scholarship, (2) exploring the potential of implied readers and readings, and (3) remembering the Christ. This sequence incorporates a deliberate process of deconstruction and possible reconstruction. The deconstructive movement explicitly addresses the methodological and substantive malaise observable in late-twentieth-century New Testament scholarship, with its deeply corrosive consequences for agreement about the nature of argument and even the very subject of study. In my constructive proposals, on the other hand, I attempt to suggest questions and directions intended to assist renewed and meaningful conversation about a common subject between different kinds of readers.

Part of my aim, too, is to question the polarizing preference of much critical biblical scholarship "to attend to what is written at the expense of what it is written about."[9] What this book proposes is no coherent approach or program for action, let

9. So the influential formulation of Kermode 1979: 118–19 (citing Starobinski 1971; cf. ET in Barthes 1974), who regards this postmodern predilection as evidence of a "powerful mind."

alone a newly conceived "semiotic cathedral" (thus the preferred terminology of Theissen 1999). Nor does it sympathize with the sort of fideistic retrenchment or ecclesiological inward turn recently fashionable in some neoconservative circles as well as some self-identified as postliberal.[10] The argument here does, however, suggest that the venerable old house of critical New Testament scholarship now requires urgent renovations by which new light and life could enter a number of vital, bricked-up windows as well as disused or barricaded doorways of communication. In allowing such long-neglected doors and windows to open, we may be surprised to find them shedding light on the sort of scene that Simon Marmion saw—and helping us watch Luke paint the Virgin.

---

10. The prefix *post* tends, ironically, to mean "neo" rather than "ex." Liberalism itself seems not to feature in the intellectual biography of many self-declared postliberals.

Alexandrian Fragments
after the fire

In those uncertain hours following our famous
conflagration, I surveyed with no small measure
of chagrin the scorched rubble, the thousand thousand

scroll rods charred and emptied of all but ashen curls,
steaming parchment, the air bitter and far too hot,
our book vaults fallen, the books reduced to cinder.

And in that moment the sun first lit our city's
eastern quarter, I found myself alone, in awe:
from that ruin, a forest had sprung up overnight,

as a wavering expanse of smoke white trees, pale
birches, original as the local laurel,
but shifting with the morning's faintest breath. They rose

to where their reaching branches twined to canopy
our broad destruction, so that each trunk expanded
at its uppermost and wove a fabric overhead—

now white, now red, now golden from the sun's approach.
Beneath that winding sheet our ravished corpus lay
razed, erased, an open, emptied volume in repose

insisting either new and strenuous reply,
or that we confess our hopelessness and turn away.

"Alexandrian Fragments," by Scott Cairns
from *Recovered Body: Poems*
(New York: George Braziller, 1998), 19.

1

THE TROUBLED FORTUNES OF NEW TESTAMENT SCHOLARSHIP

One Tuesday afternoon in June 1936, Cambridge's newly installed Norris-Hulse Professor of Divinity set out to deliver his inaugural lecture (Dodd 1936b). As he stepped up to the podium to address his distinguished audience, his subject stretched out before him in a wide-open vista, clear and uncluttered, inviting him to enter into the inheritance of a century or more of definitive scientific investigation. The man was C. H. Dodd (1884–1973); his title, "The Present Task in New Testament Studies."

At 52, Dodd was no youngster, and even after two generations the depth and substance of his remarks make it amply clear that we are dealing with a mature and seasoned master of his trade. One indication of this expertise is the accuracy with which his lecture discerned and predicted several necessary and important developments in subsequent New Testament scholarship. These included the increasing importance of Jewish studies, the inadequacy of attempting (e.g., in the history of religions school) to construe early Christian beliefs and practices simply from an "amalgam of half-digested ideas drawn from Hellenistic sources" (cf. Dodd 1936b: 15), and perhaps especially the need for renewed and serious study of the Fourth Gospel. Some of these perspectives would have found a ready audience in the Cambridge of F. C. Burkitt (1864–1935) and E. C. Hoskyns (1884–1937). At the same time, Dodd's anticipation of these developments in part already manifests a certain wariness of latent dangers they might entail, for example, for a coherently Christian interpretation of the New Testament.[1]

All that being said, it is precisely the maturity of Dodd's statement that makes the supreme ease and confidence of many of his methodological assumptions seem all the more startling after threescore and ten years have passed. A handful of examples will suffice to illustrate this point. The critical task of New Testament study, Dodd believed, must be undertaken in five successive stages. Each of these builds on the results of the earlier ones, even where those results may be preliminary or incomplete:

1. text criticism, to establish the original autograph form of the texts
2. so-called higher criticism, to address questions of *Einleitung* and historical setting
3. detailed linguistic exegesis
4. comparative study of ancient Jewish, Hellenistic, and early patristic religious beliefs
5. biblical theology, to serve as the culmination and capstone of the whole edifice

In temperamentally conservative circles, whether wedded to evangelical, liberal, or secular confessional presuppositions, some such model of New Testament studies may survive to this day. And given the size especially of a conservative evangelical constituency

1. I am grateful to my colleague James Carleton Paget for reminding me of this element of guardedness in Dodd's lecture, especially about what he saw as an emerging tendency to underplay the New Testament's coherent theological concerns by dissolving its unity into diversity (Dodd 1936b: 34–35).

in the United States, the classic "layer cake" methodology may still generate rapport in some lecture halls.[2] Elsewhere, however, this model is now widely seen to beg serious questions, to leave large lacunae, and to be generally behind the times. One might ask, for instance, whether the aim of textual criticism as the "bottom layer" should really be the reconstruction of a hypothetical *autograph*—rather than, say, to document the extended genesis of the canonical shape of the text and to trace the history of its development. Assertions about biblical theology, along with classic higher criticism's confident identifications of authors and settings or separation of sources and redactional layers, still find some support but are widely taken with a generous pinch of salt. Most contemporary interpreters will also be struck by the complete absence of any reference to the role of the reader, whether implied or stated, ancient or modern, male or female, gay or straight, rich or poor or postcolonial.

It would of course be churlish to blame our forebears for failing to address questions that have arisen only out of subsequent experience and reflection. What nevertheless seems amazing about Dodd's statement, however, is the self-evident clarity of the task as it presents itself to him. His overall argument is that work on several of these five stages has been largely completed, so that we can now move on to the later ones. He views B. F. Westcott (1825–1901) and F. J. A. Hort (1828–92) as having reliably settled the question of the New Testament text, and he celebrates the later nineteenth century's successful resolution of all the major critical issues: "The Synoptic Problem was, in principle, solved,

2. It is a well-known irony that conservative apologists have a tendency to cling to positions their opponents may ridicule as intellectually old-fashioned, but which would have seemed threateningly progressive to an earlier generation of conservatives. As this was true in the eighteenth and nineteenth centuries for evangelicalism's adoption of elements of rationalism and then romanticism, so it was for the mid-twentieth century's optimistic appeal to the all-powerful explanations of archeology (Keller 1956). One of the more recent examples may be the surprisingly enthusiastic adoption of the "historical quests" for Jesus and Paul by evangelical scholars—sometimes in connection with a newfound enthusiasm for pluralism and postmodern epistemic relativity (and still rather too often in a conversation that prioritizes the like-minded). On this postmodern "afterthought" of evangelical intellectual culture, see further Wolfe 2000, with a reply by Noll 2001.

the Pauline Corpus, within limits, fixed, and the general succession of the New Testament literature determined on lines which
all subsequent study assumes as a basis. . . . The major problems
had in a measure been solved" (1936b: 10).

Thus it has become possible to build on the certainties reliably
established by Dodd's predecessors: "The solution of the Synoptic
Problem can be stated with an artistic completeness and elegance
which charms the critical mind" (1936b: 25). What is left, therefore, is mere "tidying up" of critical issues (1936b: 11).

The higher criticism of the Fourth Gospel is one of the important
subjects still to be addressed, but otherwise the time has come to
move on from the problems of criticism to the task of interpretation proper (1936b: 31). This task involves assessing both the
diversity and the unity of the New Testament as documenting
"that significant phenomenon in history which is early Christianity" (1936b: 37; cf. 35). The newly minted professor resolved to
enter that first-century world in all its strangeness and difference
and return from it to explain its truth in the terms of our own
world (1936b: 40–41).

A Discipline in Search of Its Identity

Thus far Professor Dodd's lecture. How times have changed!
In this chapter it is not my purpose to trace the history of New
Testament studies since Dodd's day; others have done that more
competently than I could (see the surveys by Neill and Wright
1988; Riches 1993; Baird 1992–2003; and Hayes 2004). I wish
instead to shine a searchlight on the contemporary state of the
discipline by asking what someone of Dodd's stature might make
of the status quo of New Testament studies as it presents itself
a lifetime later, at the beginning of the twenty-first century. This
exercise will necessitate a sustained exposé and critique of current
problems and cul-de-sacs and of the way that the academic study
of the New Testament has come to be practiced and taught. I will
conclude by offering two more positive proposals that may assist
a constructive exit from the present malaise.

What, then, might C. H. Dodd have made of it all? To facilitate a few intelligent guesses at that question, I would like to propose a little thought experiment. We are taking Professor Dodd to a major specialist library in biblical studies. Without wasting too much time on bewildering new technologies and networked electronic resources, we begin our introduction to the current state of the discipline by drawing his attention to *New Testament Abstracts*, a thrice-yearly publication whose sole purpose is to offer brief one-paragraph summaries of about two thousand scholarly articles and one thousand books a year solely on the New Testament. Reassuringly for him, this publication is still available in print. We then allow him a day or two in the library to browse through the back issues for the last few decades and to chase up whatever references seem worth chasing. What sort of assessment might he come up with?

It seems safe to suggest that the following factors would probably form part of the picture gained from such an exercise.

The Disappearance of Method and Criteria

Professor Dodd would soon discover that his discipline no longer enjoys any agreement either about the methods of study or even about the criteria by which one might agree about appropriate methods and criteria. Only a small handful of senior authors have had the courage to face this explicitly. Klyne R. Snodgrass, for instance, fittingly begins an important article on the *Gospel of Thomas* with the words, "One of the most embarrassing facts about New Testament studies is the almost total collapse of method by which scholars do their work. No where [*sic*] is this more evident than with the study of the *Gospel of Thomas*" (1990: 19).[3] Similar comments have been voiced by outside observers, including Rowan Williams, who, writing about historical criticism in particular, comments that "it is far from clear any longer what *counts* as a serious argument" (2003: 218).

But regardless of whether particular scholars or reviewers will in fact admit to it, Dodd would soon discover a startling degree

---

3. Cf. similarly the deadlocked debate between Kingsbury 1984 and 1985 and Hill 1984 about criteria of literary criticism in Matthew.

of dissent about what is a good book and what is bad, what constitutes good evidence and argument. One and the same work can be said to be required reading, "combining the best elements of all the current approaches . . . to fashion a fair and even-handed reconstruction," while others will dismiss it out of hand for having neglected to advance this or that reviewer's favorite subdiscipline, or even as altogether unsatisfactory for "both New Testament scholars and theologians." What for one reader is "an immensely learned and comprehensive study" is for another self-evident proof that the author simply "has not done his homework."[4]

Other questions loom implicitly behind every review: what is the relationship of New Testament scholarship with Christian theology, with ancient history and the social sciences, or for that matter with any other discipline at all? What is the methodological connection of the academic study of these texts with the contemporary world in general and especially with the over two billion people who today consciously inhabit its symbolic world? In that respect, a vital but unanswered question is whether scholars of the New Testament relate to their subject matter most appropriately in descriptive and antiquarian terms like professors of Egyptology or in a more practical mode like professors of music or medicine.

Dodd might find some familiar ground among those who engage in what is now often called "diachronic" inquiry, that is, the traditional cluster of historical-critical studies along with a few newer methods adopted from fields like social history and cultural anthropology, rhetoric, and modern archeology. He would more likely find himself adrift among many of the so-called "synchronic" approaches, with their sociolinguistic, poststructuralist, or broadly literary pursuits, their miscellaneous queer or cultural studies, liberationist or postcolonialist ideological criticism, and the sometimes unabashedly partisan relativism of their hermeneutics. At the same time, he might well be impressed by the richness of fresh questions and perspectives opened up by this unfamiliar methodological avalanche.

---

4. The quotations are from published reviews of two of my own books, but in the interest of fairness and impartiality it seems best not to name the sources.

However, what would surely alarm him more than anything is the extent to which these different approaches very largely operate in splendid isolation. Once in a while a musty historical critic may doff his cap to the problems of hermeneutical relativity and perspective. Perhaps a postmodern deconstructor could, in a moment of weakness, concede that the texts may of course have originated in a particular historical setting in which questions of reference were not reducible without remainder to late modern political fashions. But after such passing mental instability, both sorts of interpreters will quickly pinch themselves and move on with renewed vigor to their respective tasks at hand, as if nothing had happened. Indeed, a number of contemporary scholars appear to welcome methodological insularity and polarization as a decidedly good thing.[5]

The Infinite Library

This extraordinary degree of isolation and fragmentation pertains not merely in matters of method, but in virtually every aspect of the discipline. By any standard it is now impossible to keep up with the sheer quantity of publications, increased exponentially by two and a half decades of word-processing technology.[6] Jorge Luis Borges's famous short story "The Library of Babel," first published before World War II, has never seemed more eerily prophetic than in the digital age.[7] The "publish or perish" mentality, long since dreaded especially by junior scholars, has become an all-encompassing output culture that is at once wholly unrealistic in its expectations and encouraging of staggering superficiality in its *Diktat* to leave no thought unpublished. In Britain, these ef-

5. See Brett 1991: 13; also Brueggemann 1993 from a postmodern pluralist perspective; more cautiously Collins 2005. Porter 2003: 371–72 (cf. 1990: 287) appears to advocate a kind of ideological Darwinism, untroubled by questions of truth or fact.
6. Contrary to widespread sentiment, however, the mass of secondary literature cannot be wholly attributed to the invention of the word processor. Adolf von Harnack (1851–1930), an illustrious doyen of the modern discipline, had already produced over ninety publications by the age of twenty-seven; see Zahn-Harnack 1936: 62.
7. "La Biblioteca de Babel," first published in 1939 and then revised in Borges 1944.

fects are further aggravated by a government-imposed "research assessment" culture, whose obsession with the regular appraisal of individual "outputs" leaves the very survival of some departments hostage to an intellectual short-termism biased against the traditional testing and maturing over time of research projects large or small.

Of course the ever-rising tide of secondary literature is a difficulty affecting other disciplines as well. As David Damrosch puts it in his influential analysis of the state of North American higher education: "In most fields scholars find themselves increasingly unable to 'keep up with,' or bear up under, the drifting accumulation of masses of specialized scholarship, across whose surface there play the shifting lights of a vertiginous succession of competing theoretical models" (1995: 4).[8] No one could reasonably take issue with that assessment, whose implications afflict all of us. In light of that, one might well dispute whether the quantity or diversity of publications is itself the problem. One important difference, however, is that most other disciplines have far more scope for the meaningful exploration of uncharted sources. In our particular case, the sheer flood of both printed and electronic publication has massively advanced the balkanization of a subject that any commonsense observer would regard as concerned with a fairly manageable source text—a mere 138,000 words.

Perhaps understandably, most specialist monographs now seem of necessity to ignore systematic engagement with the flood of look-alike commentaries. Even full-scale commentators aiming at greater breadth typically cite and endorse or dismiss hundreds of studies so summarily that one must conclude they cannot possibly have read them. To some extent this is invariably a question not only of time but also of money: nowadays even most libraries in rich countries cannot usually afford the full flood of publications, and the increasing availability of online journals and other resources has thus far proved no more than a very partial solution.

8. I am grateful to Dr. Todd A. Wilson for drawing my attention to this work.

The Great Unread

Anyone seeking to write on a mainstream topic of New Testament scholarship is thus soon trapped in Borges's library. A corollary of that previous point, however, is the extent to which New Testament scholarship's fragmentation has in recent years been further accelerated by its practitioners' increasingly restricted field of reference and linguistic competence. Scholars tend to concern themselves with primary and secondary literature only in their own postage-stamp-sized bailiwick. A generation ago, lip service was still paid to "keeping up" with scholarship in other languages, even if it was already a custom more honored in the breach than in the observance. For anyone inclined to the old-fashioned view (still widely held in the natural sciences) that serious scholarly inquiry is at least in principle a global enterprise, it can only be disheartening to observe how often footnotes in English remain remarkably untouched by directly pertinent recent publications in German, French, or Spanish—and vice versa. Rare is the scholar who bothers comprehensively with the key international publications, in part because many (formerly) distinguished institutions no longer insist that their graduate students acquire competence in the leading ancient and modern research languages.[9] Where an author's foreign-language citations are both few in number and strikingly long in the tooth, it is hard to resist the uncharitable suspicion that they have been "recycled."

Paradoxically, this linguistic atrophy comes at a time when postcolonial thought and economic globalization have emphatically drawn our attention to the fact that responsible intellectual discourse can no longer simply function as a Western European and North American pastime. The demographics of Christianity's rapid expansion in the global South and East urgently call the North Atlantic academy to a more serious intellectual engagement with the majority of the world's Bible readers. The elite Society of New

9. Betz 2003: 47–48 similarly stresses the inescapable importance of modern research languages for serious New Testament research. Cf. further Damrosch 1995: 23.

Testament Studies, whose international membership is restricted
to the leading research scholars in the field, has for a number
of years diverted some resources to the support of libraries and
conferences in Eastern Europe as well as travel funds for scholars
from the non-Western world; and in 1999 it held its annual meeting
in Pretoria, South Africa, the first time outside Western Europe
or North America.[10] Recently we saw the publication of the first
deliberately "global" attempt at a commentary on Scripture—a
genre that was, ironically, invented in Africa.[11]

But while these are welcome beginnings, they are still little more
than token efforts. In an age of globalization, it seems increasingly
imperative for the health of this discipline that its investigations
take account, however modestly or indeed critically, of where
the New Testament in fact resides in the continuous history of its
reception. It is no longer adequate to reflect merely on the intellectual context of Scripture's disappearance from public discourse
in the post-Christian West. Instead, our mental maps of Scripture's
historic footprint in the church demand to be redrawn at a time
when Christianity's remaining foothold in the Continental home-
land of biblical scholarship is dwarfed by today's thriving church
of two billion Christians, most of whom are Africans and Asians,
evangelicals and Roman Catholics.

On a more positive note, the international professional as-
sociations have helped to ensure that there is still an English-
speaking dialogue across the Atlantic (and to a lesser extent the
Pacific). This may also reflect the widely mooted shift of cutting-
edge international biblical research away from German-language
publications—although one wonders to what extent this trend is
itself reinforced by the linguistically and intellectually provincial
nature of so much scholarship. It is encouraging, in any case, that
at least an Anglophone dialogue continues despite the accelerat-
ing continental drift separating Europe and America in religious,
cultural, and geopolitical respects.

10. It was in Tel Aviv in 2000, but even the 2007 conference in Romania is in a
country due to join the European Union in that year.
11. See Patte and Okure 2004. On the Alexandrian influence on the origin of
biblical commentary, see Bockmuehl 2005a and Bockmuehl forthcoming.

Rootlessness and Amnesia

For some of the same reasons, Professor Dodd would find that his own writings, along with most works over thirty years old, seem now to be read primarily by a few scholars with statistical or antiquarian interests. It is considered an embarrassment if a dissertation fails to engage with a relevant work published eighteen months ago. The entire nineteenth century, however, can be disregarded with impunity. Scholars merrily copy each other's clichéd prejudices about Luther's interpretation of Pauline theology (a point stressed by Westerholm 2004) or Augustine's view of original sin. It is still a distressingly small number, however, who bother to crack open the apposite volumes of the respective Weimar or patristic critical editions or indeed who show any first-hand awareness of the two thousand years of Christian biblical interpretation. By the late twentieth century, the *Neutestamentler's* cappuccino had too frequently become all froth and no coffee. What further encourages this trend is that the road to the primary sources has become so thoroughly covered with slippery hypotheses that few aspiring Ph.D. students any longer feel safe to walk on it.[12]

The Persistence of Dragons

In spite of this historical rootlessness and fragmentation, or perhaps because of it, contemporary New Testament scholarship is at the same time peculiarly beholden to intellectual juggernauts unmoved by reason or evidence (a point well made by Goulder 1996 in relation to the Synoptic Problem). Too often such aging monster theories imperiously require the homage of countless young scholars until after a generation or three they may finally topple and wither away by themselves. Among this brood of dragons have been self-assured assumptions about authorship, hypothetical fragments and hymns, the so-called gospels of

---

12. Cf. Hengel 1996a: ix: "New Testament exegetes have so cluttered up the avenue to the sources with (often misleading) secondary literature that no stranger dares to approach them anymore [*sic*]." In addition to his programmatic remarks in Hengel 1994 (ET 1996b), see also his more recent essay about the crisis in New Testament scholarship: 2003a (one or two of the same points emerge in English in 2003b).

Thomas and Q; wandering charismatics and invisible "communities" playing hide-and-seek behind the text; grand power struggles
between irreconcilably divided, "suppressing" and "suppressed"
versions of faith; all manner of quasi-Darwinist speculations about
ever-ascending christologies and descending eschatologies, early
egalitarian radicalism giving way to late bourgeois patriarchalism;
and so forth. The list goes on and on. Even unbelievers in these
figments of intellectual fashion find that the attempt to ignore
them is like trying to escape after stepping into bubblegum or
dog doo: they are virtually impossible to dispel, and the aroma
lingers wherever one turns.

The Disappearing Subject Matter

If all this were not enough to make Professor Dodd begin to
doubt the words that came forth so trippingly on that June afternoon in 1936, one final consideration must surely make his hair
stand on end. Strange as it sounds, an outside observer today
would be hard put to identify any *shared purpose or subject matter* for the discipline whose transactions are chronicled in *New
Testament Abstracts* for the early twenty-first century. Never mind
assured facts, methods, or meanings: is there even an identifiable
field of study?[13]

It might seem tempting to suggest that such uncertainty is to a
considerable extent implicit in the very origins of the subject. After
all, it was only nineteenth-century Germany that first granted insti-
tutional recognition to the notion that the New Testament should
be studied separately from the Old and a fortiori in isolation from
Christian doctrine and history (cf. Hengel 1994: 324–27). Nevertheless, this questionable subject definition had found wide accep-
tance by 1936: Professor Dodd's generation took it for granted as
clear and uncontroversial; and like the present author, thousands
of academics to this day owe their employment to it.

More obvious, perhaps, would be the kinds of questions aris-
ing directly from the shape of the discipline as it developed after

---

13. On this question see already Keck 1981 and the debate in *Second Century* 1
(1981).

Dodd. For all their differences about methods and results, C. H. Dodd and his critics, or for that matter Adolf von Harnack and his detractors in the generation before Dodd, were still in remarkable agreement about *what were the basic questions to be asked*. Today we have reached a point where it is often no longer clear what the disagreements are about. Judging from *New Testament Abstracts*, is the *primary* object of this study (1) the exegesis and subject matter of the New Testament texts themselves, (2) the power interests to which those texts are or can be turned, or (3) the ancient Jewish and Greco-Roman social world, of which the texts formed but an insignificant part? And if one's work is primarily or exclusively on the second or third objects, does it matter for the subject definition if such pursuit still recognizably relates to the first? Must New Testament scholarship seek to gain some intellectually accountable sense (however vague) of what the texts intend and refer to, or is it now sufficient to offer leveraged postmodern readings that reflect above all an individual's or small group's contemporary experience and agenda? Thinking about the wider goal or purpose of New Testament study, should it acknowledge, ignore, or even deny the New Testament's historic and vital relationship with living faith communities—either in terms of a mutual accountability to Christian truth or for that matter in terms of ideological subversion? It is by no means clear that New Testament studies as an academic discipline now manifests anything approaching a consensus about even its purpose and object.

Professor Dodd could be forgiven for wondering whether such an unrecognizably altered discipline can have any future at all. At this point the good professor would no doubt thank us politely for the tour and make haste to schedule another couple of centuries of discussion with St. Matthew about the parables of the kingdom and with St. John about his use of historical tradition.

Rescue Attempts

Our thought experiment has probably taken us about as far as it will go. There is in contemporary New Testament studies an

undoubted richness of new questions, from some of which even
C. H. Dodd could have benefited. These might include, among
other things, in-depth analysis of the sociocultural setting of the
New Testament and the early Christian communities; the discoveries at Qumran on such matters as the text and interpretation of the
Old Testament, the development of Jewish apocalyptic dualism,
eschatology, and halakah; the critical study of rabbinic and mystical Jewish sources; the study of rhetoric and social anthropology;
renewed interest in theological interpretation; and reader-oriented
and non-Western approaches to the New Testament. From this
perspective, the advances since Dodd at one level offer good reason
to feel encouraged about the discipline's intellectual vitality.

For all that, however, we should not seek to downplay the fact
that the status quo does appear to many observers, both inside
and outside the discipline, to represent a serious predicament.
Here I propose to examine a number of solutions that have from
time to time been put forward. I shall argue that although most
of these proposals have genuine merit on their own terms and
potentially as part of a larger package, in the end none of them
looks particularly well placed to address the deeper crisis of the
discipline.

Renewed Historicism

Leading scholars, including Martin Hengel (1994 [ET 1996b]),
Gerd Theissen (1996; Theissen and Merz 1998), N. T. Wright
(1992a: 81–120; cf. 2003: 12–23, 736–38), and a good many
others (cf. Stanton 1985), have in recent years advocated the re-
invigorated pursuit of a more nuanced and thorough historical-
critical study of the New Testament. Such an enterprise would be
underpinned by a commitment to a wider and better knowledge
of the ancient Jewish and Greco-Roman sources and by a more
constructive, multidisciplinary account of the New Testament
texts. While the stress is on historical criticism and related methods
of sociological and anthropological study, most of these writers
would in fact include in this remit the literary and theological
aspects of the biblical documents.

It is certainly true that agreement on a rigorous study of the primary sources would help to address and stamp out a number of gross historical misjudgments and misinterpretations. Some of the most accomplished scholars are showing ill-concealed signs of exasperation with the rising incompetence and carelessness manifested even in some high-profile publications in the field.[14] The discipline's increasingly fluffy dependence on secondary and tertiary citations makes such disgruntled views difficult to dismiss out of hand. It is extraordinary, for example, how many publications in the field still restrict their range of rabbinic reference, if any, to texts discussed in the classic commentary of Strack and Billerbeck 1922–61 (a point rightly stressed by Daube 1990: 376) and their engagement with the Dead Sea Scrolls to recycling the same handful of passages that were popularized in the first wave of Qumran scholarship in the 1950s and 1960s.

Both the events about which the New Testament authors speak and the circumstances of their writing are of considerable importance for an understanding of their message. From this perspective, there is every justification for careful study of the primary sources in both their Jewish and Greco-Roman settings, with appropriate attention to ancient rhetorical, sociocultural, and literary factors. At least in this respect, the historical-critical study of the New Testament will always remain indispensable. Recent years, indeed, have seen a good deal of lively reflection about necessary changes in our historical methods—including fresh assessments of the problems of historical plausibility, critical realism, the role of memory and orality, and the place of cultural anthropology as a historical tool.[15] Much of this still cries out to

14. Hengel's later writings have taken on a notably polemical edge against the widespread ignorance of ancient sources and languages; see 1994: 339 (a knowledge of Latin and Aramaic or Syriac should be required of every Ph.D. candidate in New Testament); 1996a: vii–x; Hengel and Schwemer 1997: ix. Cf. Betz 2003: 47–48.

15. On the plausibility criterion see Theissen and Winter 2002 (and less persuasively Porter 2000); on critical realism see Wright 1992a and Meyer 1994 (who in turn followed Lonergan); on memory and orality see Dunn 2003, 2005; and Schröter 1997 (also chapter 6 below). See further the reassessment of the classic cultural anthropology approach of Bruce J. Malina, Jerome H. Neyrey, and others in Lawrence 2003 (and cf. Bockmuehl 2002 on Malina 2001).

be more carefully assimilated in discussion with historians and philosophers of history.

What is more, there remains most definitely a program of desirable primary research in this area. The last two decades of extraordinarily prolific historical-Jesus research may for the most part have run their course, at least in the form of a self-conscious Third Quest.[16] Similarly, the lack of major recent contributions or decisive rebuttals of its increasingly vociferous critics might suggest that the "new perspective on Paul" may have started to lose its head of creative steam about ten years ago, just when it seemed to be on the verge of becoming the new currency of Pauline studies.[17] Meanwhile, however, and despite the disappointing results of an extended "Pauline theology" seminar at the Society of Biblical Literature during the 1990s (Bassler et al. 1991–97), the debate on Paul has been thrown wide open by a number of vigorous new studies,[18] and there is now plenty of scope for renewed historical work on the age-old question of the balance between Paul's Jewishness and his Gentile mission—as seen not least in his Christology, his eschatology, his view of God, and his view of ethics. Similarly, and regardless of the favored Synoptic theory du jour, recent discussion suggests that further work on the identity of Jesus could now helpfully revisit such classic topics as his Jewishness and even his own implied soteriology, Christology, and ecclesiology (if any, and whether high or low or both). Beyond this, the shifts in interpretation of both Jesus and Paul once again make it worthwhile to reexamine the "Paul and Jesus" question—not merely from the old-fashioned source-critical perspective of "how much Paul knew," but by genuine comparison of Paul and Jesus

16. This terminology derives from N. T. Wright; see Neill and Wright 1988: 379–403 and Wright 1992b. Even the chronicles and typologies of this quest, let alone the contributions to it, have become legion; see Carleton Paget 2001; Powell 1998; and Witherington 1995; and note now the self-styled "new perspective on Jesus" inaugurated by Dunn 2003 and 2005.

17. It may be that N. T. Wright's forthcoming major volume on Paul will seek to address this deficit.

18. Carson et al. 2001–4; Gathercole 2002; Kim 2002; Seifrid 2000; and M. Thompson 2002. Among German authors note Stuhlmacher and Hagner 2001; Hengel and Deines 1995; and Bachmann 1999.

on newly topical issues like God, Messiah, Israel, Jerusalem, law, ethics, kingdom, resurrection, and eschatology.

A good deal of genuinely fresh work remains to be done in areas like New Testament archeology (when is someone going to dig up Colossae?); the continuing evaluation for New Testament research of the later twentieth century's extensive discoveries of papyri, inscriptions, and nonliterary remains; histories of earliest Christianity in particular regions (especially Egypt, Syria, and Mesopotamia); the further exploration of Jewish Christianity; and a host of other topics. A methodologically and textually up-dated "Strack-Billerbeck" is long overdue (1922–61); significant projects to this end are currently under way at Jerusalem's Hebrew University and at Bard College in the United States, while Instone-Brewer 2004 inaugurated a comparative project following the Mishnah's structure rather than that of the New Testament. Similarly, an accelerated publication and refined English edition of the "new Wettstein" for Greco-Roman sources (Strecker and Schnelle 1996–) seems highly desirable.

For the first time, several commentary series are in process on the Septuagint, on Josephus, and on the Dead Sea Scrolls, at last complete in the *editio princeps* (Discoveries in the Judaean Desert);[19] the recent reedition of the Apostolic Fathers for the Loeb Classical Library (Ehrman 2003a) may also reinvigorate the interest of Anglophone commentators.[20] A small cottage industry of revisers has turned its attention to trusty favorites like Bauer's *Lexicon* (now Danker and Bauer 2000) or Moulton and Geden's *Concordance* (Moulton et al. 2002), while some even favor a revised "Kittel"

19. The Septuagint series are to be edited by Stanley E. Porter for Brill and by Albert Pietersma and Benjamin G. Wright for the International Organization for Septuagint and Cognate Studies. (Note also the continuing project La Bible d'Alexandrie published by Cerf under the leadership of Marguerite Harl.) Initial volumes in the Josephus commentary series edited by Steve Mason for Brill include Feldman 1999; Mason 2001; Begg 2005; and Begg and Spilsbury 2005. The first volume of the Eerdmans Commentaries on the Dead Sea Scrolls was Davila 2000.

20. Six volumes have appeared since 1989 in the German series Kommentar zu den apostolischen Vätern, while the Hermeneia series has published volumes on Hermas (Osiek 1999), *Didache* (Niederwimmer 1998), and Ignatius (Schoedel 1985) as well as on the *Apostolic Tradition* (Bradshaw et al. 2002).

Theological Dictionary of the New Testament (Daube 1990). A comprehensive reassessment of the history of the New Testament text is gradually becoming possible through the well-funded and technologically sophisticated projects being jointly pursued at Münster and Birmingham. Fresh and thorough study of the problem of canon in the second and third centuries could help to reassess recurrent assertions about the supposed historical (or at least ideological) primacy of miscellaneous "lost" or "suppressed" gospels.[21] All this and more is doubtless good and worthy.[22]

At the same time it remains the case that new primary sources directly relevant to the historical study of the New Testament itself are few and far between, and assertions of "neglected subjects" often reveal more ignorance of the vast extant literature than genuine scholarly lacunae. While study of the Dead Sea Scrolls is set to continue for a long time, one suspects it will not be long before their significance for the New Testament will have been largely accounted for. In this respect at least, Dodd's otherwise hasty assessment may not be wholly mistaken. Without necessarily reaching agreed solutions, most of the major *historical-critical* questions one might wish to ask of the New Testament have now indeed seen a pretty good airing of the available options. It seems reasonable to suggest that our understanding cannot substantially advance without the discovery of genuinely new evidence. Until then, historical scholarship on the New Testament itself is likely to remain what Martin Hengel (1994: 334, 350) rightly calls "a science of surmises" (*Vermutungswissenschaft*) and "a merry-go-round of hypotheses" (*Hypothesenkarusell*). The continually expanding toybox of ancillary "methodologies" and "approaches" helps to perpetuate nineteenth-century myths of ineluctable "progress" and "originality" in the study of the Bible.

When the historical-critical goose has laid its egg, a crucial further question is the *place* of historical study in the overall

21. Such claims have been championed prominently and from different perspectives by writers like Crossan 1985, 1991; Ehrman 2003b, 2003c; Pagels 1973, 1979, 2003; and others.

22. See Hengel 1994 (ET 1996b) for a discussion of additional historical-critical desiderata.

exercise. Especially its methodologically conservative advocates too frequently presuppose that the interpretation of the text will take care of itself if only we get the historical problems sorted out. If only we could dispel the dreadful ignorance and methodological sloppiness of our colleagues by in-depth analysis of Dio Chrysostom's rhetoric or a precise inventory of text types in use at Qumran, the meaning and significance of the New Testament texts would very largely fall into place. And so forth. There is widespread delusion among historical critics of every confessional stripe that the results of such study are themselves self-evidently relevant to the "real" meaning of the New Testament—not just as ancient text, but even as foundation document of Christian faith.

A romantic epistemological optimism continues to underlie a surprising amount of even the best historical research. The dream of dispatching the historical-critical equivalent of a time-traveling television camera to cover episodes like the passion and resurrection of Jesus or Paul's "painful visit" to Corinth would answer all possible questions. But of course the truth is that the questions of truth and meaning would certainly *not* go away. The script is wholly predictable: the television documentary would have to conclude that some people had a religious experience or dispute; they claimed it meant one thing, and other people claimed it meant another thing. Flash in conflicting conjectures proffered by a celebrated religion expert and an Irish monk in a library, followed by a Stetson-topped Indiana Jones figure in the ruins of Qumran; then fade into the sunset with the words, "The true meaning of these events will continue to be contested and may never be known, except to the eyes of faith."

That sort of predictably safe conclusion would of course be designed to market mystique and keep the reporter's job; but it would also suitably reflect the fact that in dealing with the New Testament's inalienably theological subject matter there can be no objective history—and certainly no neutral historian. No amount of calendrical disputation in shredded scroll fragments will change that, nor will Greco-Roman statistics about the social stratification and grain supply of first-century Corinth.

Historical research at its best contributes vital and helpful clarification of the literal sense of the text. One of its great strengths, which should keep it a core element of any responsible biblical syllabus, is its potential (alongside other approaches) to contribute to a common conversation about the New Testament across faith boundaries rather than merely within particular ecclesial communities.

Historical criticism's real value, however, can be assessed only as part of an overall approach to New Testament interpretation. As Nicholas Lash (1986b) and others have long since pointed out, a coherently critical approach would need to render a credible account of the texts in relation not only to the stated or implied phenomenology of Christian origins, but also to the explosively "totalizing" theological assertions that writers like Paul and the evangelists state or imply in practically every sentence. Precisely that recognition, however, is astonishingly rare among historical critics. Without facing the inalienably transformative and self-involving demands that these ecclesial writings place on a serious reader, it is impossible to make significant sense of them—or to understand why they were written or how they survived.[23] Absent this textual dynamic, there is no reason why most New Testament teaching and research could not be farmed out as peripheral *Kleinliteratur* for the sporadic attention of classicists and ancient historians. Only the largest universities would on this account have need for the occasional specialist in what might be called the phenomenology of Christian origins, following the classic historicist proposal (popularized by Stendahl 1962) to reduce the exegete's purview to "what it meant"—as opposed to concern with "what it means." Farming out the study of Christian origins in this fashion would merely be the logical and wholly defensible consequence of adopting the detached Egyptology model of biblical studies.

Finally and most importantly, however, the historically situated New Testament documents *themselves* in fact give no encourage-

23. Commenting on the phenomenon of scholarship on the Gospels that is estranged from the church in which from the beginning these writings had their life, Nichols 1999: 168 notes how this "undermines its practitioners' judgment by neutralizing their feeling for what the texts are actually about."

ment whatever to the idea that a quest for history "behind" the texts promises access to their "real" meaning and significance. True enough, the authors deliberately allude to events outside their narrative and sometimes bring the gospel into explicit relation with wider economic or political developments that can be usefully explored. But the story they tell is inalienably theological. Their vested interpretation of the events is never an optional extra, a kind of religious topping sprinkled on a phenomenological sundae that could just as easily be consumed without it. Whatever one may decide to conclude historically, it remains a fact that the New Testament *neither envisages nor validates* any reliable access to the identity of Jesus Christ except through the apostolic witness and the life of the apostolic churches. Even Luke, arguably the New Testament author most concerned about the gospel's historical facticity and apologetic credibility, leaves no doubt about this question of access: "God raised him on the third day and granted that he should visibly appear—*not to all the people* but to us who were chosen by God as witnesses, who ate and drank with him after he rose from the dead" (Acts 10:40–41).

Final-Form Literary Approaches

Beginning about three decades ago, so-called synchronic approaches to the New Testament gained a significant foothold in the discipline. They capitalized on a simple but fertile insight of the philosophy of language: texts frequently embody a surplus of meaning that may not have been obvious to the original author or even his first readers (cf. Roman Ingarden [1893–1970] and Paul Ricoeur [1913–2005]). One can observe this in scholarly interpretation of a host of genres ranging from Dante to the American Constitution. By analyzing the literary and linguistic features and disruptions inherent within the New Testament documents, so goes the argument, we gain access to levels of meaning that may be largely independent of their historical origin and that may moreover bring the texts to life for modern readers in a far more direct and relevant way. Approaches under this heading include such methods as text-linguistics, discourse

analysis, narrative and genre criticism, and some kinds of rhetorical criticism.

Once again, the insights gained by these methods have in many
ways proved rich and varied; and some literary approaches have
shown themselves remarkably fruitful for theological discourse
and practical application to the contemporary life of faith. Perhaps this is because their concern to interpret the texts in their
final form is at times compatible with the theological and ecclesial
interpretation of the New Testament as Scripture (cf. Watson
1996b: 127). Similarly, in their explicit attention to ambiguity
and ambivalence in the text, these literary methods are, at least
in principle, amenable to a dialogue with the sort of allegorical
and spiritual interpretation that was practiced in the patristic and
medieval periods and that, after sustained neglect among even
Catholic exegetes, has begun to find renewed support in some
circles.[24] From a more ideologically leveraged, deconstructionist
point of view, some have postulated that the new literary critical
approaches are on their way to becoming "the new orthodoxy
in biblical studies" (thus Clines 1993: 82; cf. also Aichele 1995,
2001; Moore 1989; and Moore and Anderson 1992).

Even so, after a quarter century of reflection on often genuine gains, it may now be permissible to ask if the study of the
New Testament primarily as literature, narrative, or rhetoric will
not inevitably turn out to be a somewhat impoverished exercise
on at least two fronts. First, judged by any broad-based esthetic
standard, the New Testament documents never invite, and rarely
reward, interpretation from a primarily literary point of view.
They represent second-rate literature in often third-rate linguistic
forms. For good ancient literature one would surely go to Ver-
gil or Euripides; for deliberate rhetoric, to Dio or Demosthenes.
Second and more important, the texts in any case do not present
themselves as concerned with either literature or rhetoric. To view
them primarily (rather than *en passant*) in this fashion is rather

24. A leading advocate is de la Potterie 1986; cf. more recently Schürmann 1990;
Stuhlmacher 1995a; Holmes 2002; and the treatment of Romans by Cantalamessa
2002. Cf. the classic studies of medieval interpretation by de Lubac 1961–64 and
Smalley 1983; also Dahan 2000 on the development of the spiritual sense.

like using a stethoscope to examine a lightbulb: it can be done and does produce unfamiliar results, but it offers an analysis that does justice neither to the object nor to the instrument. In some manifestations, moreover, these methods do give rise to a genuine worry about methodological accountability. If many historical critics may be hermeneutically somewhat naïve, some recent appropriations of literary criticism in biblical studies presuppose a relativism that borders on the nihilistic and shows little concern for the sort of "tactful" readings of "textual intention" now urged by a number of professional literary critics.[25] The hermeneutical implications of bypassing the historical setting of the texts may often be ignored or even celebrated. What is more, poststructuralist interpreters frequently embrace a model in which the literary meaning of a text is ahistorically determined by the criteria that happen to be deemed valid by the individual interpreter and his or her particular community.[26]

On this account "texts demand nothing but yield everything under the proper caresses" (so, rightly, Lundin 1999: 41). One advocate of this strategy spells out the chillingly cynical implications of his own consumer-driven model of biblical interpretation:

> If there are no "right" interpretations, and no validity in interpretation beyond the assent of various interest groups, biblical interpreters have to give up the goal of determinate and universally acceptable interpretations and devote themselves to producing interpretations they can sell—in whatever mode is called for by the communities they choose to serve. Those who pay the piper get to call the tune. And biblical interpreters are . . . no more than pipers, playing their tunes in the service of some community or other that authorises their work and signs their salary cheques. (Clines 1993: 79–80)[27]

25. For the notion of tactful reading see Cunningham 2002; the idea of *intentio operis* is urged in Eco 1992.
26. Following Fish 1980 and others. Note the sustained philosophical and moral critique of this position in Vanhoozer 1998.
27. Cf. Porter 2003: 371–72. Note also the influential statement of the abolition of "meaning" in Stout 1982.

This corrosive intellectual context makes it easy to see why literary readings are not inherently more alert to the extratextual truth claims that are intrinsically raised by the New Testament. However accurate it may be in the case of the telephone directory, in the case of Scripture it is simply untrue that these texts "demand nothing." Even for more constructive literary approaches, assertions about such matters as the text's "irreducibly narrative" form or character emplotment seem in practice to offer precious little gain in our understanding of its creedal and theological subject matter focused in the person of Jesus Christ. There can be no subject-appropriate interpretation of the Old or New Testaments that highlights their meaning (or meanings) while neglecting the question of its truth (so, rightly, Watson 1997a: 25–26; cf. Johnson and Kurz 2002: 117, 251–52).

Ideology and Self-Deconstruction

We are immediately faced with the larger issue of reader-oriented and self-consciously ideological approaches, whose advantage lies in being able to take much more explicit account of the perspectival factors affecting any contemporary reading. This of course is a sound and in many ways vital question for biblical interpretation. And yet, having rejected old-fashioned logocentric or objective hermeneutics, a great many of the current cluster of reader-oriented approaches follow instead a nakedly explicit script about power. This is the case for many of the methods that self-consciously understand themselves as postmodern, usually characterized by an explicit antipathy to integrating perspectives (other than their own), referred to as "metanarratives" and frequently demonized as "totalizing."[28] Interpretations under this heading may draw, for example, on a range of feminist, queer, ethnic, and other liberationist approaches.

28. Early and influential primers in postmodern biblical interpretation include Aichele 1995 (on which see Moberly 2000: 26–37; cf. more recently Chapman 2002 on Aichele 2001); E. McKnight 1988; Moore and Anderson 1992; and Penchansky 1995. See further Brueggemann 1993 and, from a different viewpoint, Thiselton 1992, 1995; also *Semeia* 54 (1992).

Where the quest for truth, beauty, and goodness has been dis-membered by politically utilitarian metacritics, inevitably all we have left to talk about is a bland discourse of power—in all its tediously bulimic, self-destructive corrosiveness.[29] Of course, we did not need to wait for Michel Foucault, Luce Irigaray, or, on the other hand, Alastair Macintyre to tell us that; we could have learned it from Machiavelli, Nietzsche, or Orwell's *Animal Farm*. Self-consciously postmodern forms of ideological criticism in this regard often present themselves as a curiously undisciplined mish-mash: they tend to combine painstakingly sophisticated suspicion of the biblical writers' motives with a studied cultural and intel-lectual credulity toward their own favored (but often exegetically disemboweled) revisionist political project.

Terry Eagleton, the well-known Marxist literary critic whose textbooks on criticism shaped a generation of students of literature (1976a and 1976b), offers intriguing insights into some of these trends. Moderating his previous assaults on supporters of the "dis-credited" and indeed wholly "spurious" idea "that the truth of a text resides in the consciousness of its author," he has now ironi-cally turned his hand to autobiographic memoirs.[30] At the same time, his invective (authorially conscious, it seems) against the evils of postcolonial theory and postmodernist "amnesia" matches his declaration that he feels "ill-served by my acolytes" (see Eagleton 1999 and 2003, quoted in Patterson 2003). Some of those post-modernist acolytes, indeed, uncannily resemble a more "suspicious" version of Eagleton's scathingly caricatured (but presumably pre-postmodern) Cambridge undergraduate supervisor:[31]

If we were discussing, say, Hume's theory that reason is always a slave of passion, he would say something like "It all depends on the

29. This point is also acknowledged in Wayne Meeks's wholly nonconfessional account of New Testament studies: "The trouble is, if the warrants for our assertions become nakedly ideological, however 'good' the ideology, those warrants can only be enforced by exercise of power, not by persuasive argument" (2005: 160).

30. Eagleton 1986: 34 (in criticism of John Bayley); cf. now Eagleton 2001 (a thoroughly entertaining work to which James Carleton Paget kindly drew my attention).

31. The supervisor is called "Greenway," a cipher for Theodore Redpath.

individual," as though we were talking about a taste in broccoli.
He seemed to think that whether space was curved or rabbits had
concepts depended on the individual too. He was a naturally astute
character, but ideology had rendered him obtuse, like some gradual
wasting of the brain. He was as allergic to ideas as a wrestler or
a stockbroker. If you had presented him with a text containing
the secret of the universe, he would have noticed only a displaced
semi-colon. (Eagleton 2001: 128–29)

Within New Testament studies, Hans Weder (1996) rightly puts
his finger on the fatal weakness of the postmodern hermeneutic
of suspicion: its systemic, often studied inability to be self-critical.
However, in its fixated concern to hear what the scriptural texts
are *not* saying, the hermeneutic of suspicion often loses the ability
to hear attentively what in fact they *are* saying. Approaches of this
sort will inevitably focus on an agenda that has already become
politically familiar and emotionally domesticated, rather than on
what may be wild and fresh and scented with new life.

One of the great ironies of the contemporary cultural scene
in the West is that the supposedly inclusive metacritical stance
of this hermeneutic may in some of its manifestations exhibit
a virtually fascist suppression of genuine cultural dissent, of
what really is irreducibly Other—a point that is not lost on diverse non-Western observers.[32] Or, to put it differently: far from
being overcome, the *modernist* tendency to colonize particularities under grand universal theories is, if anything, made more
sinister in the *postmodern* program of elevating *all* competing
particularities to the same value and validity. Such a program
necessarily rules out any distinction between truth and falsehood—and thus "poisons the well," as Kevin Vanhoozer suggests (2002: 253).[33]

32. Note the celebrated Muslim tour de force of Sardar 1998; also Johnson 1996a:
95–101 on postmodern scholarship's preoccupation with a multiplication of "marginal" or "lost voices."
33. See also Gunton 1993: 70, quoted in Watson 1996a: 12 (cf. 10–11). Boghossian 1996 rightly points out that postmodern inclusivist ideology not only leaves those
in power systemically prevented from criticizing minorities, but thereby also subtly
encroaches on the ability of the oppressed to criticize the new arbiters of power.

About a decade ago the logical consequences of deconstructionist politics dressed up as scholarship were humorously and tellingly illustrated by Alan D. Sokal, a theoretical physicist at New York University. In the summer of 1996 he managed to hoodwink Duke University's prominent cultural-studies journal *Social Text* into publishing an instantly famous parody article on "a transformative hermeneutics of quantum gravity," which implicitly took the mickey out of a horde of deconstructionist readings of science from Jacques Derrida to Jacques Lacan and Luce Irigaray (Sokal 1996b). Sokal, himself a self-confessed political leftist and feminist, subsequently explained his purpose in these words:

> To test the prevailing intellectual standards, I decided to try a modest (though admittedly uncontrolled) experiment: Would a leading North American journal of cultural studies—whose editorial collective includes such luminaries as Fredric Jameson and Andrew Ross—publish an article liberally salted with nonsense if (a) it sounded good and (b) it flattered the editors' ideological preconceptions? The answer, unfortunately, is yes. . . .
>
> The editors of *Social Text* liked my article because they liked its *conclusion*: that "the content and methodology of postmodern science provide powerful intellectual support for the progressive political project." They apparently felt no need to analyze the quality of the evidence, the cogency of the arguments, or even the relevance of the arguments to the purported conclusion. (Sokal 1996a: 62–64)

The highbrow press on both sides of the Atlantic was soon abuzz with discussions of the resulting brouhaha, which spawned dozens of academic symposia and a mass of secondary literature. Unsurprisingly, perhaps, alarm was caused not only in the United States but also in France and Italy, where several of the pioneers of postmodernist philosophy evidently felt the sting of Sokal's charge rather acutely: piqued further by his additional provocative exposé in a coauthored book first published in 1997 in France under the title *Impostures intellectuelles* (ET 1998: *Fashionable Nonsense*; 2nd edition 2003), leading lights waded into the fray in

self-defense.[34] To most outside commentators, however, the whole
amusing spectacle left postmodernism's self-appointed emperors
looking mildly silly in their newfangled ideological clothes.[35] It
may be that the "Sokal Affair," with its implicit reassertion of
a modest epistemological realism, will turn out to have marked
something of a turning point for the intellectual fortunes of postmodern philosophy, at least in its claims to shed meaningful light
on scientific study (note also Sokal and Bricmont 2004).

Having said this, it is still worth considering that behind all
this stands a valid insight seriously gone to seed. Even those of
us who would still wish to distinguish "good" from "less good"
interpretations will do well to maintain a healthy distrust of naïve
or manipulative agendas operating in the minds of authors and
their interpreters. That much is indeed postmodernism's valid
identification of modernity's epistemological Achilles' heel (even
if the best "premodern" minds already had a keen eye for this).
At the same time, as Jean Baudrillard rightly points out, the effect
of Foucault's highly influential hermeneutic of social deconstruction and suspicion of power in the end unravels into another
power-mechanism to advance the interests of a temporarily countercultural elite (Baudrillard 1987: 10, cited in Thiselton 1995:
141, 144). The ideological velvet gloves of egalitarian inclusion
ill conceal the claws of a hermeneutical worldview that is in fact
far *more* totalizing and prescriptive, and far *more* stifling of free
criticism, than could have been foreseen in the more pragmatic
and perhaps naïve era of C. H. Dodd's inaugural lecture. From
an Augustinian perspective alert to the fallenness of desire and
imagination, there is indeed undoubted benefit in a searching
suspicion and critique—beginning, perhaps, with *self*-suspicion
and self-deconstruction.

What, then, is to be learned here? It can clearly be an effective
analytical tool to ask in whose interest either a New Testament
author or his interpreters advance a particular idea. To gain a
perspectival awareness of both text and reader is a vital asset in

34. Sokal keeps a full account of this ongoing debate on his website; see http://www
.physics.nyu.edu/faculty/sokal/ (accessed April 17, 2006).
35. For an initial assessment of subsequent debate, see Boghossian 1996.

the interpretative endeavor. Just as in the historical-critical enterprise, however, the usefulness of this political quest once again depends entirely on its place in the overall exercise of interpretation. Where the hermeneutic of suspicion governs interpretation as an all-encompassing agenda, its caustic epistemology will serve merely to reinforce our discipline's quandary about agreed methods and criteria. Though appearing to promise instant relevance and application to jaded or disaffected readers, the unrestrained discourse of power is in the end a false friend to any genuine quest to encounter and understand the New Testament text.

Herein may well lie the Cinderella of today's much-heralded "ethics of biblical interpretation": can we really welcome a scholarly approach to the text that seems in some ways to resemble 1960s rock stars ritually smashing their instruments on stage?[36] It is too early to risk forgetting that many of this past century's gravest injustices were the consequence of ahistorical and unhistorical misappropriations of texts for ideological purposes. From both a hermeneutical and a theological perspective, any approach primarily based on this metacritical relativism can only be regarded as discarding the exegetical baby along with the inevitable eisegetical bathwater.

Pros and Cons of Theological Interpretation

The last two decades of the twentieth century saw a hardening of opposing points of view on whether New Testament interpretation should rally around a synthetic stance of Christian faith or rather explicitly bracket out such a stance. Recent salvos in this battle have been fired on the one hand by writers like Philip Davies (1995), Werner Jeanrond (1996), Heikki Räisänen (2000a), and

---

36. Cf. Fowl 1990; contrast the radical relativism of Patte 1995 (denounced even by a cheerfully "kaleidoscopic" pluralist like Carroll 1998: 61–62, 65n19). Although writing from an explicitly feminist point of view, Mouton 2002: 252–53 by contrast rightly notes that properly ethical engagement with Scripture entails reinterpretation of contemporary moral worlds "in accordance with" and "analogous to" the perspectives of the text. Similarly, she regards such interpretation of the New Testament as requiring the interpreter to acknowledge and appropriate the "direction of the document" (253n115).

Jacques Berlinerblau (2005), who argue in different ways that as a public, university-based discipline the Bible can be treated only in strictly nonconfessional fashion as a document of religious history.[37] If theological questions are admissible in any form at all, one may speak only of discrete "theologies" of the various biblical authors or perhaps at most (with Berger 1988: 108–24; 1995b; and Schmithals 1996) of a history of early Christian theology. On this reading, the future of New Testament studies as an academic discipline in the universities must lie in regrouping around a strictly secular phenomenological study, in which a Christian theological interpretation can have no part.

A number of contrary writers, however, have in recent years taken up salient insights of postmodern hermeneutics in order to plead for the legitimacy of an unabashedly Christian theological perspective. This alone, it is argued, is most clearly in keeping with the New Testament's normative canonical function in the communities of faith for whom it was written and by whom it is received to this day. Leading scholars in this interpretative "growth industry" include Brevard Childs, Peter Stuhlmacher, Luke Timothy Johnson, Stephen Fowl, Joel B. Green, and Francis Watson, among others, although each of them manifests distinctive emphases.[38]

The debate between these different approaches has become heated and passionate and further polarized by the mutually exclusive claims of competence and authority that frequently accompany it. In the 1990s, the exchange between Philip Davies (1995; 2nd edition 2004) and Francis Watson (1996a) was somewhat indicative in this respect. Davies's original piece served

---

37. Cf. Räisänen 2000b on what he thinks is the "liberationist" convergence of global readings—aided by conventional historical criticism. A more promising approach to this latter topic will draw on more theologically articulate readings like that of Segovia and Tolbert 1995 or studies of the actual role of the Bible in the churches of Africa and Asia.

38. Childs 1984, 1992, 1995, 1997, 2002; Stuhlmacher 1992–99, 1995a, 1995b, 2002b; Johnson 1998; Johnson and Kurz 2002; Fowl 1998, 2002; Green 2002; Green and Turner 2000; Watson 1994, 1996a, 1997a. Note also the recent collections on biblical theology by Bartholomew et al. 2004 and Hafemann 2002, and cf. the methodological reflections of Morgan 1996b and Balla 1998 as well as the diverse but complementary systematic-theological perspectives offered by Yeago 1994; Vanhoozer 2002: 275–308; and Reno 2004.

up the familiar comfort food of doctrinaire bird's-eye-view secularism, which cannot allow any place for a Christian study of the New Testament in the public university context. Predictably, therefore, and yet paradoxically, Davies's perspective failed to perceive the theological and *historical* implications of the New Testament's role as Christian Scripture—a role that has always been equally important in its implicit as much as its explicit expressions. Yet even if one were to progress beyond Davies to a more "inclusively" construed metaperspective of secular pluralism, that umbrella viewpoint itself nevertheless remains constitutionally unself-critical, hospitable to that which serves its purpose but wedded to a logic of *excluding* all that seems (like religious practice or questions of truth) to call it into question (so, rightly, Watson 1996a: 12).

Davies's sparring partner Watson, on the other hand, tends in that debate (as in his other writings of that period) to downplay the significance of historical realities and seemingly to question any possibility of intellectual engagement with the Bible in other than trinitarian Christian terms. While this seems at one level coherent and attractive, it raises difficulties for aspects of New Testament study that might reasonably seem accessible from a variety of presuppositions. The shape of the text is one particularly obvious example: the *text* that Watson envisages is, quite rightly, a final-form canonical text. This position, which is also advocated by Childs (1984: 518–30) and an increasing number of other interpreters (Watson 1994: 15–16), nevertheless involves critical questions whose resolution might presumably benefit, at least inter alia, from public debate with scholars who subscribe to something like Davies's pluralistic terms.

More important, perhaps, and unlike Childs, Watson in his debate with Davies did not provide a credible account of how the irreducible historical and geographic particularities, especially of the gospel texts, can be given their exegetical and theological due without recourse to some identifiably historical questions.[39] It is

---

39. Watson acknowledges the questions (1994: 250–51) but bypasses them with a methodologically vague reference to the concept of the incarnation.

precisely *in* that particularity, rather than in spite of it, that the texts can and do raise the fundamental theological questions. Finally, one other difficulty in Watson's riposte concerns the use of the term *church*. This would not of course trouble Davies, and Watson for his part might respond differently now. Yet for all its undeniable theological energy over against the facile assumption of the New Testament text as a "neutral" space, in itself the term *church* can remain notably abstract and detached from the life and worship of any concrete ecclesial polity.[40] Whether in postliberal or evangelical guise, fashionably mellifluous talk of "ecclesial communities" may conveniently cloak tough questions both of history and of tradition. Ecclesially affirming Catholic scholars are sometimes accused of conservative subservience to an all-too-particular magisterium, even if this is usually a caricature of interpreters and magisterium alike (see Johnson and Kurz 2002; Martin 2002, 2004; and Williamson 2001, 2003). Among Protestant "theological interpreters" like Watson or Fowl, by contrast, the Archimedean point is often a kind of benignly neo-Barthian trinitarianism—though at times this may nevertheless exercise a surprisingly robust ideological subversion of the text in the service of a quite particular political agenda (rather than, say, an agenda beholden to the doctrinal or moral teaching of a particular church; Watson 1994: 6, 226, 230, and esp. 247).[41] In the context of this particular debate, Watson's welcome rebuttal of Davies never quite proceeds to an account of the church in which this ecclesial hermeneutic actually resides, offering no concrete reference to baptism or Eucharist, to local or global mission, to lay groups reading Scripture, or to bishops or priests.[42]

40. For this critique cf. already Rowland 1995; *pace* Watson 1994: 6 and chap. 15.

41. Ideological *Sachkritik* appears in comments on the "complicity" of "violently suppressing" and "viciously misogynistic" biblical texts in their subsequent interpretation; see Watson 1994: 116, 161–71. Fowl 1998: 97–127 interprets Acts 15 as generating a hermeneutic in support of homosexual lifestyles in the church; this argument, previously supported by Siker 1994 and Johnson 1996b, has also been central in subsequent Anglican debate; see Keesmaat 2004 (unqualified affirmation) as well as Goddard 2001 and Seitz 2001 (appreciative critique).

42. A point also noted by Fowl 1998: 22–23, whose talk of interpreting "vigilant communities," ironically, remains similarly vague about concrete ecclesial polities. On the other hand, Watson 2002: 211–13 is in fact considerably more forthcoming

Thus, while in the interest of a public secular discourse Davies programmatically ignored the historical identity of the Bible as Christian Scripture, Watson's consciously Christian theological reply appeared ironically to operate in some detachment *both* from the possibility of a shared public conversation *and* from specifically embedded moorings of the ecclesial reading he advocated in its place. Absent an affirmation of Christian truth as in some identifiable sense "public truth," theological interpretation inevitably falls short of providing a credible rallying point around which secular, Jewish, and Christian approaches to the New Testament could even meet for discussion and debate about the Christian claims.[43]

Watson's subsequent publications (1997a, 1997b, 2001, 2004) in this respect do reflect a turn to a more deliberate engagement with exegesis of the New Testament, especially vis-à-vis the Old— and to (sometimes bracingly critical) positions on the historical questions it raises.[44] Similarly, the relationship between descriptive and confessional interpretation also receives more explicit attention in Watson's most recent work (2002 and 2004), where historical and theological concerns are again addressed in open debate with all comers—including secularists like Davies.

The Rise and Rise of Hermeneutics

Finally, a brief word about the hope that some vest in the pursuit of biblical hermeneutics. *Neutestamentler* like Stephen Fowl, Joel B. Green, Peter Stuhlmacher, Gerd Theissen, Anthony Thiselton, Hans Weder, Francis Watson, and many others all have at one time or another taken leave of the exegetical spade work to ride off and charge the hermeneutical windmills. Assessments of this

---

about ecclesiological particularities in a subsequent response to Robert Jenson. Might the earlier deficit owe something to its polemical setting?

43. Watson 1996a: 14–15; cf. 13: "A Christian theological interpretative practice cannot do otherwise than claim that it alone can accommodate itself to the true reality of these texts."

44. Watson's intellectual development puzzles a number of interpreters (so already Rowland 1995), but he himself evidently sees less dramatic changes than some suppose; see Watson 2004: 29, 29n61.

exercise doubtless vary, but among its particular benefits in recent times has been a dawning awareness of the necessarily self-involving, corporate, and ecclesial dimensions of interpretation. Like some contemporary secular literary criticism, New Testament hermeneutics takes seriously the role of social context—whether of faith or indeed of unbelief—in the process of interpretation. It can also help to validate the reading of Scripture explicitly in a Christian ecclesial and doctrinal context.

Nevertheless, two considerations suggest that a turn to hermeneutics cannot by itself rescue New Testament studies from its current malaise. First, many hermeneuts appear in practice to find it even more difficult than historical critics to escape the ever more complex intellectual maze of their discourse in order to bring home the interpretative fruits of their labors. Some end up further from the New Testament texts than they began. There are indeed admirable exceptions to this, as in Stuhlmacher's deliberate pursuit of biblical theology (1992–99, 2002b), Thiselton's monumental commentary on 1 Corinthians (2000), or Watson's energetic return to the study of Paul and his Bible (2000, 2004).[45] Too often, however, the temptation to substitute ever more arcane critical theory for accessible, hands-on reading of texts has contributed to the fragmentation of this, as of other disciplines.[46]

Although increasingly noted and affirmed, the recovery of interpretation's ecclesial dimension has up to now not gone nearly far enough. In many cases, as we saw a moment ago, references to "ecclesial" or "interpreting communities" remain remarkably anemic and ahistorical. In practice they often tend to designate either some subset of the professional guild (what David Bleich 1988: 17 calls an "academic fraternity with a French accent"; quoted in Thiselton 1992: 532) or else the special-interest groups on whose behalf a particular interpretation is being advanced. Such talk of communities thinly disguises the all-too-common assumption that *L'Église, c'est moi*: that is to say, my "community"

---

45. Richard Bauckham is similarly notable for his breadth of continued hermeneutical, historical, and exegetical engagement.

46. Cf. more generally American Jewish novelist Cynthia Ozick 1996 on literary criticism, as quoted in O'Toole 1996.

may be like-minded academics or the black community or the gay community or any number of identity-driven polities.[47]

Ways Forward? Two Ideas for a Common Conversation

We have seen a variety of respectable and sophisticated attempts to show a way out of the current crisis in New Testament studies. More than one has the potential to contribute to a possible renewal and redefinition of the discipline. Unfortunately, none of the proposals can do so by itself. More seriously, the real problem often lies in their respective claims of methodological sovereignty or at least priority, which aggravate rather than alleviate the crisis and make it seem virtually impossible to arrive at a composite solution. The inability to see this is a weakness, for example, of the 1993 document of the Pontifical Commission on biblical interpretation, which in its zeal to shoot down the straw man of "fundamentalism" ends up offering a largely uncritical whitewash of disparate existing approaches.[48] If anything other than a strictly self-affirming conversation about the New Testament is to occur between those espousing differing methods, we must find a way of identifying forums of shared inquiry. Are there spaces where a common concern for truth makes it possible *both* to articulate and to question inherited certainties, to assess one's own and the other's deep-seated ideological commitments without immediate disqualification?

The very possibility of scholarship depends on a willingness to learn, to grow or change one's mind, to embrace truth wherever it reveals itself, and also, where we can identify it, to abandon error—even if it were to be culturally entrenched or critically de

---

47. Lack of both catholicity and ecclesial specificity is also a weakness of Countryman 2003, whose concern for a renewed common conversation I share. His purely contemporary location of the interpreter and the community in the "interpretive triangle" engaging the text is, in my view, further weakened because of its lack of attention to the text's effective history (see below, pp. 64–68).

48. See Fitzmyer 1995 (this document is read more sympathetically by Williamson 2003); contrast the more discriminating stance of Pontifical Biblical Commission 2002.

rigueur. As Brother William puts it in *The Name of the Rose*:
"Excess of loquacity can be a sin, and so can excess of reticence.
. . . The life of learning is difficult, and it is difficult to distinguish
good from evil. And often the learned men of our time are only
dwarfs on the shoulders of dwarfs" (Eco 1984: 89). "Because,"
Eco elaborates a little later, "learning does not consist only of
knowing what we must or we can do, but also of knowing what
we could do and perhaps should not do" (97).

If there is to be a viable future for New Testament research as
in any sense involving a common or public endeavor, it too will
require our conversations with colleagues in this and other disciplines to show such knowledge—both of what can and must be
done and of what an intellectually humble and hospitable quest
for truth might rightly refrain from doing.

The wealth of diversity in the contemporary field of New Testament studies is undeniable. Only by renewing conversation about
a common object, however, can the many synchronic and diachronic approaches begin to render account of their intellectual
endeavor. No one seriously suggests that we should (even if we
could) return to the splendidly "objective" homogeneity of C. H.
Dodd and the classic heyday of *neutestamentliche Wissenschaft*.
Nor indeed would it be desirable to reimpose such a conflux of
methods and results. But a workable future for New Testament
studies as a publicly defensible intellectual discipline would seem
to depend on at least a minimal agreement about *what* it is we are
studying and *why*—and perhaps even on a loose demarcation of
what might constitute argument and evidence in the adjudication
of our competing theories and interpretations.

Our present difficulty, however, lies neither in the plurality of
results as such nor even in the coexistence of competing methods.
These predicaments similarly afflict—and indeed enrich—other
disciplines, as we saw earlier. It is tempting to think that New
Testament scholarship's challenges are somewhat greater because
of our lack of consensus about the very nature of the exercise
in which we are fundamentally engaged. Do not historians at
least in some sense study the distant or recent past, geographers
land and people, and economists the production and distribution

of wealth? But perhaps even that assessment merely pines after greener grass on the other side of the intellectual fence?[49] Be that as it may: despite the seemingly self-evident reference point of a field known as "New Testament studies," many of its practitioners today paradoxically seem to enjoy no such clarity. What is more, neither a consensus nor even a converging dialogue about the subject's nature and purpose is at present anywhere on the horizon. Such partial remedies as we have encountered seem on the whole to enhance the centrifugal and fragmenting tendencies of the discipline. And so, for all the reasons given, and despite all superficially vigorous hyperactivity of conferences and publications, on a sober assessment the possibility of a common future for New Testament studies as a recognizable discipline seems in grave danger of slipping out of reach. More optimistic appraisals tend to mistake busyness for achievement and seem invariably characterized by tunnel vision or wishful thinking.

Given the complex nature of these difficulties, we are unlikely to recover a coherent subject definition, whether integrated or piecemeal. The discipline as established in late-nineteenth- and early-twentieth-century professional societies, journals, and university departments[50] seems set to continue its disintegration into a number of entirely separate enterprises. A few of these fragments may manage to persuade their respective paymasters that they are worth continuing to fund in departments of theology or religious studies or in church-based institutions. Others will be farmed out to departments of archeology, classics, social anthropology, and women's or queer studies. A fair number are likely to wither away without much lament or sympathy from anyone else—a process

49. Damrosch 1995: 9 writes, "When campuses were more socially homogeneous than they now are, scholars could assume a certain collegiality of debate, or at least a certain peaceful coexistence, even given disciplinary rifts such as those between cultural and physical anthropologists or between philologists and New Critics. Equally, the philologists and the New Critics would at least all be studying texts, and would not have to contemplate tenure decisions concerning people whose research involves analyzing pornographic films and interviewing sex workers. To date, we have responded poorly to these changes, and the result has been an increase in factionality and coterie behaviour."

50. A concise account of this development is offered in Horbury 2003b.

that, in Britain and Europe at least, is already well under way. And perhaps in some respects such a sweeping of the Augean stables should be seen as a welcome development.

An understanding of the New Testament as the church's Scripture is indispensable, *even from a phenomenological (or "etic") point of view*, for any approach that aims to do justice to the texts themselves, let alone to their historic footprint. At a time when Christianity as a global faith is growing faster than ever before, it seems safe to predict that despite unresolved weaknesses this approach really *does* have a future, both in terms of its working relationship with other theological disciplines and in terms of its potential to integrate and offer an intellectual home to a variety of different methods. While this exercise is in fact extremely well placed to justify its existence and value within the university context, it also seems clear that to guarantee its credibility and integrity this project would need to be defined in some sort of relation to a broadly orthodox and catholic ecclesial base in which these texts in fact have their life.

Having said all this, however, the terms of our discussion here do perhaps allow for a certain amount of dreaming dreams and seeing visions. If the twentieth-century phenomenon of "New Testament studies" will assuredly go down the plughole, it seems in fact equally certain that the study and exposition of the New Testament will not. And so the remainder of this chapter will offer two proposals, each of which could potentially provide a methodological focus of integration for a newly conceived task of studying the New Testament, both for those who may approach it from a deliberately Christian theological perspective and for those who do not. The first of these proposals concerns the place of the text in history; the second, the place of the reader in the text. They are part of my own ongoing reflection on this topic and are here sketched only in rough outline, although both are also given additional elucidation in later chapters of this book.

Effective History and the Spectrum of Textual Intention

My first suggestion is that New Testament scholars explicitly adopt the history of the influence of the New Testament as an integral and indeed inescapable part of the exercise in which they are engaged. Among the numerous benefits of this move would be a more historically embedded understanding of not just the background but also the foreground (so to speak) of the New Testament, including its reception and understanding in the patristic period and beyond. Instead of perpetually going behind the text, the whole battery of historical-critical and synchronic tools could usefully be applied to approaching the New Testament from its meaning and function "in front of the text," where it was in fact heard and heeded (or ignored).

New Testament studies on this view could find a focus in the study of the New Testament as not just a historical but also a historic document. Its place in history clearly comprises not just an original setting but a history of lived responses to the historical and eternal realities to which it testifies. The meaning of a text is in practice deeply intertwined with its own tradition of hearing and heeding, interpretation and performance. Only the totality of that tradition can begin to give a view of the New Testament's real historical footprint, the vast majority of which is to be found in reading communities that, for all their diversity, place themselves deliberately "within the living tradition of the church, whose first concern is fidelity to the revelation attested by the Bible."[51] And conversely, that footprint, for good and for ill, can in turn serve as a valuable guide to the scope of the text's meaning and truth. (In chapter 6 below we will see how this might enliven our understanding of the interrelation between apostolic history and the living memory of that period.)

It is encouraging to note that increasing numbers of scholars are recognizing this concern as a desideratum for the future prospering of New Testament studies,[52] even if in both method and substance we surely have a long way to go. There is still much scope for fresh research here, of a kind that would build bridges both internally between synchronic and diachronic methods and also externally

51. So the phrasing of *The Interpretation of the Bible in the Church* in Fitzmyer 1995: §3.
52. Meeks 2005: 165 in his 2004 presidential address to the Society of New Testament Studies.

between biblical studies and historical theology as well as other disciplines. "Effective history" (*Wirkungsgeschichte*) could offer a shared and focusing interest for subdisciplines ranging all the way from textual criticism to narrative criticism, from biblical theology to liberationist deconstruction. In the process it would enrich and cross-pollinate a great deal of insular academic discussion—providing a broader and less ephemeral base by reviving long-forgotten insights of exegesis and application, but without being forced to give hostages to either a one-dimensional "history of the victors" or a revisionist veneration of all that was supposedly suppressed.

It is also worth considering whether a concerted move of biblical scholars into the area of effective history might not in turn persuade *systematic theologians* to think a little harder about the formal relationship of their discipline to biblical studies. In this regard, one might want to initiate a sustained dialogue about Eberhard Jüngel's frequent dictum that systematic theology is nothing if not consistent exegesis.[53] If that has any truth to it, what might be the effect on biblical studies of reconceiving both contemporary and historical theology primarily in terms of the interpretation and application of Scripture? Critically applied, *Wirkungsgeschichte* offers a hermeneutically sensitive and powerful instrument for interpreting both the reader and his or her text.

On a more pragmatic political note, effective history would at least enable New Testament scholars to give some substance to the rather hackneyed claim that their discipline matters because the New Testament is a canonical document of great influence.[54]

---

53. Jüngel frequently employs Barth's principle in lectures (e.g., in a course the present writer attended at Tübingen University in 1981–82); see also Jüngel 1995: 221. Note further Barth's *Kirchliche Dogmatik* 1.2; 1.1.261; 2.1.523–98; Welker 1997, 1999; Härle 1995: 111–39; Mildenberger 1991–93; and Jeanrond 1993: 99 (quoted in Watson 1997a: 74). Ebeling 1947 famously characterized church history as the history of the interpretation of Scripture.

54. So the largely phenomenological and descriptive account of New Testament studies developed in the Edinburgh inaugural lecture of Hurtado 1999: additional justification for tax-funded teaching of the New Testament at public universities is somewhat optimistically sought in the tolerance that such study fosters in a religiously pluralistic world. In early-twenty-first-century Britain at least, it is difficult to see evidence that nonconfessional study of the New Testament in departments of

It is of course true that to some degree the same hermeneutical diversity and incongruity observed in conventional New Testament studies would inevitably beset a study of *Wirkungsgeschichte* as well. We would not suddenly arrive at splendid agreement about the true meaning of the text in history. The effect, say, of Romans 13 in subsequent political thought, or of the Fourth Gospel in conciliar Christology, is by no means free from the sorts of historical, literary, and political ambiguities that affect the study of the New Testament itself. But the polyvalency of our findings would not as such invalidate the project. By agreeing to include in our remit the question of how the New Testament texts have in fact been read and lived, we would at least be engaged in a common exploration that would by definition embrace historical and reader-response concerns alike. Properly defined, such a study could in turn provide a commonly accessible subject matter and pool of insights for the different exegetical and hermeneutical approaches that are always likely to coexist.

The need for such a pursuit of effective history is in fact coming to be recognized by scholars from a great variety of theological presuppositions, including Ulrich Luz (1985–2002: 1.78–82; 1994: 23–38), Robert Morgan (1996b: 128–51), Heikki Räisänen (1992 and 2000a), and others.[55] The Evangelisch-Katholischer Kommentar series, particularly in its more recent volumes on Matthew (Luz 1985–2002 [ET 1989–]) and 1 Corinthians (Schrage 1991–2000), has become an important point of reference in this regard—although it remains unclear if its conception ultimately makes the text's effective history the handmaiden of historical criticism or if the two stand in some other, more constructive relationship. In English-speaking scholarship it is good to see such issues at last coming to diverse expression in the recently inaugurated Blackwell Bible Com-

---

religious studies and theology has noticeably enhanced tolerance for biblical beliefs and practices in society at large. There are better justifications for university-based religious study as appropriately pursued from either a purely phenomenological or a faith perspective, whether Christian or otherwise.

55. Note also Mitchell 2000 as an interesting case study on John Chrysostom; and see further Coggins 1993: 172, musing about the future of Old Testament commentaries. I ventured some preliminary reflections on Philippians under this heading in Bockmuehl 1995.

mentaries, with their emphasis on reception history.[56] At the same time, much systematic reflection about more and less appropriate *methods* of writing *Wirkungsgeschichte* will be necessary if work on these welcome initiatives is not to produce mere "scrapbooks" of effects, a cacophonous postmodern catalog of "voices" without communication, in dialogue with only themselves.[57]

Implied Readers and Their Readings

Wirkungsgeschichte suitably refined, then, might become one way of harnessing several existing approaches in New Testament studies to the question of how the ecclesially and culturally embedded text of Scripture historically connects with its reader—who is, de facto at least, almost always analogously embedded. Chapter 6 below will in part examine the question of whether the earliest effective history in the subapostolic period of living memory might constitute one possible focus for the connection between readers actually addressed by the text and the readings it actually engendered. My second proposal therefore picks up the widely debated hermeneutical concept of the implied or model reader, in order to derive from this a range of criteria for appropriate spiritual and theological engagement with the text.[58] While we cannot climb into the heads of the original authors to discover their intentions, the documents as they stand do manifest a patently religious outlook and bias. What is more, both in their original setting and in their ongoing stature as authoritative religious texts, they do assume and address a certain kind of audience; this may be regarded as part of what Umberto Eco influentially terms the *intentio operis* or textual intention, which in turn imposes constraints upon readerly whimsy (*intentio lectoris*).[59]

56. The promising first two volumes are Kovacs and Rowland 2004 on Revelation and (rather differently) Edwards 2004 on John. Rowland directs the Oxford Centre for Reception History of the Bible and has widely published on the reception history of the book of Revelation.

57. I am indebted for these images to Nicholls 2005.

58. See the seminal study of Iser 1974 and subsequent developments discussed in Moore 1989: 71–107 and Thiselton 1992: 516–23. For Umberto Eco's term *model reader*, cf. Eco 1981 and the discussion in Thiselton 1992: 526–29.

59. Eco 1992: 25, in explicit disagreement with Richard Rorty.

We must concede at once that a precise identification of that implied audience may in practice be elusive on the diachronic as much as on the synchronic level. And this idea in no way attempts to reintroduce old-fashioned hermeneutical objectivity through the back door. Similarly, to affirm that the texts envisage a certain *kind* of reader in no way denies the active contribution of that reader to the act of interpretation and the generation of meaning.[60] Nevertheless, a core of basic characteristics does emerge. My proposal is here merely sketched by way of five simple theses, designed not as a package but as a somewhat eclectic collection. Yet the overall outline should become clear. (The next chapter will explore more fully what this might entail for the implied exegete of the New Testament.)

The implied reader of the New Testament has a personal stake in the truthful reference of what it asserts. Although inevitably affected by a variety of significant social and political factors, he or she is in fact interested in the New Testament primarily for its apostolic witness to God's work in Jesus Christ and ongoing engagement with the world. Not just Luke but also Theophilus and his actual or implied clientele evidently care about "the *certainty* [τὴν ἀσφάλειαν] of the things about which you have been informed" (Luke 1:4). Similarly, 1 Peter consistently implies a readership that believes the truth of Christ "although you have not seen him" (1:8). The same observation could be repeated in the case of all other New Testament authors: it matters that these things are true—and at least to that (admittedly limited) extent it matters that they are true to history. Contrary to a widespread view among post-Enlightenment critics, in this respect the assumptions of early Christian authors and implied readers differ significantly from those of many gnostic and most other ancient mythologies, whose ultimate frame of reference tended to be attached to the realm of either timeless or cyclical verities.[61]

60. Since publishing an early version of this material (Bockmuehl 1998b), I have found many of these points nimbly and lucidly discussed in Vanhoozer 2002: 239–50; cf. more fully Vanhoozer 1998.

61. Contrast the characteristic phrase of Sallustius, the friend of Emperor Julian the Apostate, in his manual of neoplatonic paganism, *On the Gods and the World* 4.9; cf. 2.1 (Rochefort 1960): "These things never happened, but always are" (ταῦτα δὲ

More specifically, the implied reader has undergone a religious, moral, and intellectual *conversion* to the gospel of which the documents speak. Regardless of whether the texts instruct, narrate, or reprove, they implicitly assume that the readers share a stance of Christian faith, that they look to the Christian gospel as both formative and normative in their lives, and that they accept a Christian way of thinking about God, the world, and themselves. This perspective could again be demonstrated for all New Testament documents and applies even in those texts that criticize their readers or assume that they are under the influence of false teaching. As will be confirmed in chapter 3, it seems that, for the implied reader, interpretation is brought into striking proximity to the practice of prayer and of Christian intellectual and practical virtues. Almost without exception, the New Testament writings presume a close intellectual link between such conversion and true interpretation.

To the extent that this is even broadly correct, it also necessarily follows that the implied reader already takes a view of the New Testament texts as authoritative. For the individual documents this may initially mean no more than that they assume their readers assign to them an a priori precedence of seniority and trusted expertise in the matters of which they speak. One should therefore not overrate this third criterion, since a similar assessment could easily be offered for a host of works ranging from *The Cloud of Unknowing* to the *Wisden Cricketers' Almanack*. Beyond that, however, the stance of the texts themselves already presupposes a kind of canonical momentum, as Thomas Söding (1996: 165), among others, argues (and as we will see more fully in the next chapter). In that sense, too, the implied reader of the New Testament *as a whole* seems indeed to take the point of view that sees in the canonical side-by-side of authoritative but individually disparate or even contradictory documents a purposeful montage or kaleidoscope of meaning. That is to say, the very fact

---

ἐγένετο μὲν οὐδέποτε, ἔστι δὲ ἀεί). I am indebted to Martin Hengel for first drawing my attention to this passage. Against the fashionable view that (ancient and presumably modern) "Gnostics" are a mere construct of "essentialist" scholarship, see the shrewd critique of K. L. King 2003 by Edwards 2005.

of a biblical canon comes to represent an implicit invitation to an interpretative synthesis, to look for what is in common amid the all-too-evident tension and diversity—between the four Gospels, between James and Paul, between the New Testament and the Old, and so forth. (In a somewhat different vein, Gerd Theissen 2004 also draws attention to the way in which precisely the *tensions* and *contradictions* within the New Testament may offer implicit guidance to a theology of the New Testament.)[62] Almost invariably, the implied readers are ecclesially situated. Even where they are directly addressed as individuals (e.g., in Luke-Acts or the Pastorals), it is clear that the readers are never undefined and unrelated singularities. Instead, they are assumed to be related to the (or a) body of Christian believers, either as full members or at least as sympathizers and hangers-on. The chronological priority of the church over the New Testament has in effect surrounded the text with a cloud of presupposed ecclesial witnesses.[63] The implied reader does not approach the text as a disembodied rational self or as the post-Christian liberalism that is still sometimes taken for granted as the natural constituency of New Testament scholarship.[64] As Robert Jenson puts it somewhat

62. Theissen highlights clashes like those between history and myth, universalism and particularism, radicalism and relativism, meaning and facticity, and determination and freedom. Such contradictions should be seen not as irrationalist but as indicating a rational structure of religion, since these contradictions are intrinsic to human existence. On his reading, the later doctrine of the Trinity can be seen as an internally consistent processing of these contradictions: faith in the Son deals with the problem of suffering, faith in the Holy Spirit with the problem of human freedom. Both together constitute the core of the theodicy problem, which in such acuteness presents itself only in a monotheistic religion.
63. Cf. Pannenberg 1996. The church's priority over Scripture is asserted in Orthodox hermeneutics (Mihoc 2005); it needs to be balanced against Protestant admonitions such as that of Webster 2003a, who stresses that the word of God stands over against the church and is not its creation. See chapter 2 below.
64. As by Meeks 2005: 163–64, although he still acknowledges the basic appropriateness of a church-related constituency. Others like Houlden 2005: 186 favor a more radical divorce from theology and religion, so that New Testament scholarship can finally enjoy "parity of esteem" with other subjects devoted to answering questions that nobody is asking—a view to which he seems to think only representatives of "the large, looming iceberg of self-contained fundamentalist and aprioristic biblical interpretation" could possibly object.

provocatively, "The Bible exists only within the church" (1995: 89;
cf. further 2003a: 27, 36). That "church" is not as yet identifiable
in the New Testament in terms of the clear catholic synthesis of
Irenaeus and later writers, but it is already orientated around a
commitment to key apostles that would in due course determine
the shape of the New Testament canon.

Finally, the implied reader is evidently assumed to be "inspired,"
in the sense of Spirit filled. The documents appear to take for
granted that their envisaged reader will in the act of reading be
empowered to receive the saving divine reality of which the text
speaks (cf. Körtner 1994). What this also implies is that access
to the text's concerns is a function less of the detached acuity of
criticism than of engaged self-involvement. The existentialist understanding of the word of God by Rudolf Bultmann (1884–1976)
had at least this to be said for it, that it took seriously the extent
to which the New Testament texts presuppose readers whose interpretation and self-involving participation are inseparable parts
of the same process. The moment of understanding is at once the
moment of response.

If this previous point in particular sounds to New Testament
scholars unfamiliar and methodologically exotic, numerous passages nevertheless confirm that this is indeed the present-tense
perspective of the texts themselves. Three illustrations may suffice
out of the multitude of possible case studies. What sort of reader,
for example, is implied in the following statements? "Let anyone
who has an ear listen to what the Spirit *is saying* [λέγει, present
tense] to the churches" (Rev. 2:7); "and we also thank God constantly for this, that when you received the word of God which
you heard from us, you accepted it not as the word of men but as
what it really is [καθώς ἐστιν ἀληθῶς]—the word of God, which is
at work [ἐνεργεῖται] in you believers" (1 Thess. 2:13); "and *I am*
[εἰμί] with you every day [πάσας τὰς ἡμέρας] until the conclusion
of the age" (Matt. 28:20).

In these three cases and many others, the implied reader is
drawn into an act of reading that involves an active part on stage
rather than the discreet view from the upper balcony. Even the
most apologetic of texts never accommodate a properly neutral

or objectivist epistemology, as we saw earlier in Acts 10. Instead, the New Testament frequently claims that the realities of which it speaks are properly accessible only to believers like the implied reader (cf. Mark 4:11–12 and parallels; 1 Cor. 2:6–16). Even if other aspects of his program may be debatable, Peter Stuhlmacher's call for a "hermeneutic of consent" (1986: 205–25; 1995a: 7–8) is at least in this respect appropriate to the *Tendenz* apparent in the texts themselves (cf. further the important remarks of Nichols 1999: 163–67, citing Saward 1996). In other words, the texts appear to envisage a reader who freely explores certain lines of interpretation while avoiding others. There is a sense in which these texts already presuppose something akin to *Lectio Divina*.

My description of this second principle might appear to erect an insurmountable barrier between confessional New Testament studies on the one hand and secular, phenomenological approaches on the other. As Paul Griffiths (1999: 182) memorably puts it, "The gaze of those who practice *Religionswissenschaft* is systematically wrenched away from what they study and toward its epiphenomena by the very practices that promised to reveal the thing-in-itself." In that case, of course, my proposal could hardly be said to foster a consensus-building definition for a common conversation, but would merely accelerate the discipline's disintegration.

However, it may be possible to formulate a less polarized and less sectarian way of looking at this matter. There is no reason why this question of the implied reader could not be addressed from a wide variety of intellectual and experiential perspectives, including the purely secular and phenomenological, the poststructuralist or liberationist. In this sense the method could be broadly inclusive, at any rate of all those approaches that are prepared to recognize the textual implication of a certain sort of reader—regardless of whether interpreters are personally inclined to read "with the grain" of the text. Most of the approaches discussed in this chapter might have relevant things to say about how the New Testament relates to these implied readers. After all, it should not be only a Christian theological perspective that can recognize and comment usefully on the text's concern with truth: a plurality of viewpoints on that question dates back all the way to the first century.

74 SEEING THE WORD

Both the questions and the answers would no doubt continue to differ widely in this exercise, and there would still be all manner of disagreement about basic historical and ideological issues, including the implied readers' context, social setting, and so forth. Nevertheless, agreement on the relevance and importance of the implied audience would at least facilitate the discipline's ability to engage in a common conversation concerned with an identifiable subject. It might even help to address the chasm that continues to divide the scholarly from the ordinary reader of the New Testament, especially within a Christian context.

At the same time, an inquiry of this kind does admittedly posit a relatively sharp distinction between interpretations that seek to hear and expound the text and those that intend primarily to subvert it, whether doggedly or glibly. Such a distinction in itself is probably no bad thing and by no means inherently invalidates radical or revisionist readings. Nevertheless, there may well be a sense in which one cannot long pursue the question of how the text's implied reader relates to its truth before one stumbles over the more delicate issue of how the modern interpreter for his or her part relates to it. Bracketing this issue temporarily may well be an illuminating exercise; sidestepping it over the long term requires increasingly taxing and implausible amounts of fancy footwork.

Ultimately the implied reader may turn out to be in a better position to understand the text than the aloof or the distrusting interpreter. From that point of view, the influential Swiss exegete Adolf Schlatter (1852–1938) was perhaps right after all to criticize "atheistic methods" of theological study for their inability to perceive what is in fact clearly in the text (1969 [ET 1996; cf. Neuer 1996a: 211–25]).[65] Or, to use a Cambridge image that would have been equally intelligible to C. H. Dodd in 1936: there are limits to how much you can usefully say about the stained glass windows of King's College Chapel without actually going in to see them from the inside.

---

65. Daley 2003: 72 develops a similar point in contrasting contemporary with patristic exegesis.

2

THE WISDOM OF THE
IMPLIED EXEGETE

How fortunate is the reader . . . along with those who
hear and keep what is written here. (Rev. 1:3)

Chapter 1 led us down a rigorously critical path to the
sobering conclusion that conventional New Testament
scholarship as conceived in the nineteenth century and practiced
in the twentieth is today in a deep and quite possibly irrecoverable
crisis. At the same time, ironically, its two billion adherents make
Christianity today more widespread and more numerous than
at any time in history; and this fact alone assures the continued
endurance of the New Testament for the church. But what might
it take to reconstitute intellectually coherent study of the New
Testament at the beginning of Christianity's third millennium? It
is to this more positive and constructive task that the remainder of
this book hopes to make a contribution, beginning in the present
chapter with the question of how, from an exegetical and theological perspective, the exercise of human reason and of wisdom

relates to the interpretative role that the text itself appears to envisage for its implied readership.

In some professional societies and departments of religious studies, it still remains de rigueur to assert, as twentieth-century scholars often did, that Christian confessional and theological convictions have no place in serious study of the Bible. (This is a position, indeed, that such departments frequently affirm with far greater zeal vis-à-vis Christianity than for the teaching of any other religion.) Until not so very long ago, academic gatherings of biblical scholars witnessed regular recitations of the mantra that biblical exegetes must "set aside their presuppositions" and read the Bible "like any other ancient book." Quite how or why one might achieve either the former or the latter was never made entirely clear.

The mantras, if not perhaps the associated methods, seem less universally normative now: academic biblical study is widely acknowledged to be in a period of greater flux and change than perhaps at any time in the past couple of centuries. Nevertheless, this newfound diversity has not yet caused the demise of antitheological dogmatism. At its 2004 annual conference in Barcelona, the international Society of New Testament Studies received a presidential address entitled "Why Study the New Testament?" That up-to-date and circumspect account rightly presented a vision of the discipline as hospitable to a wide range of historical, literary, and ideological perspectives. At the same time, however, the learned society's president singled out New Testament theology (on an "anticognitivist" pretext) as needing "urgently" to be "erased" from scholarly discourse. In this way he managed to survey multiple rationales for the study of the New Testament without ever mentioning that document's undoubtedly central concern—Jesus of Nazareth (Meeks 2005: 167–68 and passim).

Here I claim no crystal ball with which to prognosticate. It merely seems worth considering from the outset that an interpretation of Scripture determined to operate wholly without reference to the historic Christian ecclesial context is particularly prone to misapprehend the nature and purpose of its very object of study. To read Scripture primarily as a document of ancient religion, or on the other hand as an instrument of repression and exclusion, is to commit at least one of two elementary category mistakes. The former approach confuses genesis with significance (the "genetic fallacy"), while the latter finds fault with a design for how it is abused and for what it is not. The former view resembles restricting the study of a Stradivari to the alpine softwood industry of Trentino; the latter, reducing the story of the instrument to who was prevented from playing or hearing it, how it was played badly, or what was *not* played on it. That sort of analysis can be intellectually respectable and may even have a certain complementary scientific or sociological interest. But it has by definition little light to shed on the instruments actually played by a violinist like Itzhak Perlman or a cellist like Yo-Yo Ma.

So too the historic significance of the ancient biblical texts is inseparable from the space they have inhabited, and continue to inhabit, as the canonical Scripture of the Christian church. Critical readings outside that perspective are of course possible and may often provide important historical, literary, or ideological insights. Inasmuch as Scripture's affirmations are public and universal rather than private or sectarian, they invite and benefit from open debate. And there are clearly questions that a self-consciously secular or otherwise non-Christian approach may ask rather well; some of them it may even answer well. Universities have often provided fruitful analysis of all sorts of texts whose implied readers are not critical scholars. Nevertheless, what such external discussions cannot manage is a "thick" historical reading of the biblical texts that accounts for the ecclesial dynamic of life and worship in which they have in fact had their existence.[1] For that, Christian Scriptures must be read within, or in deep dialogue with, their context of Christian faith.

What, then, is the shape of the interpretative stance the New Testament presumes? What use has its implied exegete for reason and wisdom in the investigation of the text?

1. Compare François Dreyfus's illuminating distinction between scriptural interpretation "in the church" (applied) and "in the Sorbonne" (scientific), as expounded by Nichols 1994: 35–38—although the nature and historic life of these texts makes it implausible to concede, as Dreyfus does, that in their own terms these two approaches are both *independently* valid.

What Place Reason?

The unprepared reader may be perplexed to discover the Bible's lack of explicit interest in critical reason and inquiry. The period of modernity, from its seventeenth-century rationalist beginnings all the way to its logical conclusion in late-modernity or postmodernity, has consistently privileged the autonomous rational subject in its approach to both epistemology and hermeneutics. From a biblical perspective, by contrast, one is tempted to quip that this has been an extended story of putting "Des-Cartes" before "De-Rrida." Of course it is not the case that Scripture has no interest in reasoning subjects; but it remains irritating to any self-consciously modern hermeneutic that critical reason seems here to play quite such an ancillary role as a tool for interpretation and understanding.

For Scripture, reason is indeed an innate and valuable creational gift; but it is fragile and profoundly corruptible. It is what Nebuchadnezzar lost when his arrogance drove him to insanity (Dan. 4:29–37). In the wisdom literature, human reasoning is seen as largely flawed by its inability to draw close to God. The preacher in Ecclesiastes stresses humanity's failure to find out the meaning of things, despite much searching; human knowledge is partial, fleeting, and perishable (Eccles. 7:24, 8:16–17; 9:10). The book of Wisdom shares a similar perspective on the nature of reason (Wis. 2:1–2, 21; 3:10). Sirach takes a more constructive view of the place of reason in understanding, although he never assumes that the exercise of reason in itself holds a promise of either truth or wisdom.[2]

The New Testament shares this skepticism about autonomous reason. Here the Greek word *dialogismos*, which classically denoted deliberation and reflection, is used more frequently to indicate doubt, anxiety, or evil and cantankerous thoughts.[3] We find here no treatise on the place of reason in human understanding:

2. Only 4 Maccabees with its clearly Stoic outlook offers a more explicit engagement with the nature of reason (λογισμός) itself. Devout reason rules over the emotions and is the guide to all the virtues.

3. See Luke 5:22; 6:8; 9:46–47; 24:38; Rom. 1:21; 14:1; 1 Cor. 3:20; Phil. 2:14; 1 Tim. 2:8; cf. Mark 7:21 par. Matt. 15:19; James 2:4; less clearly, Luke 2:35.

the perspective seems comparable especially to contemporary Jewish apocalyptic literature. The writer of *4 Ezra*, for example, reflects on a time of divine judgment when among all manner of ecological disasters both reason (Latin *sensus*) and understanding (*intellectus*) disappear along with the doing of righteousness (5.9–10). In the New Testament, Luke and Paul are perhaps the authors most concerned to demonstrate the rationality and public defensibility of Christian life and faith. But even their most famous statements of natural revelation in Romans 1 or Acts 17 make few claims for the ability of autonomous human reason to discover God's truth. Romans 1, in fact, affirms precisely the opposite: human minds have been darkened by the failure to acknowledge God, who alone reveals truth (Rom. 1:21; cf. Acts 17:29–31).

Reason and the skills it entails, therefore, are God-given qualities that we necessarily bring to the task of interpretation and understanding. But most of the biblical writers suggest quite clearly that what we bring is insufficient because it is in significant ways flawed and in need of redemption. The gospel neither affirms nor denies human reason as such, but stresses the need for a Christ-shaped *transformation* of our minds if we are to discern and embrace the will of God (Rom. 12:1–2; Eph. 4:17–24).

The Wisdom of God

Scripture has a good deal more to say about wisdom than about reason, although its perspectives are in some ways analogous. Classic wisdom literature does indeed give considerable encouragement to the pursuit of wisdom and the quest to understand the moral and scientific workings of the world. In these writings, such understanding is indeed open to patient rational scrutiny, and those who seek wisdom and righteousness will prosper in this life, while the wicked will perish. Wisdom may be found by those who seek her. Even in relatively conventional wisdom texts like Proverbs, Job, or Sirach, however, it is already beginning to become clear that reality may be rather more mysterious. However much one mines it in deep underground shafts, wisdom's true understanding of the ways of the Lord may well elude our human grasp (cf. Job 28).

In postexilic literature, wisdom is now prayed for rather than independently sought: she is received as a special gift of grace rather than merely found (Wis. 7:7; 8:21; 9:1-2, 4, 17). That gift is increasingly understood as granted by the Holy Spirit only to the elect people of God in the Torah—and in some quarters through apocalyptic visions of the heavenly mysteries (Bar. 3:9-4:4; Sir. 24:8; Wis. 18:4; *Letter of Aristeas* 200; Mishnah, tractate *Abot* 1.1).[4] For the psalmist, the one who meditates on the law of the Lord is like a tree planted by the life-giving water channels, which help it bring its fruit in due season (Ps. 1). In subsequent exegesis this image was increasingly adopted for the teacher of wisdom and Torah (Sir. 24:30-31; cf. 1QH 16 (= 8).4-26 and Dan. 9:1-3, 20-27). Ben Sira, moreover, distinguishes carefully between two types of scribes, the ordinary and the inspired interpreter (Sir. 39:1-8; cf. Wis. 9:16-17). In his work, as in some of the canonical and postcanonical psalms, wisdom assumes a setting that is as markedly *liturgical* as it is centered on the study of *Torah* (Ps. 1, 19, 119; cf. Sir. 24:10; 39:6-8). Wisdom condescends specifically to make her revealed dwelling in Israel (Sir. 17:11-14; 24:23; Bar. 3:36-4:1)—this is a conviction anticipated perhaps as early as Deuteronomy (4:6) but now widely shared in Palestinian and Diaspora Judaism. Its development in Philo's hermeneutics went on to be particularly influential for the Alexandrian fathers.

If this conception of revealed wisdom seems strikingly particular, its formulation is hardly more universalistic in the New Testament. The focus and personification of wisdom is now none other than Christ himself. In the Synoptic Gospels, especially in Matthew and Luke, he is both the teacher and giver of wisdom par excellence; and more than once he appears as the personification of the wisdom of God (Matt. 11:19; 12:42; 13:54; Luke 2:40, 52;

---

4. See also my discussion in Bockmuehl 1990: 24-31, 57-65; cf. further Gese 1984.

7:35; 11:31, 49; 21:15; cf. also Rev. 5:12, where wisdom is most properly the attribute of the Lamb). For Paul, most explicitly, Christ himself has become the power of God and the wisdom of God, in deliberate contrast to conventional secular definitions of wisdom. In Christ all the treasures of wisdom and knowledge are hidden, and it is God's wisdom, secret and hidden in Christ crucified, that has through the Spirit been revealed to those who love God. No other access to that wisdom is possible (1 Cor. 1:24, 30; 2:1–10; Col. 2:3). And this same Christ, the wisdom of God, is himself the message of the "God-breathed" Scriptures: in the context of faith in Christ they "are able to *make you wise* for salvation" (2 Tim. 3:15).

Biblical Interpretation and Theology

How then might such a scriptural view of wisdom and reason bear on the task of biblical interpretation and its place in Christian theology? That question seems in some respects singularly difficult to address in the contemporary context. Even now, only a minority of biblical scholars even bother to ask it; and a number of those who do seem to branch out into hermeneutical metadiscourses that effectively ensure rapid marginalization in a separate subdiscipline. Systematic theology, for its part, has often been similarly egregious in its studied avoidance of any formally articulated engagement with Scripture. With painfully few exceptions, it fails to pay so much as lip service to the idea that Christian theology depends in any palpable sense upon Scripture.[5]

In a number of studies John Webster has in recent years spelled out a vitally important "dogmatic sketch" of the place of Scripture

5. James Barr 1999: 586–604 treats D. Brown 1999 (cf. 2000) as the last and seemingly consummate example of how one might responsibly pursue biblical theology; but Brown in fact goes out of his way *not* to assign Scripture a distinctive role that sets it apart from other sources of revelation. David Ford reflects on Scripture in a number of works, sometimes extensively (1999: 107–65); but he has not thus far offered a considered rationale for its role in theology beyond the desire "to explore human flourishing in some of its richest forms" (107). Note, however, Ford 2001c, and see below.

in Christian theology; this is now without a doubt the clearest systematic-theological account of its kind. Webster's success in facilitating a genuine reintegration of the study of Scripture and of doctrine will depend to some extent on whether his subsequent work offers a concretely visible interpretative *implementation* of the dogmatic principles set forth in that sketch: "Doctrine serves Scripture, rather than the other way round"; and "theology guides the church by exemplifying submission to Holy Scripture as the *viva vox Dei*. . . . Reading Scripture is not only that from which theology proceeds, but also that to which theology is directed" (Webster 2003b: 115, 128–29 [and 3]).[6] This clearly sets out an agenda of great promise and consequence. It is also a program that no one theological subdiscipline can expect to implement on its own.

In a somewhat more applied vein, one of the clearest recent statements by a British systematic theologian is offered by Rowan Williams, who articulates a desire to place the historical and literal sense of Scripture squarely back on the map of Christian theology (2000: 44–59; cf. previously 1991). This is clearly a welcome change from what has all too frequently been systematic theology's engagement with Scripture on the level of a handful of favorite texts or of a second-order discourse that assumes exegesis to have nothing further to contribute to reflection about doctrine. In this sense Williams's statement represents a breath of fresh air and more than hints at the possibility of a renewed engagement with biblical study. Unfortunately, the promise of this appreciation for the literal sense seems attenuated by a postmodern mortgaging of what that sense might represent. Williams views integrated canonical readings like those of Brevard Childs as "uncritical" and "totalitarian" (Williams 2000: 44, 44nn3–4, 48) and as summarily

6. Oliver O'Donovan has long been a marked exception among British theologians in his sustained engagement with Scripture from the perspective of moral theology (1996; cf. 1994; 2005), even if to date he has not given an explicit hermeneutical account of this approach (note, however, his replies to each of the essays in Bartholomew et al. 2002). One might also mention the stated commitment of Gunton 1990 to "be read by Scripture"; but in practice this rarely surfaces in his theological writings (his systematic theology is said to be forthcoming in a posthumous edition by Robert Jenson and Christoph Schwöbel; this may in part redress the lacuna).

refuted by James Barr.[7] Those who resist the definitive foregrounding of conflict as their hermeneutical lens, and who do not "refuse to take the homogeneity of the canon for granted," are guilty of a "reaction against the literal" that leads to a "new totalitarianism of canonical context" (or else "arbitrary pluralism," which presumably is not Childs's problem). "Canons," we are assured in a restatement of Barr's exquisitely oxymoronic assertion, "do not give us hermeneutical guidance" (1983: 67, quoted approvingly in Williams 2000: 48n14).[8]

Williams's version of the *sensus literalis*, by contrast, privileges the principle of inner-canonical conflict by prioritizing ideological tension between biblical texts and between the allegedly suppressed voices of their redactional layers. By denying any hermeneutical precedence of canonical texts over this stratification of their textual genesis, like many biblical critics Williams on this account defers scriptural meaning in quasi-Derridean terms.

In itself, his emphasis on an *eschatological* hermeneutic of Scripture and theology is immensely valuable. In fact, however, most of the biblical evidence he adduces in support of his conflictual account lends itself just as fittingly to a dialectic of biblical theology read in the more explicitly teleological terms of the church's creedal (and exegetical) rule of faith, with no patent loss of hermeneutical "thickness" or "excess" of meaning. In that sense, Childs and other "canonical" or historically catholic readers would not perhaps have as much difficulty with Scripture's undoubted polyphony as Williams supposes. Even Walter Brueggemann, though he deliberately rejects the hermeneutical role of a rule of faith, rightly stresses that precisely the polyvalency of the *final form* generates ever-fresh exegetical riches.[9] In that sense, to regard the

---

7. Barr 1983 is the definitive critic of canonical criticism *tout court*, including explicitly its leading advocates Brevard S. Childs and James A. Sanders.

8. Quite what a canon might be intended to achieve other than to offer hermeneutical guidance is not spelled out.

9. "The interpretive project that constitutes the final form of the text is itself profoundly polyvalent, yielding to no single exegetical outcome, but allowing layers and layers of fresh reading in which God's own life and character are deeply engaged and put at risk" (Brueggemann 2002: 15). At the same time, Childs 2004: 315–17 (cf. 294nn3–4) offers a discerning critique of Brueggemann's assumption that a rule

literal sense as (for all its disruptions or tensions) "a resource of problem-solving clarity" and "simple truthfulness" has a rather better ecclesial pedigree than Williams's association of it with "the fundamentalist" (2000: 58) might imply—especially when one hears it in keeping with the apostolic rule of faith (which admittedly many Protestant fundamentalists do not).[10]

The Reformers and Protestant scholastics, too, read Scripture predominantly in that expectation of truthfulness, as did Thomas Aquinas (see below; cf. also Williams 2000: 47–48). Even someone as nonliteral as Origen evidently assumed some sort of "problem-solving clarity" to ensue from a programmatic statement such as "that alone is to be accepted as truth which differs in no respect from the ecclesiastical and apostolical tradition" (*First Principles*, preface).

Williams may of course be right to see the less conflict-driven hermeneutics of "at least some" (which?) canonical readings and of (all?) "fundamentalists" as either "totalitarian" or arbitrarily pluralist (2000: 48, 58). It is not clear, however, how the rejection of canonical coherence inherently facilitates a theologically superior, richer exegesis. To *prioritize* the ideological antagonisms in Scripture, rather than to *recognize* and *receive* them canonically, cannot in the end compensate for other, deeper deficits. Does not a hermeneutic explicitly predicated *against* the canonical grain inevitably entail the loss of a dogmatically articulate account of Scripture, as in any serviceable sense revealing the Word of Life? To acknowledge conflict within the canon, both diachronic and synchronic, is indeed to be faithful to its literary topography. To turn such conflict into the key hermeneutical driver, however,

of faith necessarily and unduly constricts the freedom of good interpretation (with reference inter alia to Brueggemann 2001).

10. In a personal communication (Sept. 23, 2003), Williams elaborates his conviction "that the questions we bring to Scripture are commonly far less important than the new world into which Scripture introduces us," which may entail "bafflements" no less than faith. The concern for "problem-solving clarity" is for him "manifestly a way of not taking time or growing through the process of exposure to Scripture." This is a helpful clarification, although it remains unclear to me why the desire for world-opening exposure to Scripture should be deemed absent in canonically minded readers trusting it, at least in principle, to address them with truthfulness and clarity.

threatens to starve an otherwise laudable and theologically elegant "discipline of Scripture" of its organic lifeblood.

In other writings Williams speaks memorably of a theological "grammar of obedience." In this discussion of the Bible, however, he does not appear to tether that obedience to a concrete *object*—be it a particular canonical (i.e., "nondeferred") doctrine, a positive moral command, or even a specific divine person to be *encountered and loved* through its pages (2001a: 11; note also 6–7).[11] To read Scripture in faith is indeed "reading it as moving towards or around a unifying narrative moment, the story of the work of Jesus" (2000: 56). Yet where classic accounts often resort to incarnational or sacramental analogies in relating the divine and human dimensions of that story,[12] Williams explicitly prefers the postmodern analogy of the competitive or subversive production of deferred meanings: the "literal sense" of Scripture teaches that "the unity of Christ . . . is learned or produced *only* in . . . the history of counter-claims and debate" (2000: 58 [emphasis added]; cf. 2001b). The Chalcedonian duality of Christ may be expressed in the fact that he is both "produced" in and through this history of conflict and yet also present to the believer as an unstable, "gratuitous and unpredictable moment" of that process.

This in turn, however, would seem to create certain difficulties for the imposition of "limits to pluralism." How can the preferential option for conflict escape its own dissolution into the sort of process-driven Hegelian dialectic that Williams explicitly disowns (2000: 56, 58)?[13] A phenomenological answer to that question soon self-deconstructs: if conflict is the essence rather than an unfortunate affliction, it soon makes little sense to see limits just because no known "historic Christian communities" de facto taught X or Y (thus Williams 2000: 56). Nonpractitioners of

11. A similar point about the apparent unspecificity of divine persons (and of core ecclesial assertions) is made by Jenson 2002: 368 in his review of Williams 2000.

12. Cf. p. 89n20 below.

13. Williams's resistance to final-form interpretation is further articulated in 2003: 220–23, with citation of Derrida on 220 and an explicit denial of both hermeneutical "genealogy" (the authenticity of the earliest form) and "evolutionism" (the normativity of the final form).

singular baptism or regular Eucharist, like other à la carte or "post-catholic" creeds ancient and modern, tend almost by definition to become non-"historic" (and unknown). Conversely, however, in the absence of limits to biblical pluralism it was precisely the "historic" Christian arguments that were the first to come to grief in late-twentieth-century Protestant conflicts and deferrals of meaning about issues ranging from the priesthood to nuclear weapons, from global trade to variosexual concubinage.

One is reminded of Cyril of Alexandria's conviction that to demonstrate the harmony of Scripture where others see only con-tradiction is the mark of a "peacemaker" who imitates the Son of God.[14] Williams adapts Ambrose's well-known dictum: "It was not by dialectic that God was pleased to save his people" (non in dialectica complacuit Deo salvum facere populum suum; On the Faith 1.42)—but Ambrose himself pointedly continues in the very next sentence: "For the kingdom of God consists in simplicity of faith, not in conflict of discourse" (regnum enim Dei in simplicitate fidei est, non in contentione sermonis).

We have drawn particular attention to Rowan Williams (and to some extent John Webster) as outstanding among leading dogma-ticians for his explicit and articulate attention to the problem of giving an account of Scripture's place in theology. More typically, one finds that the general neglect of this problem does not appear particularly troubling to the majority either of systematicians or of biblical scholars. David Ford's recent survey of British theology, for example, acknowledged Williams's unrivaled eminence in the field but tellingly confined its comments on biblical studies to a fleeting and patchy list of primarily New Testament practitioners (Ford 2000a: 426–27; cf. 2000b and 2000c).[15] (In a subsequent

14. Cyril of Alexandria, *Commentary on Matthew* frag. 38 (on Matt. 5:9) (ed. Reuss 1957: 164–65): "The peacemaker is one who demonstrates to others the sym-phony of the apparent conflict between the Scriptures [ὁ τὴν ἄλλοις φαινομένην μάχην τῶν γραφῶν ἀποδεικνὺς συμφωνίαν], as between the Old and the New, the legal and prophetic, or between the Gospels. For this, as one who imitates the Son of God [μιμησάμενος τὸν υἱὸν τοῦ θεοῦ], he will receive a spirit of adoption and be called a son of God." Also cited in Simonetti 2001–2: 1.88.

15. Francis Watson's absence is particularly surprising in the context, given works such as Watson 1997a and 1997b. James Dunn, Craig Bartholomew, and Andrew

public exchange with a leading exponent of Radical Orthodoxy, Ford rightly raised the place of Scripture as "the most radical question" [2001a: 397–99] to be asked of that movement. Despite its stated urgency, that highly apposite question did not appear to fall on hearing ears.)[16] Among leading German and American systematic theologians, too, it is still only a minority who continue to affirm the centrality of Scripture explicitly. Thus, Michael Welker is among those who follow Karl Barth in understanding dogmatics as "consistent exegesis" (konsequente Exegese; see p. 66 above), while Robert Jenson (1999), Gabriel Fackre (1984–87), and a few others (Jones and Buckley 1998; Soulen 1996; Greene-McCreight 1999; and Placher in Brueggemann 2002) affirm and practice this discipline in America—even if it rarely finds explicit articulation.

Biblical scholars, to be sure, are hardly in a position to exercise intellectual one-upmanship. Their professional societies frequently remain content to ignore the question of Scripture's witness to the truth. Whether deliberately or by default, most of their members perpetuate the eighteenth and nineteenth centuries' separation of Scripture from Christian doctrine and of the Old Testament from the New. In reading against the grain of catholic faith, moreover, biblical scholarship tends to take for granted a sectarian ecclesiology, presupposing unbridgeable discontinuity between the church who first believed and the church who now believes (so,

---

Lincoln are among a number of other unmentioned leading players with an arguable interest in Scripture and theology; more have emerged since 2000.

16. See Pickstock 2001, about whose reply Ford 2001b: 424–25 is charitable. Cf. similarly Nichols 2001: 289 on Radical Orthodoxy's neglect of Scripture's importance for Aquinas. Given the surprising insistence with which the historicity of the passion narratives is put to theological use in Milbank 2001, the possibility of a belated turn to Scripture cannot of course be ruled out. Other pronouncements, however, suggest that this may have merely illustrative effect, serving argumentative expediency for a point that would have been made in any case—purely from Jean-Luc Marion or Giorgio Agamben, if need be. Certainly no account or rationale is given of Scripture's place in theology; and subsequent pronouncements reinforce the impression of expedience rather than normativity (e.g., Milbank 2003, where "this biblical view of idolatry and sex fails to be radical enough," just as its insistence on worshiping "Israel's god, not other gods" shows the Bible "at its weakest"). Others note this apparent deficit; see Bauerschmidt 1999.

rightly, Jenson 1999: 98; cf. Green 2002: 10).[17] Once again this
is reminiscent of Adolf Schlatter's observations about academic
theology's "atheistic" methodological presuppositions (1969 [ET
1996; cf. Neuer 1996a: 211–25]).

Much theological and biblical scholarship does not now pay
even lip service to the once universal conviction that Christian
theology is at its heart an *exegetical* discipline, "whose defining
activity is exegetical reason" (thus Webster 2003b: 135). The early
church, by contrast, held this truth to be self-evident. For its theologians, the study of Scripture was both source and destiny of their
reason and wisdom: "Biblical interpretation was not a stage on
the way to the real work of thinking. Thinking took place through
exegesis, and the language of the Bible became the language of
Christian thought. Christian thinkers returned again and again as
to a bountiful spring from which, says Ambrose [*Epistle* 63.78],
flow 'rivers of understanding, rivers of meditation, and spiritual
rivers'" (Wilken 2003: 77; cf. 102, 53, 72).

Within academic biblical and theological studies, the departure
from this fundamental concern with the object, the *Sache* or *res*
of Scripture, finds its most striking illustration in the textbooks
we write, the course syllabi we teach, and the exams we set our
students. At a time when even to sympathetic outside observers it
often seems that modern theology is primarily the study of modern
theologians and New Testament studies is similarly preoccupied
with rearranging the deck chairs of New Testament scholars, it
could be a fruitful exercise to take time out and ponder what has
gone amiss. We have lost sight of the real thing: we are accus-
tomed and indeed trained to confuse text and commentary, the
Word and the words, contentedly submerging the former under
the deluge of the latter.

17. Jenson insists that "whatever hermeneutical gaps may need to be dealt with
. . . , there is *no* historical distance between the community in which the Bible appeared and the church which now seeks to understand the Bible. . . . The text we call
the Bible was put together in the first place by the same community that now needs
to interpret it" (1998: 98, emphasis original). This sort of "sectarian" ecclesiology is
nicely illustrated in a standard textbook like Malina 2001: 24, who treats the biblical
authors consistently as "a group of foreigners somehow dropped in our midst." Cf.
Bockmuehl 2002.

As a Protestant, the present writer may perhaps be permitted to observe that he has found no more theologically attractive statement of this quasi-sacramental place of Scripture in the church's faith than that of the 1994 *Catechism of the Catholic Church* (§§102–4):

> Through all the words of Sacred Scripture, God speaks only one single Word, his one Utterance in whom he expresses himself completely. . . .
>
> For this reason, the Church has always venerated the Scriptures as she venerates the Lord's Body. She never ceases to present to the faithful the bread of life, taken from the one table of God's Word and Christ's Body.
>
> In Sacred Scripture, the Church constantly finds her nourishment and her strength, for she welcomes it not as a human word, "but as what it really is, the word of God" [1 Thess 2:13]. "In the sacred books, the Father who is in heaven comes lovingly to meet his children, and talks with them."[18]

We must hasten to add that this position is not universally held even among Roman Catholic exegetes.[19] Neither, however, is it peculiarly Roman Catholic, but it expresses the spirit of historic Christian thought and life from its inception.[20] From that point

---

18. The concluding quotation is from *Dei Verbum* 21. The context of 1 Thess. 2:13 concerns not Scripture in general but the apostolic proclamation. Cf. also n. 20 below.

19. Among the range of more liberal Catholic views, contrast Schneiders 1991: 174, who prefers to describe the interpretation of the "revelatory" text as a more attenuated, "conscious effort toward life-integration through self-transcendence toward the horizon of ultimate value."

20. Note also the discussion of revelation and sanctification in Webster 2003b: 11–30. He approvingly quotes (28n26) the application to Scripture of the familiar Lutheran sacramental formula in Wenz 1996: 303, but never quite makes that analogy explicit himself (cf. Webster 2003b: 9). His carefully reasoned rejection of the "incarnational analogy" (22–24) is a significant contribution to current debate, especially when allied (as in the Pontifical Biblical Commission's 1993 document *The Interpretation of the Bible in the Church*; in Fitzmyer 1995) to a preference for historical over other kinds of critical methods. Webster's proposal would, however, need to be further articulated vis-à-vis the patristic and medieval pedigree of the *christological* analogy documented by Ayres and Fowl 1999 in their critique of the 1993 document; an important eighteenth-century advocate was Johann Georg Hamann. (Like the authors of

of view, to read Scripture is never some jumping-off point from which to abstract or develop the "real" intellectual or theological task: in its historic ecclesial setting Christian thought has intrinsically been a movement of the exegesis of Scripture that, in the context of eucharistic fellowship, invigorates believers and interpreters with the One who is the very Bread of Life. From an analogous but somewhat different point of departure, Jim Fodor uses another traditional variation on the feeding metaphor to characterize this text's life-shaping effect upon readers within the implied ecclesial *Sitz im Leben*: "By being read, Scriptures work themselves into the lives of the faithful just as yeast is kneaded into dough" (2004: 150). All this again points to the need for a "joined-up" approach to New Testament study to operate on a rather larger canvas than we have been used to, whether we claim to operate from a position of Christian faith, of another faith, or of no faith at all. To understand how the New Testament "works" requires one to take seriously where it resides, whom it addresses, and of what it speaks. That is no self-subsistent mellifluous dogma but a question open to public and interfaith engagement.

At the same time, it may be that Western Christian interpreters in particular are answerable to a singularly urgent ecclesiological imperative in all this. British church demographers, for example, suggest that on present trends, verily, some of us shall not taste death before they see the light of Christianity extinguished upon these islands (Brierley 2000). The Church of England's so-called Redundant Churches Division (*sic*) reports that nearly 1,700 of its churches were closed down between 1969 and 2004.[21] Where such sanctuaries are placed in the care of the Churches Conservation Trust (rather than sold for redevelopment as yuppie flats, shops, or nightclubs), visitors sometimes encounter tidy wall plaques inscribed with the devastatingly symbolic an-

---

that document, Ayres and Fowl 1999: 527–28 do continue to affirm a christological analogy of Scripture's two natures, *pace* Webster 2003b: 23n21.) The Eastern Orthodox view of Scripture's *sacramentality* is discussed in Mihoc 2005: 42–47.

   21. See http://www.cofe.anglican.org/about/churchcommissioners/redchurches (accessed April 17, 2006).

nouncement that "this church is no longer needed for Christian worship." Things are no better in much of Continental Europe, and depressing figures could equally be adduced for some parts of North America. As intellectuals, of course, we know that we all have knowledge, and we are well immunized against "lies, damned lies, and statistics." We can decide to sit back and wish away such an unpleasant demographic prognosis, evaporating it under a thousand qualifications. Nevertheless, it remains the case that for Christian theology in the West this may be a moment of truth. While secular and interfaith biblical study will inevitably have their own valid dynamic and agenda, Christian expositors at present face the more peculiarly pressing challenge of how to heed Scripture's self-presentation as revealing the Word of Life for the people of God.

The Implied Disciple: Hermeneutical Temptation and Discovery

For biblical and patristic writers, the interpretation of Scripture is itself subject to the hermeneutic of the Spirit. In their view prophetic truth is never just a matter of individual interpretation (2 Pet. 1:19–21; 1 Cor. 2:6–10), and the Bible in every part is imbued with the Spirit's "unfinished business." So also the meaning of the sacred text is understood not primarily by intellectual genius or once-and-for-all scientific dissection, but by the interplay of divine gift with human welcome and delight. In his extensive reflection on divine revelation in Psalm 119, for example, the psalmist applies to his object of study no transitive verbs of manipulation or deconstruction but only words of delight and discovery—of "invention" (*invenire*), in its original sense not of a creation de novo but of a "finding" that engages and transforms the "inventor." "I rejoice at your word," he says, "as one who has found [Vulgate *invenit*] great spoil" (119:162). God's word has become a lamp and a light for this interpreter's path (119:105).

Both Testaments of Scripture clearly presuppose such an interpreter. The implied interpreter of the Christian Scripture is a *disciple*, just as that disciple's implied reading of the text is its witness to the Christ.[22] In rabbinic Judaism, the most celebrated Old Testament encapsulation of this posture was Israel's response to the word of God at Sinai: "We will do and we will heed" (Exod. 24:7; cf. Babylonian Talmud, tractate *Shabbat* 88a). The object of biblical interpretation, in other words, is the interpreter as much as it is the text, and it is *performative* as much as it is hermeneutical.[23] Taking a cue from John Webster, one might even say that this presumption of discipleship involves the interpreter in the kind of theological anthropology that the New Testament itself envisages: it presumes to engage an exegete whose very interpretation serves, is judged by, and is *converted* to the evangelical truth that inheres in Scripture's witness.[24]

Part of theology's predicament, of course, has always been that even sincere interpretation of Scripture can be false as well as true; and this hermeneutical contest in turn goes to the very heart of the struggle between good and evil. It is here that transformed reason and Spirit-given, Christ-centered wisdom are essential to the Christian interpreter's task.

It is highly instructive to illustrate this point from Scripture's two pivotal stories of temptation—the temptation of Adam and the temptation of Christ. Both turn on hermeneutics,[25] to wit: a hermeneutic of suspicion, detachment, and *Sachkritik*. Interpretation in each case reduces the divine address to an object for an analysis as if from an Archimedean point outside, by staking a pseudoempirical claim to objectivity.

22. This is not to deny the complementary insight of those like Green 2002: 20 who stress the role of Scripture in effecting the interpreter's theological conversion. Note similarly Vanhoozer 2002: 255–56; cf. further Hays 1999 on the hermeneutical theme of a "converted imagination," and Williams 2000: xvi, who writes eloquently about "the inescapable place of repentance" in all theology.

23. This of course is widely acknowledged; cf. Lash 1986a; S. Barton 1999; and Gunton 1990.

24. See Webster 2003b: 88–89, 101; cf. 2003a: 124 and 2003c: 254. The inherency of evangelical truth in Scripture is also stressed in Brueggemann 2002: 11.

25. Cf. also the apposite remarks by Oakes 2001 about Fish 2001 on Milton.

The Temptation of the First Eve and Adam

Enter the serpent in Genesis 3. Step one is to eliminate the ecclesial reception of the word of God and to place interpretation in the hands of the autonomous reasoning subject, isolated from the worshiping community: the serpent speaks to Eve, not to Eve and Adam, let alone to their fellowship with the Lord God himself who walks in the garden. Thus the living word of God is rendered harmless as the object of solitary analysis, a mere cadaver except as energized by the expert's alchemy of method (cf. Lundin et al. 1999: 41).

Step two is to eliminate the *sensus literalis*. When in doubt, relativize. The tempter caricatures *what* God said in order to expose it as rationally suspect: he muses provocatively, "Did God indeed say, 'You shall not eat from *any* tree in the garden'?" (Gen. 3:1). Eve rises to the bait. Responding with cavalier forgetfulness of God's actual words, she produces a garbled and legalistic rendition of the divine command that all but eliminates divine grace and greatly exacerbates the severity of this prohibition. What God *really* commanded was to "eat *freely* of *every* tree in the garden,"[26] which presumably includes the tree of life, set explicitly "in the midst of the garden" (2:9), and excepting only the tree of the knowledge of good and evil, which is not (2:16–17). Eve's mangled version is that while "we may eat of the fruit of the trees," God has forbidden "the tree that is in the middle of the garden"—not only to eat, but even to *touch* (3:1–2). Oh, but that seems altogether unreasonable, plainly unmasked for what it really is: a coercive, controlling, authoritarian imposition! Reduced to autonomous reason, Eve finds the devices and desires of her own heart seductively co-opted by the serpent's hermeneutics.

Having safely established the external viewpoint from which the divine command is exposed as extreme and repressive, the serpent now turns to allegorize and demythologize the judgment that supposedly follows disobedience: "Surely you will not die; God himself knows . . . that your eyes will be opened and you will

---

26. The Hebrew of Gen. 2:16 stresses "every tree of the garden" (*kol 'ets*) and the emphatic infinitive absolute "you will surely eat" (*'akhol to'khel*).

be like God" (3:4–5). In this hermeneutical Wonderland, words do not mean what they appear to mean, let alone *more* than they appear to mean. Instead of signifying, they represent something different altogether. Expertly massaged by the parasitic allegory of deconstruction, "texts demand nothing but yield everything under the proper caresses," allowing us to play them whimsically as a computer game and thus, as Roger Lundin puts it, "to feed off tradition without replenishing its stores, to consume the spiritual and ethical harvests of past ages without planting new crops for future generations" (1999: 41).

Part of this allegorical deconstruction involves the substitution of an immanent consequentialism for divine judgment, a classic reductionist move in moral hermeneutics ever since. Things are wrong not because they violate a sacred principle or divine mandate, but only inasmuch as their immediate consequences can be shown to be unpleasant or undesirable.

Step three is simply to move in for the hermeneutical kill. Eliminating the divine command in this fashion enables the reprogramming of the human moral subject along the classic lines of a lust for a forbidden object—material consumption of it, esthetic possession of it, and knowledge of it as power: "Seeing that the tree was *good for food*, and a *delight to the eyes*, and *desirable to make one wise*, she took of the fruit and ate" (3:6). Adam is simply content to follow the impeccably footnoted precedent, supported by the unanswerable weight of public opinion—and the rest, as they say, is salvation history.

The Temptation of the Second Adam

Contrast this with the scriptural interpretation in the temptation story of Matthew 4. The recurring pattern in the tempter's approach is chilling. Step one: challenge the individual interpreter as autonomous reasoning subject, isolated from the ecclesial corrective of the chosen people reading Scripture. After fasting forty days and nights, Jesus is famished. Only *then* the devil comes to him. For Jesus too the wilderness is a place of vulnerability, but it is not inherently the devil's domain: as Luke (4:1, 14) makes even clearer than Matthew or Mark, it is in fact the Spirit in fullness who leads Jesus into (literally "in") the desert and the Spirit in power who leads him out of it. In Jesus's case, sanctified solitude may also habituate him to hear the word of God *over against* the community.

And then the familiar step two: eliminate the plain sense of the divine word by expropriating it for a seemingly more objective (but in fact only more self-interested) viewpoint. "*If* you really are the Son of God . . ." (Matt. 4:3). A divine Son surely is and does all that pleases him! Never mind that the baptismal heavenly voice in fact affirmed Jesus to be the Son who is and does all that pleases *the Father* (3:17). But unlike his foremother in the garden, this Son does *not* rise to the bait and does *not* produce the invited distortion of what God has "really" said. Instead, the Word himself turns to find in Scripture the true representation, the textual icon, of God's life-giving and all-nourishing presence: "Man . . . shall live by every word that proceeds from the mouth of God" (4:4).

Having failed on that score, the tempter nevertheless raises the stakes. He rolls steps two and three into one, all the while flattering the human craving to know and be like God. First is an attempt to hijack Jesus's own hermeneutics. Resorting to Scripture is a game at which the slanderer and distorter too can play: "If you are the Son of God, throw yourself down" from the house of God (4:6): let yourself go, for Scripture itself promises you the power to do so. Jesus resists this blatant estrangement of the *sensus literalis*, which seeks to make God's word deny itself and malign its author: "Again it is written, 'Do not put the Lord your God to the test' " (4:7).

All else having failed, the appeal to Scripture is now quietly abandoned: ultimately the tempter knows that by patient and persistent attention to Scripture his point will never be winnable. He returns therefore to the appeal that clinched his victory in the garden: the human lust for power, for material and esthetic possession: "All the kingdoms of this world and their splendor" I will give you (4:8–9).

But just when the tempter's ever grander self-deification dispenses with Scripture altogether, Jesus dismisses him by the simple

truth of its most basic affirmation: "It is written, 'You shall worship the Lord your God and serve him only'" (4:10).[27]
By this hermeneutical reversal of the fall, faithfully sustained through the depths of Gethsemane and the cross, the risen Jesus has become the key to Scripture itself. This is recognized by all the New Testament and patristic writers. And it receives its most explicit affirmation on the road to Emmaus, as Walter Moberly recently argued (2000: 45–70). "Beginning with Moses," the crucified and risen wisdom of God shows "all that the prophets declared" by the Spirit to speak the one word of God in Jesus Christ (Luke 24:25–27). Here Scripture and theology cohere in an interpretation that gives life to the people of God, causing their hearts to burn within them (24:32). Only reason thus renewed by the Spirit can behold the beauty of God.[28]

Aquinas as a Disciple of Scripture

Lest all this sound a little remote to exegetes and dogmaticians alike, it may be helpful to close with a picture of one who was both—and who has regained increasing importance in recent theological debate. A Flemish engraving depicts a scene first mentioned in the early-fourteenth-century lives of St. Thomas by William Tocco and Bernard Gui:

> Once when Thomas had wrestled with the meaning of a certain passage in Isaiah for three days of prayer and fasting, one night his friend Reginald heard two men speaking with him. After they left,

27. All three of Jesus's responses are thus quotations from Deuteronomy: 8:3; 6:16; and 6:13.
28. Basil of Caesarea (ca. 330–79) writes: "The mind that is suffused with the Godhead of the Spirit [ὁ μέντοι τῇ θεότητι τοῦ πνεύματος ἀνακραθεὶς νοῦς] . . . gazes on the divine beauty, as far as grace grants it and its nature receives it. . . . The judgment of our mind is given us for the understanding of the truth [δέδοται ἡμῖν τὸ τοῦ νοῦ κριτήριον εἰς τὴν τῆς ἀληθείας σύνεσιν]. Now our God is truth itself [ἡ αὐτοαλήθεια]. So the mind's primary purpose is to know our God—to know him, that is, insofar as it is possible for the infinitely great to be known by the minuscule [ὡς δυνατὸν γνωρίζεσθαι τὸν ἀπειρομεγέθη ὑπὸ τοῦ μικροτάτου]" (Epistle 233.1–2 [Courtonne 1957–66]).

Cum pro senfu loci alicuius in Ifaia triduo ieunijs et orationibus inftitiffet, nocte quadam focius eius Reginaldus duos cum eo loquentes audiuit: quibus abeuntibus, focio ad fe vocato, commentaria in eum locum expedite admodum dictauit. Quo facto obnixe eum Reginaldus rogauit; vt qui illi fuffet, cum quibus tanto tempore locutus erat, aperiret: victus Thomas ait fuffe fanctifsimos Petrum et Paulum Apoftolos, qui eum vna cum Deipara Virgine in dubijs faepius edocere foliti erant.

Thomas called his friend and promptly dictated the commentary on that passage without difficulty. When this was done, Reginald pressed him to explain with whom he had spoken at such length. Thomas conceded that they had been the holy apostles Peter and

Paul, who along with the Virgin Mother of God often used to teach
him in difficult questions.[29]

For all the evident hagiography of this portrait, it does embody
several aspects of the interpretative stance that I have argued the
New Testament text itself elicits. Our portrait embellishes this
stance in relation to a theological giant whose commitment and
towering importance *as an interpreter of Scripture* has too often
been ignored. This picture shows a master of systematic theologians employing renewed human reason in the demanding and
persistent labor of exegesis, a task that does not yield its treasures
to the fair-weather inquirer in ready-made confessional sound-
bites. When the intellectual going gets tough, Thomas the exegete
is not free simply to fabricate the conclusion he needs or favors.

29. This paragraph is the summary caption accompanying Veen 1610: pl. 18,
as reproduced in Thomas Aquinas 1966: iv (my translation). See the longer accounts
in the lives by Tocco (chap. 31) and Gui (chap. 16), which date around 1319–25 (cf.
Foster 1959: 6–11). Aidan Nichols kindly drew my attention to Gui's version in Foster
1959: 38–39 (cf. also 70–71nn47–48), reproduced here for convenience:

> On one occasion it was an obscure text of Isaiah that puzzled him, and so much
> that for many days he could get no farther with it, though he prayed and fasted
> assiduously, begging for light to see into the prophet's mind. At last, one night
> when he had stayed up to pray, his socius overheard him speaking, as it seemed,
> with other persons in the room; though what was being said the socius could
> not make out, nor did he recognize the other voices. Then these fell silent and he
> heard Thomas's voice calling: "Reginald, my son, get up and bring a light and the
> commentary on Isaiah; I want you to write for me." So Reginald rose and began
> to take down the dictation, which ran so clearly that it was as if the master were
> reading aloud from a book under his eyes. This continued for an hour, and then
> Thomas said: "Now go back to bed, son; there is little time left for sleep." But
> Reginald fell at his feet and said: "I will not leave this room until you tell me who
> was speaking with you." And this demand he made calling on the name of God.
> Yet did Thomas refuse it; to grant it, he said, would serve no purpose. But Regi-
> nald continued urging and begging him, until at last Thomas—not wishing even
> to seem indifferent to the Name by which Reginald was adjuring him—said, while
> tears ran down his cheeks: "My son, you have seen the distress I have suffered
> lately because of that text which I have only now finished explaining. I could not
> understand it, and I begged our Lord to help me, and tonight he sent his blessed
> apostles to me, Peter and Paul, whose intercession I had also begged for; and they
> have spoken with me and told me all I desired to know. But now, in God's name,
> never tell anyone else of this as long as I live. I have told you only because you
> adjured me so strongly."

What is called for is patient observation and attentiveness: for the disciple there are methods to embrace and methods to shun. Notably, too, Thomas here engages the text of the *Old Testament*, reading it as Christian Scripture.

This picture of the saint, then, shows Thomas as an ideal interpreter, exemplifying the wisdom of the implied exegete. He evidently "burns the midnight oil" at his desk—in a kind of sanctified *solitude*, like that of Christ or of Saints Anthony or Jerome in the wilderness. At the same time, paradoxically, Thomas is prompted and accompanied in this evidently *communal* and *ecclesial* task by the twin apostolic witnesses to the Jews and to the Gentiles—Peter and Paul, regarded since antiquity as having jointly laid the foundation of the church and thus as representing the historic link with Christianity's origins. Even in the critical solitude of his study, in other words, Thomas works not in splendid detachment but as a disciple in the company of the saints who preceded him as readers (and writers) of the sacred text.[30] In that work, finally, he is further encouraged and prompted by the testimony of a third fellow disciple—the Mother of God, the new Eve whose faithful, self-giving ministry of pointing the world to her Son both illumines and exemplifies the implied exegete's task.

---

30. Cf. also S. Barton 1999: 199–202 on the saints as fellow "performers" of Scripture.

3

HUMPTY DUMPTY
AND THE RANGE OF
IMPLIED READINGS

I n chapter 2 we examined the nature of interpretation and the interpreter, as they are envisaged by the New Testament itself. Our conclusion was that the implied reader of the New Testament is a disciple, and that wisdom and theology are on that supposition a function of scriptural exegesis within, or in correspondence with, a strongly ecclesial frame of reference.

With this in mind, in the following pages we now turn more briefly to a kind of postscript on a subject that the last chapter repeatedly flagged up but did not explicitly address. Even if we grant that the New Testament itself assumes a Christian reader, do not the tensions and conflicts between its different authors make a mockery of the notion that a canonical reading could meaningfully guide interpretation and theology, or indeed that a New Testament theology is possible as anything other than a chronicle of revision and dissent?

In the halls of postmodern learning it has long been de rigueur to assert that classic Christian affirmations like the canon or the creeds are mere symbols of the victors in a political battle for supremacy—a battle fought "with considerable strong-arm tactics," using oppressive power to silence "marginal voices" and "lost Christianities."[1] Inasmuch as they bother with historical questions at all, interpreters of the New Testament have been brought up to insist that any proper understanding depends on a recognition of the sociopolitical controversies and literary dependencies that lie behind the genesis of each biblical document. These are home truths so familiar, so basic that they slip down effortlessly, like James Bond's unstirred martini; we teach our students to recite them with their prayers before they go to bed at night. Surely no one in their right mind could possibly question them?

Nagging doubts have, alas, begun to intrude upon my reflection on this seemingly self-authenticating consensus.

As far as the creed is concerned, can we *really* believe it to be of significant consequence to congregations from Little Snoring to Lusaka that seventeen centuries ago the momentous formulations of Nicea happen also to have flattered the convictions, and the undoubtedly mixed motives, of the party that eventually triumphed in long-forgotten feuds? For all the interest of its historically contingent, socially fraught, and politically dubious origins, might it not rather be the case that the creed came over time to be all but universally adopted in the church precisely because successive generations found it to be the most serviceable expression of essential Christian doctrines—that is to say, truths accepted as being of transcendent and abiding significance rather than exclusively tied to a particular culture, clique, or context?[2]

1. So Rodd 1997 about the Nicene Creed; note also the titles of Ehrman 2003b and 2003c.
2. The content of the ecumenical creeds was regarded as "apostolic, indeed as the apostolic legacy par excellence and as the quintessence of Holy Scripture" (Harnack 1935: 190).

And if this is even vaguely true for the creed, must not an equivalent judgment apply a fortiori to the case of Scripture? At the end of the day, when everything is said and done about the genetic vagaries of the New Testament canon's formation, it remains an equally *historical* phenomenon that the church catholic came to recognize in these twenty-seven books the normative attestation of its apostolic rule of faith (cf. similarly Stuhlmacher 1992–99: 1.34, also cited in Balla 1998: 11). What if the storms and contradictions, while of course still visible as if in the tree rings of the New Testament canon, have their real significance precisely not in themselves, but only in the settled deposit of the final product, which the Great Church accepted in toto as definitive revelation of the Word of Life for the people of God? And what might be the implications of such ecclesial realism for the exercise known as New Testament theology? Here we will consider these and related questions by offering first a brief historical reminder of "how we got here" before turning to the question of whether the shape of the New Testament itself may outline an implied interpretation of its own theology.

All the King's Horses and All the King's Men

A search for publications on the New Testament whose titles contain the word *theology* would soon uncover a proliferation of works on the theologies of individual authors and particular documents or even of the various layers of a hypothesis called Q. Talk of a "whole New Testament" or "whole Bible" theology, by contrast, is still widely suspected as a retrograde attempt to put the clock back to a point before "biblical theology" shattered, rather like Humpty Dumpty, into a thousand pieces. Our studied desire to privilege the diversity of "voices," heard or unheard, leads us to see the New Testament as a cacophony of irreconcilably conflicting interpretations and pleas for power. And even though a number of "horses and men" have in recent years been seen trying to put such theology back together, it seems fair to say that centrifugal pressures and expectations remain in the ascendancy. The dominant assumption continues to be that if it is possible at all, the legitimate exercise of New Testament theology can amount at best to a phenomenological (and historical) chronicle of discrete New Testament theologies.[3] The logic of that position naturally leads to the notion that even a "Pauline theology" must give way to theologies of individual Pauline letters, as the Society of Biblical Literature attempted somewhat unsuccessfully to show in the 1990s (Bassler et al. 1991–97; cf. Bockmuehl 1997: 41–42).

But how did we get to this point of apparently irretrievable disintegration? When it was first introduced, the term *biblical theology* identified a project that was regarded as the crown of biblical studies: beginning in mid-seventeenth-century Germany, "biblical" or "exegetical" theology expressed the Pietist-led concern to show the biblical foundations of the classical loci of Christian doctrine, in part as a critical tool against the dominant interests of the Protestant scholastics. The eighteenth century then reinvented this same project in terms of a need to study the biblical texts in explicit *isolation* from the body of Christian doctrine. Thus the famous 1787 inaugural lecture of Johann Philipp Gabler (1753–1826) programmatically distinguished the strictly descriptive, historical discipline of biblical theology from the didactic task of dogmatic theology.[4] This program undeniably had a liberating effect on serious study of Scripture. Yet before the eighteenth century was out, scholars were on these same grounds calling for the separate study of the Old and New Testaments. By the time of F. C. Baur (1792–1860), the theology of the New Testament was rapidly being reduced to the history of the doctrines discernible within its various documents. This "farewell to theology" was raised by William Wrede (1859–1906) to the level of a program-

3. Following Bultmann 1951; cf. Berger 1995b; Kümmel 1974; Räisänen 2000a; Strecker 2000; and Hübner 1990. The program of Stuhlmacher 1992–99 and 2002b, by contrast, develops a historical treatment that nevertheless attempts to overcome the problems of piecemeal phenomenology. Similarly, Caird 1994 proposes a constructive "conciliar" approach to the different authors of the New Testament; this is more recently pursued in an interesting "dialogical" direction by Vouga 2001.

4. See Sandys-Wunsch and Eldredge 1980 for translation and commentary on this piece. Cf. also the discussion in Stuckenbruck 1999.

matic agenda[5] and lent additional historical pedigree by Walter Bauer's widely accepted arguments about the ubiquity of heresy (see ET in Bauer 1972, originally published in 1934, with 2nd edition in 1964). This perspective in fact remained dominant throughout the twentieth century, even if some lamented what they regarded as the inadequate implementation of Wrede's program.[6] It has been a virtually normative assumption that New Testament theology is possible only as a serial compilation of its authors' diverse theologies. This of course is simply in keeping with Werner Georg Kümmel's justly famous account of modern New Testament scholarship, which insists that "it is impossible to speak of a scientific study of the New Testament until the New Testament became the object of investigation as an independent body of literature with historical interests . . . without dogmatic or creedal bias" (1973: 13).

True, the 1960s saw a number of short-lived attempts to revive a unitary biblical theology along various thematic lines;[7] but by 1970 it had become clear that in its synthetic bird's-eye view of biblical history this effort was dead in the water, on both historical and theological grounds (cf. Childs 1970). Several important efforts at a "biblical theology of the New Testament" have indeed been published since then,[8] but their sometimes unusual and in any case mutually incompatible hermeneutical presuppositions have not thus far won widespread support.

There are good reasons to consider a *return* to the classic expressions of biblical theology neither possible nor desirable. That

---

5. See Morgan 1973; the quotation is from Räisänen 2000a: 21.

6. So Räisänen 2000a: 21–27, 142–50, although he acknowledges the achievement of Theissen 1999. Cf. the discussion in Balla 1998: 10–11 and Matera 2005.

7. A search for "biblical theology" in titles of books published in the 1960s will reveal numerous examples; among the better known authors were G. Ernest Wright, Leopold Sabourin, Robert C. Dentan, Krister Stendahl, Xavier Léon-Dufour, Joseph Blenkinsopp, and William S. LaSor.

8. Childs 1992 (cf. also the compact program outlined in Childs 2002); Stuhlmacher 1992–99, 2002b; and Hübner 1990. Scobie 2003 offers the most recent attempt at a constructive "whole-Bible" theology, while Alexander and Rosner 2000 even propose a full-scale dictionary. See further Hafemann 2002 as well as Green and Turner 2000 for an assessment of the current state of play in New Testament theology.

movement's blanket historical judgments failed in practice to be
sufficiently alert either to the Bible's historical diversity or to the
perspectival (and equally historical!) question of how a given
individual's unprecedented modern construct relates to the Bible's
reception in the church's life and doctrine.

It may be possible to parry postmodern attacks on the "grand
narrative" or "metanarrative" that is almost by definition implicit
in any approach to biblical theology, even to allow Scripture's
story of noncoercive divine self-giving to turn such charges back
upon a philosophy whose inability to be self-critical can appear
distinctly imperial in its ambitions. Indeed, postmodernism's attack on biblical theology may with the passage of time turn out to
be as ill fitting and ineffectual as the supposedly fatal threat once
posed to it by modernist programs of demythologization.[9]

Be that as it may; for both modernist historical criticism and
postmodernist political deconstruction, the question of the New
Testament's unity tends to be endlessly deferred in favor of ever
more disparate analyses of its diversity. Meanwhile the continuing
assumption even in theologically conservative circles often appears
to be that biblical theology necessarily involves a kaleidoscopic
montage of Scripture's individual building blocks, each assessed
in its own particular historical context and setting.

Humpty Dumpty Sat *Where*? The Setting of New Testament Theology

How, then, might we begin to look forward? One continuing
approach in recent years has been to *welcome* the subordination
of New Testament theology to the more manageable phenomenology of early Christian communities, their settings, writings, and
beliefs. This sort of study from an "etic," outsider's perspective has

9. One such critique of the postmodernist challenge, focusing on Nietzsche,
Heidegger, and Derrida, is that of Ingraffia 1995. Although Bultmann's demythologiz-
ing program won relatively few wholehearted adherents in Britain, liberals like A. R.
Vidler (1965: 94, cf. 88–95) joined in celebrating what they believed to be the fatal
wound it had dealt to "the fashion of biblical theology" as expounded in Britain by
E. C. Hoskyns and others.

the advantage that it could take its place alongside other worthy efforts such as social history, text-linguistics, and deconstruction, all of which seem less obviously hamstrung by the problem of diversity. Thus John Barton continues to stress: "Despite the best efforts of biblical theologians and canonical critics to show that the Bible exhibits, or can or should be read as if it exhibited, an impressive unity, anyone who has engaged in the detail of modern biblical study is likely to have a stronger sense of its variegated and untidy character" (2003: 26).[10]

To sweep unity under the carpet of diversity offers the additional benefit that it more readily placates the contemporary champions of a patently anachronistic but surprisingly resilient idea discussed in chapter 1 above: questions of the text's metaphysical reference and confessional relevance must have no place in a university-based study of the New Testament writings (Davies 1995 and Räisänen 2000a).

To be sure, careful phenomenological study plays a vital and indeed theologically indispensable role in highlighting the distinctive contributions of each of the biblical documents. Only by faithfully observing and following the contours of the scriptural map can we expect to understand what it represents; and a fear of tension or contradiction can have no place in a high view of Scripture. Literary and reader-oriented synchronic approaches have in recent years offered significant new (or newly rediscovered) interpretative insights in this respect, not least about the intrinsic polyvalence of the biblical text (cf. Brueggemann 2002: 15, quoted above).

Much of this concern is good and true. Here, however, I wish to suggest that it may be time to consider a complementary, balancing approach that is no less historical or phenomenological.

10. This statement's implied slight on the professional competence of authors like Brevard Childs seems both unmistakable and incomprehensible. I am similarly puzzled by Barton's recruitment of the rabbis to his cause: Ben Bag-Bag's counsel about the Torah, to "turn it and turn it, for everything is in it" (Mishnah, tractate *Abot* 5.22), is said to signify the sort of delight in the Old Testament's "sheer diversity" (presumably at the expense of its unity) that is in fact without patristic or indeed rabbinic parallel (J. Barton 2003: 22, 26).

There is in fact a strong case that the New Testament text itself begs to be read *systematically*, whether as a canonical whole or in its constituent parts. This is not inherently a novel idea: among recent writers on New Testament theology, Peter Stuhlmacher (esp. 1992–99, including his summary: 2.309–11), Ferdinand Hahn (2002), and others (e.g., I. H. Marshall 2004 and Matera 2005) stress such coherent diversity. Here it seems worth reiterating this concern as something to which the New Testament *itself* points as its implied reading.

This is in a sense a corollary to the argument we developed in chapter 2: not only does the New Testament imply a certain kind of reader, but in fact the shape of its own text elicits at least the outline of a certain kind of *reading*. Within the limited confines of this chapter, we will focus specifically on how that implied reading might affect the search for a New Testament theology. Far from being haphazard or a historical accident, the shape of the New Testament as we find it turns out to be highly pertinent to that problem.

One Gospel and the Shape of the Canon

The first thing to note is that the constituent parts of the New Testament canon appear remarkably *uninterested* in what distinguishes them from other biblical theologies, even where they occasionally show themselves to be aware of them. Examples range from Luke's prologue via Paul's discussion of other apostolic workers in 1 Corinthians 1–4 or (more controversially) Philippians 1 or Galatians 1–2 all the way to the Petrine reflection on Paul in 2 Peter 3:16. These canonical writers claim, in all their diversity and at times overt disagreement, to be concerned with *the same gospel* as their fellow apostles (and despite their rejection of derivative false teachers).

This point may at first appear straightforwardly naïve and trivial—and perhaps of little obvious relevance. Canonical theologies have of course been much in vogue in some circles and may be thought to have advanced such claims ad nauseam. But whatever one wishes to make of it at the historical level, even the macrostructure of the New Testament canon can be seen to give important pointers to its implied meaning as a received whole. A few illustrations of this may be in order.

In the traditional order of the books, the fourfold gospel emphatically separates Luke from its historical-critical connection with Acts, John from the Johannine Epistles, Matthew from James, and perhaps Mark from Peter. Each one of them is presented not as the book or Gospel "of" Matthew or of Mark and so on, but as *the Gospel* (τὸ εὐαγγέλιον) *according to* Matthew, Mark, Luke, and John.[11]

But there is more. In its present shape both the fourfold gospel and the entire New Testament share certain formal features that appear to confirm this impression of overall coherence. Matthew 1:1 ("the *book* of the beginning") fittingly opens the fourfold gospel. That four-gospel codex concludes with a strikingly apposite scribal codicil, appended in the first-person singular after the first-person plural conclusion of the Fourth Gospel—but without being necessarily or intrinsically Johannine in flavor (and interestingly absent from the uncorrected Codex Sinaiticus): "But there are also many other things that Jesus did; if every one of them were written down, I suppose that the world itself could not contain the books [plural!] that would be written" (John 21:25).

At least in their final form, Mark and Luke similarly contribute their own subtle literary signposts to the concord of plural Gospels. Luke implies that the multiple accounts of "what has been accomplished among us" are held together by the unity of "the word," the object that unites the apostolic witnesses, and by the trustworthy content of the Christian instruction (Luke 1:1–4). A plausible case has been made, too, that the fourth and probably latest gospel relates to Mark, the earliest one, in a similar way, for instance by taking the reader's familiarity with Markan characters for granted while pursuing a clearly independent narrative line (see Bauckham 1998b).

The inauthentic longer ending of Mark 16:9–20, finally, constitutes an early second-century conclusion that completes the

---

11. This point is particularly stressed by Hengel 1985, 2000, 2004. On Luke and Acts, cf. also Bockmuehl 2005c on Rowe 2005.

earliest of the Gospels with the latest of the conclusions, providing what Mark 16 either lost or else never had. While its continued textual uncertainty for several centuries is not in question, what is particularly interesting about this secondary ending is that it provides an additional account of three resurrection appearances drawn from material found in the three other canonical Gospels (cf. Kelhoffer 2000). In that sense, there is something a little unreal in fashionably ultra-Kermodian theories about this ending-less Gospel supposedly composed in a code of infinitely malleable literary plasticine. David Parker rightly questions the peculiarity of the claim "that we can now read Mark with its Short Ending as though we had never read it with its Long Ending. We are . . . not in a position to say that the Long Ending can be forgotten. The fact is that it stands as the ending which has been dominant for the reading of Mark for most of the text's history" (1997: 147; cf. 124–47).[12] Such a surface reading of the longer ending coheres remarkably well with the second-century affirmation of the fourfold gospel. As church father Irenaeus shows so clearly, that catholic tradition was solidly established even at a time when certain "marginal" Jewish Christians accepted only their own form of a single Gospel of Matthew, and while other groups were still busy producing a multiplicity of new gospels. The case for dating the fourfold gospel tradition no later than the first half of the second century is cogently demonstrated in recent discussion of Irenaeus, Justin, and others (Stanton 1997), even with tenuous reference to a first codex possibly containing all four Gospels (cf. Skeat 1997).

Elsewhere in the New Testament canon, Paul's letters are obviously grouped together. But the compiler's primary interest is in the apostolicity of this correspondence about the gospel: the final order is based on length, not on historical setting or chronology; and despite occasional claims to the contrary, no allowance is made for either circulars or letters of joint or doubtful Pauline

12. The continuing influence of Kermode 1967 and 1979 on Markan literary criticism is illustrated most recently in works like Gaventa and Miller 2005; cf. Hooker 2005.

authorship.[13] The form, canonical setting, and content (2 Pet. 3:1) of the Petrine Epistles all declare their apostolic complementarity, despite their contested historical origin. In the final form of the canon, even Matthew 1:1 and the concluding verses of Revelation (22:18–21) came to constitute a similarly suggestive canonical fastener around the New Testament as a whole.

Taken by themselves, such observations are of course highly problematic and could easily incur the charge of an anachronistic and almost superstitious biblicism. The final shape of the canon was gradually consolidated over several centuries, and surface observations of this kind therefore necessarily part company with a "genetic" line of thought that would want to limit the meaning of the texts to that which they had in their originally disparate historical settings.

And yet, the notion of a canon is not just a contrived fourth-century clampdown by authoritarian churchmen. For all that is good and true about protestations to the contrary from F. C. Baur to M. D. Goulder (1994 and 2001), the issue of *unity* in the midst of complex diversity is already strongly implicit in many of the individual documents in the New Testament. Ferdinand Hahn is in this sense not just dogmatically but *exegetically* right to structure the approach to New Testament theology in terms of historical diversity *as well as* theological unity.[14] What is more, in certain respects the canon of the New Testament *itself* manifests a striking and by no means incidental interrelation of form and content, to which David Trobisch, among others, eloquently draws attention.[15]

13. The point is sometimes made that P[46], a Chester Beatty papyrus containing the earliest extant collection of the Pauline corpus, lacks the Pastoral Epistles. But it is in any case only an excerpted corpus, with no one letter copied intact, and with 2 Thessalonians and Philemon also absent (but portions of Hebrews included). And there could be other, more mundane explanations of the lacuna for the Pastorals, as Duff 1998 suggests.

14. The two volumes of Hahn 2002 are entitled *Die Vielfalt des Neuen Testaments: Theologiegeschichte des Urchristentums* and *Die Einheit des Neuen Testaments: Thematische Darstellung.*

15. Trobisch 2000: 78 (on Acts as linking Paul with Peter), 137–38 (on the Markan connection of the Gospels with Acts, Paul, 2 Timothy, and 1–2 Peter). See also Trobisch 1994 on the Pauline corpus.

The gospel was thought from the outset to be reliably repre-sented in diverse apostolic witnesses, and despite their disagree-ments and the fluidity of the tradition the different writers were thought, perhaps paradoxically, to be at one in the gospel. Even their fierce (if somewhat overrated) confrontation at Antioch (Gal. 2) does not prevent Paul's unquestioned affirmation of Peter (1 Cor. 1:12–13), five years or so later, as a fellow steward of God's mys-teries (4:1), a senior missionary colleague (9:5), and a definitive apostolic witness of the resurrection (15:5). Paul says very directly about the apostolic witnesses, "Whether then it was I or they, so we proclaim and so you have come to believe" (15:11). Various Pauline or deuteropauline passages already point explicitly in the direction of an identifiable corpus of Paul's writings (2 Cor. 10:9–10; 2 Thess. 3:17; cf. Col. 4:16); and even the Petrine tradi-tion refers explicitly to "all his letters" as though a known Pauline collection exists (2 Pet. 3:15–16).

For all their tensions and apparent contradictions, then, the New Testament writers are agreed that there is fundamentally only one gospel faith, "once for all entrusted to the saints" (Jude 3).[16] Following a long succession of jaded critics, we may of course dismiss such claims as wishful thinking. Is this not polemical make-believe, which may suit the particular writer's vested interests but quickly runs aground on a rudimentary comparison with other New Testament authors? Are there not clear tensions between Acts and Paul, James and Galatians? On the face of it, these are entirely reasonable objections. Nevertheless, and however irritat-ing it may be to critical minds, in many of the New Testament documents a unifying canonical impulse is in principle already a given—and from a perspective that is well aware of competing alternatives (so, rightly, Söding 1996: 165). For example, the au-thors readily admit that outsiders may preach a different gospel, make false messianic claims, or assert that Jesus Christ did not come in the flesh. But such competing allegations are for them not equally valid alternatives. In the end, there is apostolic truth

16. Cf. Eph. 3:5; 4:20–21; 1 Cor. 3:11; 8:6; 15:11; and note further the numerous passages that mention "the faith" or "the gospel."

and there is falsehood, and the two are not the same. Only "the truth will make you free" (John 8:32), and "no lie comes from the truth" (1 John 2:21).[17]

Regardless of how *successful* one judges the collection of New Testament books to be in uniting around an identifiable common vision of truth, there is little question that both authors and framers of the canon *intended and expected* the individual texts and the collection to be understood in this fashion. The differences between the authors are indeed highly instructive for understanding both the historical origins and the present contours of Scripture. But the fact is that New Testament interpretation can disregard the *integrating vision* in the texts only on the explicit assumption that the apostolic project has in fact failed.[18]

The Church's Gospel

One further observation is worth recalling from chapter 2. From the outset, both the authors and their implied readers evidently agreed in assuming not only the unity of the apostolic gospel of Jesus Christ, but also the necessarily and unmistakably *ecclesial location* of the interpretative task. In spite of its foundational significance for Christianity, the New Testament does not *create* the church but rather *presupposes* and confirms it at every turn. As Pannenberg 1996 also notes, in this sense nonecclesial and nontheological interpretation is from the start handicapped and ill-suited to the evident intention of the New Testament itself—and thus necessarily to the orientation of its implied readers.

The very survival of these documents reliably indicates that scholarly speculations about their *origin* will make an inadequate

17. The Johannine corpus in this respect affirms a conviction strikingly echoed by George Orwell's Winston: amid the fog and confusion of enemies within and without, "there was truth and there was untruth, and if you clung to the truth even against the whole world, you were not mad" (1966: 173 [part 2, chap. 9]).

18. Liberal interpreters classically fail to grasp this point, which is clearly understood both by orthodox Christian theology and by its more radical critics. Cf. also pp. 87–88 and n. 17 above on the subject of New Testament criticism's characteristic assumption of a sectarian ecclesiology. Note further the robustly textual case for an early canon mounted in Trobisch 2000.

guide to their actual meaning as historic documents. The New Testament survives not as a ragtag collection of disparate tracts with ill-concealed political agendas and hopelessly incompatible conceptions of the church—much as these and other factors may of course have been at play in their historical genesis. Instead, the New Testament as a whole and in its parts *presupposes* an implied readership and a *Sitz im Leben* in which it functions as the abiding deposit of the apostolic witness to the gospel. Its defining function and setting as part of the church's united two-testament canon derives in the first instance from being creedally *posited* rather than critically validated (however much critical study can shed valuable light on its historical genesis).

The Practice of New Testament Theology

How, then, might these observations be applied? If the Humpty Dumpty approach leads to unsatisfactory results, how else should one go about the study of New Testament theology? To be sure, the attempt to find a single overarching theme of biblical theology has too often floundered on its apparent inability to account for the diversity in Scripture—whether that theme be "salvation history" (Oscar Cullmann and Gerhard von Rad), "the mighty acts of God" (G. Ernest Wright), or more recently "the end of exile" and "the return of Yahweh to Zion" (N. T. Wright). Such reconstructions are perhaps too often wedded to contingent claims of historicity and original meanings that are rarely verifiable, and they cannot readily support the interpretative theological weight imposed upon them. This is quite apart from the fact that many of these grand objective visions have classically failed to acknowledge their own perspectival location and thus fall foul of the postmodern deconstructive project. (Is it significant that no one has ever seen this or that supposedly central theme before?)

How else, then, might we proceed? Taking the implied canonical consensus seriously, there would appear to be considerable scope for an approach from three directions, corresponding respectively to the New Testament's shared canonical concern for truth, the diversity of its theological voices, and its ecclesial and historical *Sitz im Leben.* One step would be to reconsider the elusive quest for the *central kerygma* of the New Testament. Despite widespread scholarly skepticism on this front, there is in fact plenty of scope for further work, not least because the New Testament itself cries out to be read in relation to its own stated central concern. In 1930s Cambridge, C. H. Dodd presented important work on this subject in *The Apostolic Preaching and Its Developments* (1936a), while five years earlier his colleague E. C. Hoskyns had argued for a unified core of theological conviction in *The Riddle of the New Testament* (Hoskyns and Davey 1931, a book and an author to which we shall return in chapter 5 below). Since that time, remarkably few others have followed their lead; among the exceptions are articles published almost twenty years ago by Eugene Lemcio, which demonstrated a heavily theological, christological, and response-oriented convergence in the New Testament (Lemcio 1988, 1990). This subject is obviously beset with methodological difficulties similar to those of the "grand unified theories" just cited. Nevertheless, the quest for a shared central kerygma, however limited in scope, is a valuable analytical task—and it is appropriate to the claims of the New Testament itself, as we have seen.

The "unity and diversity" question is one that any contemporary New Testament theology can avoid only to its own detriment, almost regardless of social location. On the one hand, neither diachronic nor synchronic approaches will succeed in providing a viably coherent interpretation while bracketing out differences between the evangelists or between Paul, Peter, James, and John.

Having said that, there are clearly different ways of addressing this question, some more and some less constructive. In the contemporary context of resistance to metanarratives, there would seem to be a good deal of potential in a further exploration of G. B. Caird's image (1994) of an "apostolic conference" of the different New Testament authors on shared central themes—an approach also fruitfully pursued in recent work by François Vouga (2001). This would differ from the pastiche or montage model of postmodern and other recent work, in that theological unity within diversity would be assumed to be both real and desirable in principle, as well as a shared aim in practice. For all the real debate that should undoubtedly ensue, the fact that the envisaged conference is "apostolic" would have clear implications for the source and nature of its authority. What is more, the primacy of the subject matter (the *res*) might well shape the aim and scope (the *telos*) and the outcome of the deliberations.

Aidan Nichols pointedly queries the postmodern celebration of diversity at any price: "Not only the integrity of the Canon but its essential unity of content is crucial to a truly ecclesial exegesis. . . . The desire to see and celebrate difference wherever possible, including in the New Testament Canon, is not something self-evidently right and proper, either in itself or as a way of tuning in to the Scriptures" (1999: 166–67).

It is easy to see here the continuation of themes explored in the last chapter, where we discussed strengths and weaknesses of imperturbably conflict-driven approaches such as those embraced by many of Caird's critics, often in conjunction with an indefinite deferral of meaning.[19] The "apostolic conference" model, by contrast, might indeed provide for an honest and imaginative dialogical negotiation of differences. It would do so, however, on the consensus of the apostles—and their implied readers—about their shared central kerygma, all the while retaining an awareness for the inalienably ecclesial locus of their interpretation. Unlike the view of apostolic testimony as immured in unforgiving antagonisms and naked grabs for power, this perspective could more credibly accommodate the textual interdependence of New Testament theologies, both internally as between their different authors and in relation to the Old Testament.

Finally, this same textual interdependence has necessary consequences for the New Testament's place in historic *Christian theology*. The historical setting of both the text and its interpreter could be more usefully harnessed for theology by an approach that takes seriously the place of Scripture in Christian faith. This

---

19. Notably Houlden 1995; cf. 1991: 57–58 and Goulder 1994. See also chapter 2 above.

is not of course to undermine classic critical questions like the background meaning of central New Testament terms: historical theology begins, after all, with the New Testament itself. And yet it is also to recognize, for example, that the reference and meaning of the term *son of God* is not exhausted by its place in Jewish messianism or in the Greco-Roman emperor cult, but reaches forward to include the active role of New Testament Christology in the formation of Christian doctrine. As suggested in chapter 2 above, that exegetically constructive function of doctrine represents a living dialogue with the New Testament's own "effective history," not least in the Christian mainstream's emerging *regula fidei* and indeed in documents like the Nicene Creed.

It is not just Scripture but its interpreter, too, who must be understood in his or her historical context, inevitably indebted to the interpreters and indeed interpretative "performers" of the text who have gone before. Any subject-appropriate interpretation of Scripture is a task with inescapably ecclesial and theological dimensions; from a Christian perspective this means that it is to be carried out in common loyalty to fellow Christian authors (so, rightly, Berger 1995a) and in dialogue with the living tradition to which they gave rise. In that loyalty to the "communion of the saints" affirmed in the creeds lies the abiding importance both of the apostolic text's (often multivalent) intention and of its ecclesial setting and address.[20]

20. The intrinsic polyvalency of the literal sense is highlighted by Fowl 1998: 34–40, not least with reference to Thomas Aquinas. In practice, however, and not just in relation to Thomas, Fowl significantly underplays authorial intention by subordinating it, almost without remainder, to the authority of interpreting communities—however "vigilant" or "virtuous" (62–96) (a similar criticism is made by Cummins 2004: 184). Fowl (1998: 23–28, 38) explicitly distances himself from the concern for the literal sense in writers like Brevard Childs and Francis Watson, preferring instead the positions of Hans Frei, George Lindbeck, and Kathryn Tanner. Dismissing the concern for the discrete voice of the Old Testament (Childs 1997 and by implication the development of this theme by Seitz 2001: 5), Fowl is happy to endorse an avowedly supersessionist Christian reading of the Old Testament (1998: 129–30), in which the Spirit functions as the agent of ecclesial abolition and innovation. Seitz (2001: 67–69) tellingly exposes this common caricature of the Spirit as "a taboo-toppling, new truth revealer" (also quoted in Cummins 2004: 192). Studied denial of the theological value of historical study of the Bible (Fowl 1998: 185–90) may be a plausible corollary of this approach (though related issues seem discussed more cautiously and lucidly in

This is no mere pious or dogmatic postulate. The Bible's theological *Wirkungsgeschichte* is by no means immaterial to the quest for the theological kerygma of the New Testament itself. Robert Morgan argues that the unifying center of the New Testament and the doctrinal norm of Christianity coalesce in the acknowledgment of God in the historical particularity of the crucified God: the divinity of the Christ is itself the central theme of New Testament theology, with the Fourth Gospel at its center. And this in turn establishes for Morgan an essential unity between the theology of the New Testament and that of the ecumenical councils of the church: "The conciliar definition of Jesus . . . is based on the *whole* New Testament witness and is sufficiently true to its intentions to test the claim of any modern theology or piece of biblical interpretation to be Christian in a traditional sense" (1996a: 216).

The presuppositions and conclusions of biblical interpreters are themselves inescapably carried along by the effective history of the very text they are seeking to study (so Luz 1985–2002: 1.79; cf. the discussion in chapter 6), even where they aim to resist or subvert its effects. If this is true, then it immediately becomes *historically* appropriate (*pace* Houlden 1991: 56–57) to hear the New Testament speaking not only on those theological or moral issues that historical critics deem the authors to have explicitly addressed. Instead, a historically aware and theologically fruitful engagement with the New Testament's theology will also recognize many of the great themes that have arisen as a direct *result* of the New Testament text's continuing theological voice in the church. New Testament interpreters could be kept profitably busy by returning to exegetically neglected Christian theological and ethical loci like the Trinity, sanctification, judgment, the inspiration of Scripture, or the doctrine of heaven.

Fowl 2002: 205–11). In the face of approaches that place Scripture at the disposal of "interpreting communities," Webster rightly questions the adequacy of "hermeneutical virtues" to prevent the captivity of Scripture "in self-enclosed worlds of readerly psyches and habit-forming communities" (2003a: 125)—thereby losing any sense in which, through the canon, God sets "the judgment of the apostolic gospel" before "an unruly church" (126).

Somewhat ironically, perhaps, the threshold of the third Christian millennium presents the Humpty Dumpty of biblical scholarship with a novel and life-giving challenge: to revisit New Testament theology afresh in light of the recognition that the text, in its unity and its diversity, invariably intends believers' instruction, encouragement, and hope. To do this consistently, whether from an insider or outsider perspective, could turn out to be a pioneering adventure of rediscovery for the coming generation of New Testament study.

4

THE ICON OF PETER AND PAUL BETWEEN HISTORY AND RECEPTION

In chapters 2–3 we repeatedly encountered the challenge and the problems inherent in conflict-driven readings of the New Testament. Chapter 2 approached this issue from the point of view of the text's implied readers, while chapter 3 attempted to investigate what might be said about the range of such readers' implied readings—or in other words, about New Testament theology. We found that alongside the undoubted plurality and diversity of the New Testament witnesses there is a significant internal coherence in the theological subject matter under discussion. The distinctly canonizing implications of this coherence seem, moreover, to draw additional reinforcement from certain external features apparent in the collation and correlation of the different documents, as we saw.

Where the last chapter sketched one alternative to primarily conflict-centered models from the point of view of New Testament *theology*, we now open a further perspective by focusing on a particular historical paradigm of *Christian origins*, whose immense influence has made it a kind of watermark in the pages of many New Testament publications to this day. This is the assumption that the Christian mission to the Jews and to the Gentiles, as represented above all in the two great apostles Peter and Paul, was irreconcilably divided from the start—and that this conflict draws perhaps the early church's most basic line in the sand.

The relationship between these two apostles and their respective missions is still widely assumed to encapsulate fundamental hermeneutical and theological contradictions between opposing models of Christian theological thought. More specifically, we will here explore certain aspects of the sharp dichotomy between the profile of that relationship in Scripture and tradition on the one hand and in contemporary New Testament scholarship on the other.

A picture is said to be worth a thousand words. Adjacent is an example of a classic, widespread icon of the embrace of St. Peter and St. Paul, which in this particular case dates from the sixteenth century and comes from the Chapel of St. Athanasios at Mount Athos. The artistic juxtaposition of Peter and Paul dates back at least to the early fourth century,[1] while the idea of Peter rushing to embrace Paul on his arrival in Rome is found in Pseudo-Marcellus's *Passion of Peter and Paul*, whose date may be somewhat later.[2] In the Middle Ages this particular theme appears to have gained in popularity, especially in the East, although a form strikingly reminiscent of our icon occurs in late-twelfth-century wall mosaics in the Byzantine style at the Palatine Chapel of Palermo and at Monreale Cathedral.[3] The motif further served to encourage fifteenth-century

1. See the bas-relief now in the Museum of Early Christian Antiquities at Aquileia; for an image see http://www.museoarcheo-aquileia.it/aquileia_eng/museo_paleoeng/pop/p_pop2.htm (accessed April 17, 2006).
2. See Schneemelcher 1991–92: 2.279. Waldmann 2001 goes well beyond even the optimistic proposals of Lipsius and Bonnet 1891: 1.119–77 in asserting a first-century date. For a recent (relatively skeptical) survey of apocryphal Petrine Acts literature, see most fully Baldwin 2005.
3. See Demus 1949: 296 and figs. 43a (Palatina) and 83a (Monreale; top right); Kitzinger 1992: 2.36 and fig. 134. Note also Sauser 1994: 409.

hopes culminating in the ill-fated reunion of Eastern and Western churches formally proclaimed at the Council of Florence on July 6, 1439.

But how is it relevant today? Western readers often find this sort of image artistically and culturally alien; but might the esthetic astigmatism be ours rather than that of the icon painters? Seeing things through other cultural eyes may offer excellent assistance in the notoriously difficult task of changing our mind.

The pictorial icon here reflects a verbal icon. The basic drift of its interpretation of the two great apostles is relatively straightforward. Their feet are planted at some remove from each other, and their dress and appearance are clearly distinct. Unlike the famous Rublev *Trinity* or many icons of the Virgin and Child, this one has neither character looking directly at the other. Clearly they are diverse in role and personality, and in posture and expression one can see hints of a relationship that may in some respects be a complex and uneasy one (a point also noted—and perhaps overinterpreted—by Sauser 1994 and 1999). Nevertheless, the overriding impression is that of their embrace: they are united in Christian charity and in their service of the gospel.

And yet such a picture cannot but be an affront to the sensibilities of self-respecting historical critics. Two centuries of New Testament scholarship have unequivocally taught us that this picture is a historical impossibility, a case of pious myth-making devoid of solid evidence.

Ostensibly, our discipline has taken its cue from the early Christian texts themselves. Galatians 2 clearly shows Paul engaged in a notoriously bitter feud with Peter over the fundamental nature of Christian faith and the integrity of the Gentile mission. In the rest of the Pauline correspondence, Peter appears as an almost marginal figure, from whose ministry Paul repeatedly distinguishes his own—specifically in Galatians (1:18; 2:9, 11) and 1 Corinthians (1:12; 3:22). Peter is said to represent "the gospel to the circumcised" (Gal. 2:7); and Paul at times ill conceals his intense exasperation with certain individuals ostensibly associated with that mission (Gal. 2:4; 5:12; 2 Cor. 11:13; Phil. 1:15; 3:2). Peter himself is never mentioned in Paul's letter to Rome, where subsequent tradition at least since 1 Peter always assigned to the Prince of Apostles a vested interest and presence. Despite their otherwise evident harmonizing tendencies, Acts and the so-called deuteropauline letters (however delimited) similarly omit any mention of Peter from their account of Paul's conversion or subsequent mission and ministry. In some of the later supposedly Petrine circles, a comparably uneasy memory persisted of Peter's dealings with Paul. One indication of this has been thought to surface in the distinctly faint praise in 2 Peter 3:15–16, even if the supposed anti-Paulinism of documents like the *Pseudo-Clementine Recognitions* could be seen as late, muddled, and hardly conclusive.

It is this rendering of the apostolic evidence that is reinforced by the dominant trends in contemporary New Testament studies. With a few notable exceptions, many leading lights of twentieth-century New Testament scholarship continued to adhere to several key presuppositions of the nineteenth-century Tübingen scheme of Christian origins (see Harris 1975 and Kaye 1984). On that reading, Paul's law-free mission of preaching justification by faith alone to the Gentiles was conducted in explicit and ongoing antithesis to a rival Judaizing mission spearheaded by Peter and especially the Jerusalem church under the leadership of James. This construct was exemplified by twentieth-century giants like William Wrede, Rudolf Bultmann, and Ernst Käsemann in Germany, and at least in modified form it is still widely encountered in contemporary scholarship there (see the surveys in Wechsler 1991 and Böttrich 2002). It has similarly enjoyed a large following in the English-speaking world. Contemporary sympathizers include C. K. Barrett (1963, 1997) and Michael Goulder (1994, 2001) among the older generation, but also a number of younger scholars (Pate 2000: 438–44; Sim 1998; Smith 1985; and Campbell 2002 [a nuanced but enthusiastic review of Goulder 2001]). Major commentators on the book of Acts routinely dismiss signs of accommodation between Paul, Peter, and Jerusalem as Lukan wishful thinking—just as to German writers of an earlier generation they were unmistakable symptoms of the cancer of "early catholicism." Nowadays it tends to be watered-down versions of Baur's theory that persist, often tacitly ("baurite" rather than "Baurite," as one advocate likes to put it [Campbell 2002; cf. Campbell 2005: 21]).

Aside from periodic (but not nowadays widely embraced) attempts to identify a single Petrine anti-Pauline front in 1–2 Co-

rinthians (so, e.g., Goulder 2001), the classic test case continues
to be the Antioch dispute of Galatians 2. As Andreas Wechsler
persuasively suggests in his history of scholarship, one's exegetical
judgment of that episode largely determines one's view of early
Christian history as a whole—and vice versa (1991: 281). This is
true especially, but by no means exclusively, where it has been allied
with Protestant theological assumptions—in which the instinctive
typology of the Pauline Reformer versus the Petrine Pope has perhaps not always been consciously resisted.[4] And thus the Antioch
episode is often used to reinforce the belief that the leading players
in early Christianity represented implacably polarized factions of
charismatic freedom versus hierarchical institutionalism—rather
than, for example, as some younger scholars even in Germany
have begun to suggest, at once "rivals and partners"[5] engaged in
a "managed conflict" of shared but differently prioritized loyalties
(so Böttrich 2001, 2002, 2004).

For our present discussion there is no time, and probably no
need, to provide full documentation of this scholarly debate; others have done so admirably.[6] F. C. Baur himself was influenced by
the late-eighteenth-century work of David J. S. Semler and Johann

---

4. This was explicitly true for Baur (1878: 112), and perhaps more implicitly for
Bultmann and his students; Wechsler 1991: 285 similarly notes Hans Lietzmann and
Karl Holl and rightly concludes: "Diese Auslegung scheint auch durch hermeneutische
Voraussetzungen des Protestantismus geprägt, weil sie sich einseitig hinter Paulus stellt
und Gefahr läuft, dem Paulus-Verständnis Luthers untergeordnet zu werden." Cf. Lohse
1991: 433 on Baur's influence on interpretation of the Antioch incident: "Although
these ideas have been very stimulating for historical research one may raise the objec-
tion as to what extent these perspectives have been of a special Protestant character
seeing Protestantism as a later branch of Paulinism and catholicism as an expression
of what could have been called Petrinism." Today even a conservative German critic
of Baur like Martin Hengel can still devote the entire conclusion of a major volume
on Paul to a comparison of the apostle with Martin Luther, united in their unflinching
devotion to the great doctrine of "justification of the godless by grace alone" (Hengel
and Schwemer 1997: 311–13). This treasured Reformational typology may suggest
why the "new perspective on Paul" has been so fiercely opposed in Lutheran and
some other Protestant circles.
    5. Note the title of Wechsler 1991; also cf. Gnilka 2002 and Doering 2002.
    6. See Wechsler 1991 for the most complete history of research on the Antioch
dispute; also Kieffer 1982 and Karrer 1989 on the view of Peter in Pauline Christianity.
See Kümmel 1973: 127–43 and Harris 1975 for the history of the Tübingen school.

Schmidt and more generally by G. W. F. Hegel's (1770–1831) dialectical philosophy of history. After his first programmatic essay about Peter and Paul appeared in 1831,[7] he worked out his powerful intellectual paradigm more fully over a number of years; but it was left to his students (notably Albert Schwegler, whose work Baur endorsed)[8] to pursue it to its logical conclusions in a variety of directions. Despite intermittent voices of more sober historical caution,[9] it is this bipolar construct whose influence continues at least indirectly to resonate in much current discussion 175 years later. It may be useful to refresh our memory by citing a few representative paragraphs from Baur's 1878 *Church History of the First Three Centuries*, first published in 1851.

Baur claims that Jesus harbored within himself two contradictory instincts—the moral universal and the Jewish national messianic idea—and that his followers naturally attached themselves to one or the other of these ideas (1878: 1.49). Within Baur's nineteenth-century cultural and philosophical context, such a claim appears reasonable, even if its idealizing universalism now seems quaint. Given Paul's background in a cramped nationalistic Judaism, his conversion strikes Baur as nothing short of miraculous: "And the miracle appears all the greater when we remember that in this revulsion of his consciousness he broke through the barriers of Judaism and rose out of the particularism of Judaism into the universal idea of Christianity" (1.47). Pretty soon, the two tendencies in early Christianity became polar opposites. After Paul's short visit with Peter in Jerusalem, he turned his back on Judaism forever (1.49) and "so decided an attitude of opposition did the two standpoints now assume: on the one side was the apostle Paul refusing with immovable firmness to be shaken even for a moment in any point which his principles required him to maintain, or to yield any compliance to the proposals addressed to him: on the other side were the older apostles clinging tenaciously to their Judaism" (1.54).

7. His major book on Paul is Baur 1845 (ET 1873, reprinted 2003).
8. Baur himself cites Schwegler 1846 alongside his own work in Baur 1878: 136n1.
9. Wechsler 1991 names above all Bernhard Weiss and Theodor Zahn.

In particular, this apostolic polarity divided Peter from Paul, a division permanently sealed in the Antioch incident:

> The words and the whole tone of the apostle bear witness how sharp the personal collision between him and Peter must have been, and we are not surprised to find that the scene at Antioch made a deep impression on the mind of the age, and left very lasting effects behind. Throughout all the Epistles of Paul we do not find the slightest indication that the apostles ever drew nearer to each other in after years. The Acts passes over the occurrence at Antioch with a resolute silence, which shows clearly enough how far what was remembered of the subject was from harmonising with the reconciling tendency of this work. From a work written in the second half of the second century, the pseudo-Clementine Homilies, we gather that even then the Jewish Christians had not yet learned to forgive the harsh word which the apostle Paul had spoken of the man whom they regarded as the chief of the apostles. (1.55)

To Baur, as to his later disciples, there can be no doubt that the factionalism facing Paul in Corinth was due to the same party polarities that played themselves out in Antioch and Galatia. The Cephas party and the Christ party (cf. 1 Cor. 1:12) were both essentially those who lined up with Judaizing factions pressing the claims of Jerusalem over against Paul's law-free gospel:

> Judaizing teachers had made their way into this [the Corinthian] Church also, and had unsettled the faith of the apostle's converts in his Gospel. Several divisions and parties had arisen; but the main controversy about which they were ranged originated in a party which bore the name of Peter, although there can be no doubt that Peter never was at Corinth at all, and set itself in opposition to those members of the Corinthian Church who remained faithful to the principles of Pauline Christianity. (1.61)

In other words, then, "what determined the course of the development was not only the opposition of two radically different tendencies, but also the division of the two apostles who stood at the head of them" (1.148).

Thus far the influential views of F. C. Baur. His partly Hegelian notion of the early church's history as a struggle impelled by the deep division between Paul and Peter (and of course between Paul and James) has continued to exercise a huge influence in New Testament studies.

Conventional historical criticism in Baur's wake suggests that our icon of Peter and Paul must be a case of pious myth-making, with no basis in reality. Nevertheless, there can be no doubt that its visual interpretation does in fact represent the mainstream Christian position, or at any rate a mainstream view that has consistently prevailed since the late first century. Throughout the early church, only extremists—like the Marcionites, on the one hand, and the Ebionites, on the other—are attested as adopting a different view, the former adopting Peter as their villain and the latter Paul. The martyrdoms of Peter and Paul were remembered together ever since the first century and came before very long to be commemorated on a joint feast day: June 29. Beginning with Clement of Rome (*1 Clement* 5.1–6), Ignatius of Antioch (*To the Romans* 4.3), and Irenaeus of Lyons (*Against Heresies* 3.1.1; 3.3.2), Peter and Paul were pictured as having jointly (or at any rate equally) laid the foundation of the churches of Antioch and Rome (see Knoch 1981). They were apostles of the same Christ to different people, as Irenaeus stresses. The third and fourth centuries similarly take this picture of Peter and Paul entirely for granted, as emerges not only in the patristic writers but also from nonliterary material like third-century commemorations and Pope Damasus's fourth-century inscription at the catacombs of San Sebastiano (see Chadwick 1962 and Brändle 1992). The widespread popularity and ideological appeal of this image can be seen, moreover, in the many artistic representations of the two apostles on sarcophagi, coins, glass, and mosaic, where they seem increasingly to displace the mythological motif of the twin demigods Castor and Pollux in Greco-Roman art (Bisconti 2001; Donati 2000; also Davis-Weyer 1961 and Testini 1973–74 on the *Traditio Legis*).

Once again, it seems, history and theology are at loggerheads—history's Saul of Tarsus and Simon bar Jona versus the St. Paul and St. Peter of faith, one might say. Little would be gained from an attempt to dodge the genuine historical problems at stake here—from the Antioch dispute, famously important for Marcion and debated between Jerome and Augustine (Jerome, *Epistle* 112.4–18), to observant Jewish Christianity's gradual demise over a number of centuries. Similarly, and despite frequent exaggerations and scholarly clichés about gnostic Paulinism and Judaizing anti-Paulinism, one cannot but note the preference for Peter in documents like the *Pseudo-Clementine Recognitions* or, on the other hand, the famous recognition in Tertullian (*Against Marcion* 3.5.4) and others (Irenaeus, *Against Heresies* 5.9.1) that it was Paul who tended often to become *haereticorum apostolus*, the apostle favored by the heretics. Nevertheless, it remains worth thinking for a moment whether we might not usefully till the soil between two entrenched and seemingly irreconcilable positions—historical-critical deconstruction on the one hand and ecclesial hagiography on the other. When it is interpreted in relation to the New Testament's earliest reception history in the tradition of the postapostolic period, the synthetic view implied by this icon might after all turn out to be surprisingly fertile ground for the rethinking of long-cherished critical certainties.

Literary Perspectives on the Partnership of Peter and Paul

We may begin by illustrating this potential from the sort of final-form perspective that was proposed in the previous chapter. F. C. Baur pointed out that Acts tends to make Peter look Pauline and Paul Petrine (1.133); and whatever one may think of Baur's historical hypothesis, this is also a valid insight on the literary level. Although it is obviously something of a simplification, there is some truth in the designation of the "Acts of the Two Apostles" and in a comparison with Plutarch's studies of *Parallel Lives*.[10] Peter and Paul are protagonists at work for the same gospel of Jesus, which from the beginning of the book is destined for the "ends of the earth"; both receive visionary insight into this global

10. Note the titles of Boismard et al. 1990– and of Clark 2001 (who sees parallels between Paul and other apostles too); and cf. already Rackham 1901.

mission and are empowered by the Spirit; both preach great pro-grammatic sermons and work great healings and exorcisms; both give an account of their mission to the church in Jerusalem; and in both cases persecution and danger lead to deliverance and an open-ended conclusion.

Within the Pauline correspondence, although Baur and his acolytes rightly put their finger on the problem of Petrine and Pauline factions at Corinth, 1 Corinthians 1–4 rhetorically culmi-nates on the theme that Paul, Apollos, and Cephas are united in their role as servants of Christ and stewards of God's mysteries. Even the hotheaded harangue addressed to the Galatians recalls Paul's extended visit specifically to befriend Peter (1:18), affirms that they share *koinōnia* in being entrusted with the same gospel (2:9), and rebukes Peter's lapse in Christian praxis precisely by an appeal to *common ground* in shared Christian doctrine (2:14–17).

At least on this literary level, Petrine documents in turn show that this assumption of unity is not merely the result of Pauline political "spin." Despite dissenting voices, there continue to be fresh arguments that the Gospel of Mark shows familiarity with *both* Pauline and Petrine teachings (Rolland 1992).[11] The Gospel of Matthew, for all its residual aversion to Gentiles and to anti-nomian trends in the church, highlights Peter as the key-holder for a church that is in fact very clearly commissioned to reach and embrace the nations—not as Jewish proselytes but as disciples of Jesus. The first letter of Peter shows the apostle welcoming pre-cisely such Gentiles into God's own people with the help of Paul's own former assistant, Silvanus. As for 2 Peter, mentioned earlier, this canonical latecomer clinches its argument in the concluding paragraph by an appeal to Paul as "our beloved brother": his writings, far from being erroneous, must be respected like the other Scriptures and not twisted by ignorant and unstable interpreters (3:15–16).[12]

11. Marcus 2000 affirms scholarly preference for a Paulinist Mark vis-à-vis criti-cisms like those of Martin Werner.

12. On Peter and Paul in 2 Peter see, however, Vögtle 1981, who suggests that the remarks in 3:15–16 may have as much to do with the pseudonymous author's

Finally, and in keeping with the observations of the previous chapter, even the most basic literary reading of the Christian New Testament as a whole cannot fail to notice one obvious but by no means trivial fact, which belongs to the historical footprint—the *effect* of canonizing Paul's relationship with Peter. Despite the undeniable tensions that even the overall narrative itself throws up, the covers of the New Testament bind together, in one formative codex, writings in the name of both Paul and the Jerusalem "pillars" Peter, James, and John. The implied interpreter of that canonical decision hears the polyphony of its voices as witness to a common subject, which is the gospel.

Reading a Postmodern Partnership?

On another level, these postapostolic effects of the New Testament's literary form may give rise to further insights of a very different kind. As I intimated in chapter 2, "effective" history allows a roundtable discussion with a variety of diverse approaches and methods. From a postmodern perspective of ideological criticism, for example, one could discern in our icon the unlikely symbiosis of two males who appear to embody diametrically opposed ideas of power. Leaving aside the later ecclesial constructs associated with them, even Scripture pictures Peter as endowed with the keys of heaven and the dominical mandate to bind and to loose—and yet in turn, it seems, as remarkably submissive to the authority of James and the church in Jerusalem. Paul, by contrast, has no conventional mandate and seems to lack both formal authority and formally accountable obedience to an ecclesial center—and yet he repeatedly scores rhetorical points on a theme of authentic Spirit-filled power as manifested in weakness. Regardless of whether these impressions are in any way true to life, our verbal and pictorial icon mounts an intriguing challenge to a received image of the church that has so often pitted the charismatic politics of innovation ("Paul") against the episcopal politics of an authorized establishment ("Peter").

---

concern to counteract his opponents' deeschatologized interpretations of Paul as with the deliberate concern to honor Peter and Paul side by side.

Against the inherent volatility of this construal of their relationship, it may be that the uneasy unity of Peter and Paul simply reveals the extent to which the life and health of the church has always, at its worst no less than at its best, depended on the creative negotiation of precisely that same tension between charismatic and episcopal polity. To dismiss one in favor of the other is always to court either the tyranny of convention or the tyranny of revolution. By the same token, Scripture's canonical whole bears powerful testimony to the political sophistication of the apostolic tradition that refuses to dissolve that volatile tension between Paul and Peter by choosing between them. A sympathetic but ideologically critical reading may well ask usefully probing questions of any attempt to take the icon, or the biblical texts that it represents, merely as convenient extensions of a fiction of unclouded ecclesial harmony culminating in the observer's own community. (Such fiction may in some traditionalist quarters subsist all too conveniently as a sort of doctrinal Darwinism, for which the status quo's superiority over defeated rival points of view always seems splendidly self-evident—if not indeed "infallible.")

Other readers of this apostolic footprint might note the dominant masculinity in this icon and its underlying symbolism, in keeping with Western postmodern concerns about questions of gender, power, and inclusion. On that note, the gendered particularity of the human body stimulates further interpretative potential in this traditional orthodox picture's cordial but circumscribed embrace between a married man and a celibate man whose supposed sexual orientation inevitably strikes post-Christian culture as ipso facto ambiguous (even if one would not regard him in Bishop Spong's terms [1988: 151] as a repressed homosexual).[13] The interdependent tensions and synergies of Christian friendship, modesty, and chastity find rich illustration in this icon of reconciliation and embrace (a theme explored in Volf 1996).

At the same time, postmodernism is by no means alone in the ability to observe or indeed to generate a different perspectival spin

13. The masculine tenderness and sublimated eroticism of this iconographic type is also raised by Sauser 1994: 412; cf. 1999: 43.

on this embrace of Peter and Paul. We mentioned at the outset two Byzantine mosaics of Norman Sicily, created in the 1170s or 1180s in Palermo and Monreale under the auspices of King Roger II. Both offer strikingly similar examples of the image as part of a sequence on the life of Paul—the present episode being the apostle's arrival in Rome. Yet just as striking, perhaps, is the difference in their interpretation of it, as witnessed in the explanatory text accompanying each picture. The Palermo mosaic offers an interesting variation on the Vulgate of Acts 28:15: Peter rushes to embrace Paul as he comes from the city with the other Christians to meet and encourage Paul at the Forum of Appius and the Three Taverns (*S[ancto] Paulo Romam advenienti inde S[anctus] Petrus cum paucis Christianis occurrit usque ad Appii Forum ac Tres Tabernas; quos cum vidisset Paulus, gratias agens Deo, accepit fiduciam*). At Monreale, Paul comes to Rome and "makes peace with Peter" (*Hic Paul[us] venit Romam [et] pace[m] fecit cu[m] Petro*). The difference is eloquent.

Once again we can see how a consideration of the New Testament's earliest effective history has long since offered *exegetically* fertile ground for a conversation between historical, theological, literary, and ideological approaches.

Conclusion

One could obviously continue in this vein for some time, but for present purposes one final point seems worth stressing here. We have seen how the "synthetic" reading exemplified in our orthodox icon might furnish intriguing points of conversation with a number of more recent and emerging approaches to the New Testament. At the same time, however, such concern with Scripture's ecclesial impact both past and present (its Christian *Wirkungsgeschichte*) will in turn encourage us to renew a more comprehensively *historical* engagement with the New Testament text—a perspective that will always be an indispensable part of understanding what the text was written to communicate.

Effective history's synthetic contribution matters, first, because every one of the reader-oriented and literary points observed actually points to important *historical* corollaries. Thus, for example, the emergence of the canon as we have it is itself a vital factor in understanding Christian origins and the document we know as the New Testament; and the same could be said about its real and implied readers who spoke of ecclesial foundations laid jointly by Peter and Paul.

But second, even at the more basic level of the historical Peter and Paul, it is possible to show that the evidence supports a rather more nuanced and symbiotic view than the received bipolar paradigm would have us believe: ironically, it shows that paradigm to be insufficiently historical and insufficiently critical. What chiefly divides the two apostles at Antioch is neither a matter of basic gospel doctrine nor straightforwardly of halakah, but rather the theologically *and* halakically articulated arbitration between different but equally passionate ecclesial loyalties to the gospel of Jesus Christ.

The negotiation of their differences, therefore, can become for the conscientious interpreter precisely that: a negotiation of differences, or (as Christfried Böttrich 2002 puts it) a case of successful relational "crisis management." It is in any case highly revealing that Paul himself goes on to speak warmly of Peter as a fellow minister soon afterward in the Corinthian correspondence (1 Cor. 3:22), appealing to the authority of his example as a married man (9:5) and, above all, citing him as the leading witness of the resurrection (15:5; cf. Lohse 1991: 433). I see no reason why sympathetic historical criticism could not give a qualified and nuanced endorsement to the mainstream patristic view of the two apostles as it is consistently documented since the later first century.[14] With Franz Mussner (1976: 133) and others (Wehr 1996) it may well be appropriate to conceptualize the apostles' creative tension as "poles of unity,"[15] between which would emerge a church that was both catholic and apostolic.

14. See in this respect the important studies of Lohse 1991 and Mussner 1976 and the fuller study of the effective history of the relationship in Wehr 1996.

15. Cf. further Chadwick 1959 on the history of early Christianity as moving from a "sphere" with its center in Jerusalem to an "ellipse" with dual foci in Jerusalem

F. C. Baur was quite right to suggest that the turbulent events and personalities of apostolic history resist simplistic answers and in fact propelled miscellaneous opposing fragments of tradition in different directions. And it is indeed not difficult to see how gnostic interpreters, as well as Ebionites and Elkasaites, might come to trace their descent from an organic link with Jesus and with the apostles as viewed through their particular lens. Still, we must note that the synthetic view adopted by the emerging consensus of the catholic rule of faith came to be the strongest of those earliest trajectories. More to the point, perhaps, it is one that stands up remarkably well in comparison with others—not least in correlation with the texts themselves.

In previous chapters, I expressed the hope that by including the implied reader and the text's effective history in our deliberations we may be able to renew discussion between diversely oriented conversation partners about a shared object of inquiry in New Testament studies. Musings like these cannot of course stem or reverse the centrifugal forces; nor would it be desirable to let them sweep under the carpet the necessary debate about genuine historical problems. Nevertheless, the icon of Peter and Paul may prompt our rediscovery of the fact that the only exegetically coherent New Testament study is in the end in some sense systematic—just as the only theologically viable systematic theology is in the end exegetical.

---

and Rome—although the Western church subsequently once again reduced this to a single focus on Rome.

5

WHAT'S UNDER THE MICROSCOPE?

E. C. Hoskyns and the Object of New Testament Study

In the previous chapter, the relationship between Peter and Paul in history and effective history served as one case study of what it might mean to consider implied readings of the New Testament. Our second case study examines the concern for implied readings at the hands of an influential but now little-known twentieth-century British New Testament scholar, whose encounter with Continental theology enlivened his passion for the connection between the New Testament text and the theological reality of which it speaks and to which it points.

If we briefly recall Brother William's idea, cited earlier, that "often the learned men of our time are only dwarfs on the shoulders of dwarfs" (Eco 1984: 89), one obvious corollary must be that we cannot usually tell the giants from the dwarfs until they are fully grown. In the case of biblical interpreters in the church or the academy this means, more often than not, that we may not know their true measure until well after they are dead.

A number of such giants of New Testament scholarship in the early twentieth century arguably retain untapped potential for responding to the discipline's present quandaries both within and vis-à-vis the post-Christian academy. Here, we will consider the contribution of a scholar whose characteristic combination of astute critical scholarship with a vibrant concern for the object of this study holds considerable promise in relation to the questions here under discussion.

Sir Edwyn Clement Hoskyns (1884–1937) is rightly described as "the most inspiring British NT teacher" (Morgan 1999) of the period between the last century's two world wars, when, together with G. K. Chesterton, he was perceived as one of "the two outstanding names" (Smyth 1938: vii) in Christian thought in England.[1] Leading New Testament scholars still alive at the time of this writing owe their careers to his influence. In 1933, Christopher F. Evans and Reginald H. Fuller were among the last students whom Hoskyns sent to Tübingen to study under the likes of Adolf Schlatter (1852–1938), Gerhard Kittel (1888–1948), and Karl Heim (1874–1958). According to C. K. Barrett, it was quite simply Hoskyns who (with F. N. Davey) "set me on my way" and "did more than any others to create in me a determination to study the New Testament" (1995: 55, ix; cf. also Wakefield 1981: 44).[2] Another leading theologian significantly shaped by this "most lovable man" was Michael Ramsey, Archbishop of Canterbury (1961–74); he learned from Hoskyns, "more vividly than from anyone else, that the study of the New Testament is an exciting adventure, and . . . it is not made less scientific if the student brings to it his own experience of faith."[3]

1. C. F. Evans, however, regards this as a "ludicrous overstatement" (personal communication, Jan. 24, 2003).
2. Reginald H. Fuller took his Cambridge B.A. in 1937. Cf. also Cobham 1958a: 286, who names Evans, Fuller, Richard Gutteridge, and himself among the students Hoskyns sent to Tübingen. In 1982 Evans returned to Cambridge for a lecture to mark the publication of Hoskyns and Davey 1981; see C. F. Evans 1983.
3. So Ramsey in his foreword to Hoskyns and Davey 1981: xi–xii. In a personal communication (Dec. 23, 2003), Gordon Plumb kindly draws to my attention Ramsey's

Damnation of Memory?

But Cambridge University's Faculty of Divinity has sometimes been less than kind to its heroes. Although he had been on friendly terms with the Norris-Hulse Professor F. C. Burkitt (1864–1935), in faculty discussions Hoskyns was frequently in a minority of one (C. F. Evans, personal communication [Jan. 24, 2003]). Within a decade of his death, Hoskyns's nearly twenty years of work in Cambridge were already largely dismissed or ignored by leading liberal colleagues like Charles Raven, F. S. Marsh, and especially the Lady Margaret's Professor J. F. Bethune-Baker (see Wakefield 1981: 27, 72–73), even if the great C. H. Dodd (1884–1973), a fellow Johannine scholar, explicitly acknowledged a debt to him (1938: 92). Raven had it in his power to exclude Hoskyns's talented students Francis Noel Davey (1904–73) and Charles Smyth (1903–87) from a renewal of their Cambridge lectureships, and he acted firmly to do so—largely on the grounds of "old animosity," as more than one observer has thought.[4]

While this was undoubtedly "one of those pieces of illiberalism that the professional liberal can sometimes resort to" (C. F. Evans, personal communication [April 10, 2003]), as an exercise in *damnatio memoriae* ("erasure of memory"), its success remained perhaps less than wholly comprehensive. A generation later, for example, memories were briefly revived by Christopher Evans's 1981 guest lecture on Hoskyns in the Faculty to mark the long-delayed publication of *Crucifixion-Resurrection* (see C. F. Evans 1983).[5] But the virtual absence of friends and students from the Faculty meant that Hoskyns's heritage did inevitably fade. After

---

personal copy of *The Riddle of the New Testament* (now at Lambeth Palace Library; cat. no. E2361.H6), which was heavily annotated and supplemented at the end with several pages of handwritten notes on lectures by Hoskyns.

4. So Barrett 1995: 60; C. F. Evans, personal communication (Jan. 24, 2003); also Wakefield 1975: 569 and (more tentatively) 1981: 74; cf. MacKinnon 1987: 197, 206 (he compares Davey favorably with Bethune-Baker). Others with long Cambridge memories have told me much the same. Dillistone 1975: 205, 210 implies that Raven's enmity was directed less explicitly at Hoskyns than at "the epigoni," viz., Davey and Smyth (whom Evans knew personally).

5. In a personal communication (Jan. 24, 2003) C. F. Evans describes it as "the most difficult thing I ever had to do."

my own first arrival in Cambridge half a century after his death, I heard reference made to Hoskyns at most once or twice during nearly two decades before I embarked on this study—and that invariably from members of Hoskyns's own Corpus Christi College. Nothing much has been written about Hoskyns since a slender monograph by Richard Parsons in 1985; and it is probably fair to say that he is now largely unknown among New Testament scholars and theologians alike. Nevertheless, I suspect the time may be ripe to revisit an unfinished conversation. Here I wish to suggest that his compelling integration of catholic ecclesiology and evangelical conviction about Scripture continues to hold timely and suggestive stimuli for our own dialogue about Scripture and theology.

Scholar, Priest, and Teacher

Hoskyns embodied a potent combination of *Lux Mundi* Anglo-Catholic piety with a biblical theology of evangelical vibrancy[6] and a keen personal interest in Continental scholarship. He was born as the eldest son of the vicar of St. Clement's, Notting Hill in London on August 9, 1884; his father, a baronet, later became bishop of Southwell. After an undistinguished school career he read history at Jesus College in Cambridge, achieving a second-class result in his finals in 1906.[7] The eminent F. J. Foakes Jackson (1855–1941), who was then still dean of Jesus College,[8] sent the young Hoskyns to Berlin for a year's formative exposure to German theology; he encountered Adolf von Harnack (1851–1930), Adolf Schlatter (1852–1938), and the youthful Albert Schweitzer (1875–1965).[9] After preparing for ordination at Wells Theological College, he served as curate of a mining parish in Sunderland (1908–12) and warden of the Church of England hostel at the University of Shef-

6. Cobham 1958a: 282 aptly stresses his "evangelical catholicism"; cf. further below.

7. Several of the dates given by Fuller 1984: 323 are erroneous.

8. Foakes Jackson moved to Union Theological Seminary in New York in 1916.

9. On Hoskyns and Schweitzer cf. Barrett 1975: 4 and Parsons 1985: 36.

field (1912–15). Although he was then appointed to a fellowship and college lectureship at Corpus Christi College, he first spent the war as a greatly loved and decorated army chaplain in the Middle East, India, and France before returning to Cambridge in 1919. From then until his untimely death at the age of fifty-two (June 28, 1937), he served as lecturer in theology in the university and at Corpus Christi as dean of chapel, director of studies in theology, librarian, and (for a time) president. His wide interests embraced Cranmer, lexicography, and the manuscripts of the Parker Library; he preached on all three subjects in the chapel at Corpus Christi (Hoskyns 1938a: 89–150, 204–17).[10] He also supported college rowing, sang Schubert's *Lieder* for hours on end, and must have been the only *Neutestamentler* who faithfully, and with benefit, read the weekly *Farmer and Stockbreeder*.[11] All in all, he was a surprisingly unstuffy churchman.

Hoskyns's enormous influence in that Cambridge post seems inversely proportional to his few (and largely posthumous) publications and formal academic qualifications.[12] It shows something of the academic flexibility of a bygone age that he never held an earned degree in theology, although the University of St. Andrews awarded him a D.D. His most important early writings include essays (1926 and 1930) about Jesus and the Gospels in the 1920s, along with his best-known work, *The Riddle of the New Testament*, copublished in 1931 with his student Noel Davey (Hoskyns and Davey 1958). Remarkably, this was the first and only book published during his lifetime. Although its thesis of a unifying christological kerygma of the New Testament predictably irritated certain theologians within and beyond Cambridge,[13] it went on to be widely reprinted for decades; and it was soon translated in Germany and France.

10. Anglican sermon topics included the Homilies and the Thirty-Nine Articles (on which cf. Cobham 1958b; also MacKinnon 1987: 206–7).
11. Cf. Kenneth W. M. Pickthorn's obituary, quoted in Smyth 1938: xxii; also Barrett 1995: 59.
12. A complete list, including reviews, takes up barely three pages; Hoskyns and Davey 1981: 369–72.
13. Note the criticisms voiced by O. C. Quick 1933, Regius Professor of Divinity at Oxford.

This book's remarkable international acclaim can be seen in other ways. It was, for example, one of the small handful of contemporary theological books that Dietrich Bonhoeffer selected to read in prison during the last two years of his life (Bethge 1983: 1053). Leading German scholars Julius Schniewind and Gerhard Kittel asserted in the preface to the German translation that "no other book so succinctly and impressively summarizes the state of New Testament scholarship after a century of historical-critical work"—a judgment still echoed in part by Werner Georg Kümmel several decades later.[14] At the same time, it is interesting to note that the rather loose German rendering of Hoskyns's work arguably led Kittel and Schniewind to miss Hoskyns's main point, which is in the end less concerned with the ultimate *elusiveness* of the "riddle" than with its *solution* in the person of Jesus Christ. It may be that the choice of the German term *Rätsel* conveyed to Continental scholars a sense of intrinsic metaphysical inscrutability and mystery that is arguably absent from Hoskyns's less existentially ponderous and more detective-like understanding of the English term *riddle*.[15]

Hoskyns's other books include his translation of Karl Barth's epoch-making commentary on Romans (Barth 1933) and his masterful but unfinished commentary on the Fourth Gospel,[16] to which we will return below. Then there are two volumes of sermons (1938a and 1960) and a fragmentary torso on New Testament theology and ethics under the title *Crucifixion-Resurrection* (1981). This latter work was authored jointly with Noel Davey and first advertised as forthcoming in 1937 (so MacKinnon 1987: 196); but its publication was delayed until its edition by Gordon Wakefield in 1981.[17] (Cru-

14. So Schniewind and Kittel in the preface to Hoskyns 1938b: v (my translation). It is worth noting both the partly analogous comments of Kümmel 1973: 400, 403 and the critical deflation of that judgment by Hoskyns's own student (C. F. Evans 1983: 74). Links between Hoskyns and Schniewind are difficult to document, but note Fuller 1984: 330.

15. In his commentary, Hoskyns 1947: 131 similarly speaks of "solving" the "riddle" of the Fourth Gospel.

16. The treatment of John 6:31–21:25 remained unfinished at the time of Hoskyns's death and was published in unrevised form; Hoskyns 1947: 9, 294.

17. C. F. Evans received the manuscript as "a torso" on Davey's death, but found himself "unable to discern . . . just which way the exposition would go" on the subject of resurrection; but he believes Hoskyns or Davey never regarded it as fragmentary

cifixion-resurrection was a favorite theological slogan of Hoskyns, which he regarded as uniting all the witnesses of the New Testament [so also Wakefield in Hoskyns and Davey 1981: 365]. It came to be inscribed on his tombstone in the churchyard at Grantchester, where he is buried with his wife and one of their five children.)[18] Although Hoskyns neither followed nor started an identifiable school,[19] he did cultivate a particular critical appreciation for Continental scholars like Gerhard Kittel, Adolf Schlatter, and the rising Karl Barth (1886–1968), who was just two years his junior. With Kittel he shared a keen, perhaps over-keen, fascination with the theological vocabulary of the New Testament; and it was Hoskyns who first drew the budding *Theologisches Wörterbuch* to the attention of English readers.[20] Both of them were manifestly if understandably ignorant of linguistic philosophy, although not perhaps in every case as semantically misguided as James Barr later supposed.[21] For Kittel, the *Wörterbuch* documented the Jewish and Christian history of ideas, which

(personal communication, Jan. 24, 2003). MacKinnon 1987: 196, however, also speaks of *disiecta membra*; cf. similarly Parsons 1985: 138.

18. Lady Hoskyns (1895–1994, née Mary Trym Budden, granddaughter of Lord Kitchener of Khartoum) was a mathematics don at Newnham College whom Sir Edwin married in 1922. After being briefly associated with a loosely Anglican (but increasingly creedless) group of scientific mystics called the Epiphany Philosophers, she soon became involved with Dorothy Kerin's foundation of Burrswood, a "Christian hospital place of healing" near Tunbridge Wells (cf. http://www.burrswood.org.uk/). This, along with her own ministry of healing and her involvement with the Board of Women's Church Work, accounts for her epitaph: "True Christian mathematician and healer." (For this insight I am grateful to C. F. Evans [personal communication, April 10, 2003] for relating to me a conversation with Hoskyns's son Anthony.) Evans also communicates an unsourced recollection that Hoskyns attributed to his wife's judgment his insights on the ancient mathematical significance of the 153 fish in the commentary on John (Hoskyns 1947: 553–56)—though he merely concludes with Jerome that, rather than being symbolic in itself, the number represents the disciples' "perfect catch of fish, one of every kind."

19. Many of his students did of course acknowledge his distinct influence on them, but they constituted no identifiable group or movement.

20. Kittel (1933b: vii) appreciatively mentions Hoskyns in the preface to *Theologisches Wörterbuch zum Neuen Testament*.

21. For Barr on Hoskyns see Barr 1961: 125–26, 195–97, but note the nuanced modification offered by Horbury 2003b: 88, 91–93; also Barrett 1995: 58. Hoskyns's early pupil R. V. G. Tasker criticized Hoskyns's excessive use of concordances in the desire to find biblical unity (cited in Parsons 1985: 65).

Hoskyns appropriated in an almost mystical commitment to
the language of the New Testament as expressive of the power
of the gospel.[22]

A certain Tory predisposition and lack of political premonition
undoubtedly blurred Hoskyns's understanding of the full dangers
of Kittel's Nazi sympathies, and for this his judgment has been
frequently criticized. Nevertheless, at least until *Kristallnacht*
(November 9, 1938) and World War II (1939–45), such blithe
political naïveté arguably characterized not just Germanophile
Tories like Hoskyns but also the untiring humanitarian optimism of liberal pacifists like Charles Raven.[23] After accepting
an invitation to lecture at Tübingen, Hoskyns reciprocated by
having Kittel invited to Cambridge in 1937. Kittel's affection
for his English friend may in fact have cooled as early as 1933,[24]
perhaps in part because of the latter's somewhat alarmed with-
drawal of support at the publication of Kittel's *Die Judenfrage*
(1933a).[25] In any case, Hoskyns's untimely death spared him the
embarrassing controversy caused by Kittel's distasteful public
appearance wearing his Nazi party badge—though even here
it is worth noting that the lecture made no political points
and remained strictly a scholarly account of the making of the
Wörterbuch.[26]

22. Thus his gushing exclamation in a 1928 sermon: "Can we rescue a word,
and discover a universe? Can we study a language, and awake to the Truth? Can
we bury ourselves in a lexicon, and arise in the presence of God?" (Hoskyns
1938a: 70).

23. The enormous and remarkably long-lived popularity of Chamberlain's 1938
Munich agreement is a salutary reminder of the British public's persistent state of
denial about the true nature of National Socialism.

24. Cf. Wakefield 1981: 65–66, 66n1. On the other hand, Kittel's Cambridge
lecture expressed warm appreciation for a recently deceased friend (1938b: 3).

25. Cf. Wakefield 1975: 574 on Hoskyns's reaction. This point is conveniently
ignored by MacKinnon 1987: 204–5, whose dislike of "blind" Toryism apparently
causes him to attribute even what he sees as Hoskyns's "exaggerated sense of the
unity of the New Testament writings" to his inappropriate regard for "Kittel and his
associates." On Nazi-era biblical interpretation see also chapter 7 below.

26. This is clear from the published version (Kittel 1938b) and is further confirmed by personal memory in Barrett 1995: 59, who also comments that Hoskyns's
sympathies were certainly not Nazi so much as "universal," expressing the sort of
attitude that insists on "fair play even for . . . enemies."

Hoskyns's relationship with Schlatter, the physically diminutive but intellectually powerful Swiss theologian,[27] is a little more difficult to gauge. They had met as early as 1906, and their personal contacts were apparently few but formative. In a letter to family members shortly before Christmas 1929, Schlatter speaks fondly of the unity in the Scriptures he experienced during Hoskyns's three recent visits in order to read and discuss the Fourth Gospel together. For his own part, Hoskyns was so moved that before leaving Tübingen he made a point of buying every one of Schlatter's books (Neuer 1996b: 690; cf. also Kittel 1938a: 10). His copy of Schlatter's 1930 commentary on John was found at his death to be worn out from constant use in the unfinished work on his own commentary. Hoskyns follows his Swiss colleague's then highly unusual emphasis on the Fourth Gospel's Jewish setting (Wakefield 1981: 56; cf. Gutteridge 1964: 57n27);[28] he consistently cites this and no other commentary by a dedicated abbreviation (*D.E.J.* = *Der Evangelist Johannes*). For all their methodological and cultural differences, the two scholars shared a deep conviction about the observation of history as crucial to the theological task (cf. C. F. Evans 1983: 81–82).[29]

But at the end of the day it seems equally clear that Hoskyns's primary influence was less through publications than as an inspiring teacher. Both from explicit testimony and from reading between the lines, one realizes that his students invariably came away with a sense "that theology really mattered" (C. F. Evans 1983: 84–86) and "that the study, interpretation, and proclamation of the New Testament was both the most exciting and the most responsible task" anyone could undertake (Barrett 1995:

27. In personal conversation before a seminar held in Cambridge on November 26, 2002, to commemorate the 150th anniversary of Schlatter's birth, C. F. Evans recalled how Schlatter's striking appearance and slender stature seemed to him to resemble "a pocket Abraham" when he visited Schlatter's house for an open evening in 1933.

28. Parsons 1985: 139–40 is certainly misguided in his denigration of Schlatter's "Jewish" influence on the commentary, which was in this respect well ahead of its time.

29. At the same time, it is right to note with Stuhlmacher 2003: 267–69 and others that Schlatter's work did not consistently heed his own call for historical reading of the Bible, but acquiesced in a good deal of harmonization.

62). This assessment of Hoskyns's (and Davey's) teaching is retained even by those who, like C. F. Evans or C. K. Barrett, eventually followed a rather different theological trajectory: Barrett, reminiscing about Hoskyns's lectures, muses, "It is memory rather than the written page that rekindles the fire and revives the enthusiasm" (60).

Hoskyns on the Bible and Theology

In the literature one sometimes finds Hoskyns described as a "liberal catholic" (so Morgan 1999; C. F. Evans 1983: 72; cf. also Cobham 1958a: 280 on Robinson 1954: 13). Traits of such views arguably emerged in his early years, when he showed sympathies for the religion of Dostoevsky's *The Idiot* and for the rationalism of Catholic modernists like Alfred Loisy.[30] But this does not reflect the maturing theology of his Cambridge years, which moved in a far more biblical and theological direction under the influence of Barth, Kittel, and Schlatter.[31]

The same shift is evident in the changing definition of New Testament theology. From his postwar concern for the phenomenological development of the experiences and theologies of the early Christians, his focus ten years later had shifted to a dominant interest in the faith and behavior of those Christians and indeed to a kerygmatic theology of the word of God.[32] C. K. Barrett recalls

30. In 1915 Hoskyns interpreted the doctrine of incarnation to mean that "when fundamental human nature is revealed it is in fact the Nature of God" (quoted in Wakefield 1981: 48). On this early period cf. further Parsons 1985: 18–25; C. F. Evans 1983: 72–73; Smyth 1938: xvi (quoting J. O. Cobham); and MacKinnon 1987: 198.

31. Cf. Wakefield 1981: 54; C. F. Evans 1983: 73; Barrett 1995: 57; and Parsons 1985: 32–33 (on his critique of Loisy), 44–75 (on further developments). The trend is well under way in Hoskyns 1926 and 1930—the latter is an essay that C. F. Evans (personal communication, Jan. 24, 2003) regards as particularly important, both because of its delicate handling of messianism in certain Synoptic logia and because its inclusion in a landmark volume "meant that Hoskyns had arrived. . . . He was now definitely playing with the big boys, whatever Cambridge might think."

32. Cf. C. F. Evans quoted in Wakefield 1981: 49. Wakefield 1981: 71 writes: "Hoskyns . . . moved from a religion of experience to one of revelation through history received by faith." Similarly J. O. Cobham quoted in Smyth 1938: xvi–xviii; and Barrett 1995: 57.

an analogy that the later Hoskyns used to illustrate what this meant for New Testament study: "You look down your critical microscope at the New Testament text with a view to describing the religious life of the first-century Christians, and you find that God is looking back at you through the microscope and declaring you to be a sinner" (1995: 57). To study the New Testament is no longer to trace the social history of an ancient religious sect, but to discover the place of an arresting encounter with the living God. The exegete has become the object as much as the subject of analysis and interpretation.

There is no doubt that Hoskyns consistently disliked pietists and fundamentalists, an attitude partly in keeping with his high-church Tory sympathies.[33] But he was at least equally annoyed with liberal (and indeed liberal Anglo-Catholic) disdain for Scripture.[34] He passionately believed that only the preoccupation with Scripture can protect us from simplistic religion—whether of the subjectively pietistic, the hidebound conservative, or the gnosticizing liberal sort (cf. Hoskyns 1960: 64). Contrary to evangelical pietism, he wholeheartedly embraced the critique of religion and religious experience that is so characteristic of Barth's commentary on Romans,[35] and he followed Schlatter's emphasis on theology as irreducible to the merely conceptual, or experiential.

But Hoskyns's attack on fundamentalism was tempered by his even more trenchant rejection of the dogmatism of liberal critics in the biblical guild. Although born in the same year as Bultmann (1884) and imbibing from the same sources of German Protestant liberalism, the mature Hoskyns's sympa-

33. Fundamentalists were not the only ones to incur Hoskyns's displeasure. In a personal communication, C. F. Evans tells me (Jan. 24, 2003) that when his name appeared on the Student Christian Movement's term card as the college's undergraduate representative, Hoskyns summoned him and told him that the SCM had no place at Corpus: students wanting to learn about Christianity should attend college chapel!
34. C. F. Evans (personal communication, Jan. 24, 2003) rightly suggests to me that such disdain was at that time less typical of Anglo-Catholicism.
35. It is true that Hoskyns appears to have thought more highly of Barth's early exegetical work than of the first volume of the *Church Dogmatics*, on which he is reported to have commented somewhat skeptically. See p. 160n49 below.

thies had moved in a direction increasingly opposed to that of
Bultmann and indeed of New Testament scholarship's emerg-
ing liberal paradigm, which was to mark the generation after
World War II.

Much as he despised its intellectual obscurantism, Hoskyns
insisted that fundamentalism had in fact held on to a vital truth
that liberalism had thrown out with the creedal bathwater. Fundamentalism *properly* conceived, Hoskyns argued, is simply
"the claim that the biblical language does contain within it the
truth of religion, and if we steadily refuse to blaze forth that
language, we shall inevitably miss the truths which it generates, and which it enables us to hear" (1960: 66, also quoted
in Wakefield 1981: 52). The guild of biblical critics had instead
succumbed to the intolerably dogmatic "tyranny of a rather su-
perficial doctrine of evolution claiming the right to interpret and
remould the truths of the Christian religion": if fundamentalism
were no more than this, "it would be exceedingly difficult for
us not to side wholly and convincedly with the Fundamentalists in their insistence on the necessity of a return to the Bible,
and to refrain from pointing out that the Church is inevitably
Fundamentalist in this sense" (1960: 66). The problem in that
sense is not fundamentalism so much as the fundamentalists
themselves when they rule out any truth other than the Bible,
putting it in place of Christ.

Hoskyns was a great believer in the importance of historical criticism and in the ability of many other fields of study to
shed light on the importance of Scripture in its focus on Christ.
Indeed, he believed too deeply in critical inquiry and intellectual
freedom to be satisfied with the tidiness of the classic liberal approaches: he refused to be circumscribed by their banal desire
for a culturally palatable Christianity, or for that matter by their
concomitant tendency to explain away historic lines of continuity from Jesus to the Gospels and the church (cf. Wakefield
1981: 55–56).

In his New Testament scholarship Hoskyns was invariably scath-
ing about any study of Scripture that treated it merely from the
perspective of Christian origins, whether in literary or in historical

mode (1960: 55, 61). Nor, for that matter, did he have any time for mainstream biblical scholarship's separation of the Old and New Testaments (89).

It suited his Anglo-Catholic churchmanship to stress the obvious fact that the New Testament uses the term *church* far more frequently than the term *Christian*, which to him meant that the individual believer's being was clearly constituted in *belonging*. As the church, we bear witness "that the revelation of God . . . occurs, acts, is energetic and effective through" the Bible, the sacraments, the creeds, and the Christ (Hoskyns 1938a: 78, quoted in Wakefield 1981: 53).

At the same time, the influence of Barth shows in Hoskyns's growing insistence that the church itself must stand under the judgment of Scripture (so, rightly, Cobham 1958a: 281, 295). In that sense, too, he is most accurately described as an evangelical catholic. This is a point passionately advanced by one of his students, J. O. Cobham:

> The position he reached made him the severe antagonist of Liberalism in all its forms. That is why I hope that you will drop the phrase "Liberal Catholicism." He was concerned to give Catholics a sure basis in the Gospel. But he was no less concerned to recall Evangelicals to the Gospel. . . . I think there is danger in stressing too much Hoskyns as an Anglo-Catholic, lest Evangelicals within the Church of England fail even now to realise that Hoskyns was for many years fighting the cause of Evangelicalism almost single-handed.[36]

This evangelical catholicism emerges nowhere more clearly than in Hoskyns's persistent conviction that the "riddle" of New Testament study is its disclosure of the apostolic gospel in organic continuity with the church's faith.

36. Cf. J. O. Cobham quoted in Smyth 1938: xvii–xviii. C. F. Evans (personal communication, Jan. 24, 2003), while appreciating the reasons for this judgment, considers Hoskyns to have remained a liberal catholic—largely on the grounds that his letter for Barth's Festschrift praised Barth's renewal for Anglicans of what Edward Pusey had once done in exegeting the text. But while this is indeed a recognizably Anglo-Catholic perspective, it is hardly liberal.

Although Anglo-Catholic by temperament and affiliation, Hoskyns's low tolerance threshold for any preoccupation with either pietism or ritual also echoes Corpus Christi's transformation in the 1920s and 1930s from an evangelical college to being deliberately Tory and restrained high church, a place where services were a "scarf and hood affair" and "strictly Book of Common Prayer" (C. F. Evans, personal communication, Jan. 24, 2003).[37] By contrast, on a walk through Cambridge with Noel Davey and Christopher Evans, Hoskyns once wandered into Little St. Mary's Church, known for its elaborate Anglo-Catholic incense, images, and statues; provoked by the absence of any lectern with an open Bible, he quipped, "You see, it might be a temple of Serapis!" (Wakefield 1981: 50–51). He is reported to have joked that the annual sacrifice of a bull in the college court might usefully remind everyone of the crude presuppositions of much Christian ritual (so Ramsey 1974, cited by Peter Bottomley in *Hansard*, March 2, 1992: 128). Catholic ecclesiology, chastened and reinforced by an evangelical fervency for scriptural interpretation, may again explain something of the force and independence of his stance.

This combination of commitment and nonalignment is amusingly illustrated by an anecdote related by Christopher Evans (personal communication, April 10, 2003), which also reflects something of the controversies of the day within the Faculty of Divinity at Cambridge. An annual meeting of the Faculty was convened to consider the question of which preachers should be invited to give the university sermons at Great St. Mary's Church. J. F. Bethune-Baker, the liberal Lady Margaret's Professor and Hoskyns's leading opponent, passionately attacked the university statutes that at that time restricted the choice of university preachers to Anglicans. He proposed to revise them in the hope of inviting dissenters and non-Anglicans. When Hoskyns's turn came to speak, to everyone's surprise he began by expressing his wholehearted agreement with the Lady Margaret's Professor—and

37. William Horbury, a Fellow of Corpus Christi, also confirmed this interpretation to me in conversation.

went on to propose the (Roman Catholic) Abbot of Downside. "Oh no, no, no!" protested Bethune-Baker, "that is not what I meant at all!"

The Riddle of the Fourth Gospel

It would take a great deal more space than we have here to examine in detail Hoskyns's implementation of this approach in his commentary on the Fourth Gospel. When it appeared in 1947, that work was widely acknowledged as a masterpiece of its genre; Ernst Käsemann reputedly said that it did for John what Barth did for Romans.[38] This seems in one sense a considerable overstatement, in terms both of its impact on the history of theology and of the sheer pace and programmatic force of Barth's treatment. Taken for what it is, however, it is possible to argue that Hoskyns's expository achievement in some respects outstrips that of Barth: 135 tightly reasoned preliminary pages introduce a commentary that is often bracing in its sheer theological energy, while equally as attentive to philological and historical issues as to issues of Jewish context and patristic reception. Among the latter are matters such as the fathers' christological reading of Siloam in 9:7 (Hoskyns 1947: 354–55), their disputes with Arians about 14:28 (462–63), and the liturgical place of foot-washing in the ancient church (443–46). For a work of its time, the commentary is especially remarkable in the breadth of its interaction with ancient Jewish sources, including the Apocrypha, Pseudepigrapha, Philo, Josephus, and rabbinic writings; it also covers an impressive range of patristic and Greco-Roman literature, including newly discovered papyri. Hoskyns was up-to-date and conversant with the best scholarship in English, French, and German. He read, but shows himself largely unimpressed by, Bultmann's efforts to reassemble the sequence of the Gospel and interpret it in Mandean terms.

38. So C. F. Evans 1983: 81 (although he signally dissents from Käsemann's judgment). MacKinnon 1987: 199 suggests that while Bultmann's commentary later attended to some of these same issues, that was all the more tribute to Hoskyns's insight.

And yet, Hoskyns manages to engage with all this detailed philological and historical work without for a moment losing the theological wood for the trees. The purpose of his commentary, he insists, is to "hear and set forth the Meaning" that the evangelist himself has concretely heard and seen in Jesus of Nazareth (132). Although Hoskyns was interested in the Fourth Gospel's use of Synoptic and other Jesus tradition (82–83), he flatly refuses to disentangle history from interpretation: the two are intertwined, and to attempt to separate them would render the gospel unintelligible (132). Hoskyns's Johannine scholarship is in that sense at once comparable and yet decidedly more highly ecclesial and theological than that of the Congregationalist C. H. Dodd, his exact contemporary (born 1884; cf. J. King 1984).[39]

The commentary does, to be sure, manifest certain tensions in its understanding of the relationship between theology and history—or at any rate of historicity, which may not amount to the same thing.[40] The treatment of the raising of Lazarus in John 11 is often noted as a key case study of this difficulty, since Hoskyns here allows for John's use of tradition but seems to dodge the issue of historicity just where this might clash with the consensus of historical-critical orthodoxy (see Hoskyns 1947: 395; cf. 84).[41] (Similar problems arguably attend the overly brief treatment of the resurrection accounts in *Crucifixion-Resurrection*, further complicated by that work's composite nature as a patchwork of writing by Hoskyns and Davey later quilted together by Wakefield.)[42]

39. Dodd's inaugural lecture as Norris-Hulse Professor, which we discussed extensively in chapter 1, was delivered the year before Hoskyns died.
40. This is a point repeatedly made by reviewers of the commentary; see also J. King 1984: 5–6, who cites Dodd's critique of the notion that "nonhistorical truth" must be revealed in "nonhistorical form."
41. J. King 1984: 6 writes, "Despite his knowledge that the Evangelist stresses the historical nature of the event, Hoskyns did not grapple with the question of historicity at the very point where it presses most strongly upon the reader of the Fourth Gospel."
42. Hoskyns and Davey 1981: 279–92, on which see also MacKinnon 1987: 199. At times this erratic volume shows a curiously uncharacteristic, almost Bultmannian slippage in the meaning both of the word *history*, which includes "the records of the inner experience of godly men and women" (297), and of *resurrection*, in which the disciples saw God's power working not visibly (and bearing no "observable fruits in

But even if, for all its subtlety, the exegetical implementation at times leaves something to be desired, the theological poignancy of Hoskyns's stance can be usefully illustrated in several striking programmatic passages on the Fourth Gospel's integration of history and theology.[43] For Hoskyns, the Gospel's Christology of Word made flesh also holds the key to the entire problem of gospel history and interpretation: to the extent that it downplays history, the Word is a meaningless myth; but unless Jesus is in fact the Son of God sent into the world, then all the history of Jesus and all the piety of the church is in fact darkness, misunderstanding, and blasphemy: "There is no escape from history possible for the author of the Fourth Gospel, just as there can be no historical materialism in the presence of Jesus" (85; cf. 83–84).

Hoskyns's christological and kerygmatic emphasis is perhaps unsurprising in view of his reception of Karl Barth, even if his insistence on the indispensability of history hints at limits of that influence. Nevertheless, in the opinion of one prominent reviewer of *Crucifixion-Resurrection*, "what Hoskyns learnt from Barth enabled him [to] present, as very few of his generation, the epistemological problems lying at the heart of Christian belief" (MacKinnon 1987: 198–99; cf. 201).[44] Indeed, Hoskyns presses the question of how to interpret and understand the gospel in a strikingly pneumatological and trinitarian direction: "Mere historicity, mere reminiscences, would bury the truth irrecoverably in the earth; for the truth which Jesus *is* and *was* can be made known only by the Holy Spirit of

---

time and space") but only "to the eye of their faith" (305, 307). Does this slippage tell us much about Hoskyns, or does it reveal more about the editorial hand of Wakefield, who interpolated the chapter from which these quotations are taken (and whose epilogue tacitly endorses a view of resurrection as "metaphor and symbolism" and indeed "myth"; 354–55), or for that matter about that of Davey, who composed the chapter? Wakefield seems to acknowledge what the answer must be (355–56): "But Hoskyns would have been hostile to any view that seemed to lay primary stress on the subjective and the experiential, ambiguous as these terms are. Had he lived he would have found himself increasingly unsympathetic to Bultmann." For him, the resurrection was indeed "not simply something which the disciples felt had happened."

43. See chapters 4 ("The Historical Tension of the Fourth Gospel"), 5 ("The Authority of the Fourth Gospel"), and 8 ("The Theological Tension of the Fourth Gospel").

44. MacKinnon was Norris-Hulse Professor of Divinity in Cambridge, 1960–78.

God, who is the Spirit of Truth" (Hoskyns 1947: 129 [emphasis original]; cf. 131).

And for Hoskyns it is this encounter with the reality of God's eternal life that inextricably ties the historical Jesus to the historical church created by the witness of the apostles. The resurrection and the gift of the Spirit necessitate an understanding of apostolic Christianity that is irreducible both to mysticism on the one hand and to mere historicism on the other (131–32):

> With the mention of the name "Jesus," a strict historical emphasis moves into the centre of the Johannine picture of the Church, an emphasis that inevitably carries with it the authority of the witness of the original disciples who saw and heard and touched. Once the name of Jesus has been spoken or written, their authority, far from being submerged by the vigorous faith of later Christians, becomes central. . . . For this reason, the authoritative witness of the original disciples, of the strictly apostolic "we," governs the whole edifice of the Christian community and alone is able to bring into being the authoritative first person plural of the general body of Christians. (91)

Once again we find here the basic idea governing *The Riddle of the New Testament*, which is this: the New Testament witnesses in all their diversity agree on a fundamental conviction about Jesus of Nazareth that stands in organic continuity with the apostolic faith of the church.

Limitations and Enduring Stimuli

A great deal more could fruitfully be said about Hoskyns's significance in his own time, but others have done this better than I can. In the remarks that follow, therefore, I wish in conclusion to focus on what might be seen as some abiding merits of Hoskyns's approach to Scripture and theology.

Twenty years ago Reginald H. Fuller attempted to resist the seemingly self-authenticating liberal assumption that "Hoskyns and his biblical theology were merely a detour" (1984: 334).

Fuller's answer was to try to show that Hoskyns's work anticipated various trends in postwar liberal critical scholarship, with perhaps predictably wearisome and unsatisfactory results. Updating Hoskyns after the fact does not seem a promising project. Here I want instead to suggest that several of his forgotten theological emphases may in themselves provide a timely reminder about the nature of Christian New Testament study. While a Hoskyns revival would be inappropriate, several of his emphases could still prove energizing for the development of an evangelical catholic reading of the text in our own time.

Hoskyns's work undoubtedly has numerous shortcomings. His early death left it a torso, and important questions remained unanswered or even unasked. In many ways he inhabited a rather old-fashioned world of Oxbridge collegiate clericalism. More to the point, perhaps, critics rightly question his lack of a hermeneutical and philosophical awareness (Morgan 1999; Fuller 1984: 325; MacKinnon 1987: 199–200), a problem that is often characteristic of English biblical scholarship. On the other hand, for a text-centered catholic approach to Scripture this is perhaps less important: it could be argued that an explicitly ecclesial and doctrinal framework of engagement with the Bible may itself deliver particular hermeneutical strengths and disciplines. In any case there is little point in scolding parents for their ignorance of the innovations of their children.

Aside from a certain tendency to make rather florid assertions about the language of the New Testament, Hoskyns ran the risk of letting his kerygmatic exuberance get the better of his scholarly caution.[45] While affirming *The Riddle of the New Testament* to be well ahead of its time, even a sympathetic critic like C. F. D. Moule comments on the repeated impression of glibness and haste in handling complex or detailed evidence (1961: 145–46). After sitting at the feet of Germany's self-possessed scholarly giants of biblical *Wissenschaft*, Hoskyns had perhaps become overly optimistic about critical New Testament study and its ability to deliver

45. Even a fellow contributor to *Essays Catholic & Critical* (Selwyn 1926) wondered about "Barthianism . . . pushed to extremes": "Yet surely the Bible itself cannot be quite so Biblical," wrote the baffled O. C. Quick (1933: 109 and n. 1).

not only "assured results" but also a picture of Christian origins that could be easily rendered congenial to a catholic theological stance. This confidence in the power of critical scholarship remains even at a time when the tidiness of his earlier understanding gave way to a more turbulent and red-blooded engagement with what he called the "strange, restless, and unfamiliar" complexities of Scripture (1947: 20).

While bearing in mind these and other limitations, I would like here to suggest Hoskyns's three abiding contributions to a biblical scholarship prepared to bring a self-involving intellectual seriousness to the study of the text's implied readings.

History and Theology

Hoskyns's first key contribution is the focus on an integrated historical-critical reading of Scripture that is at once keenly theological and concerned for the organic lines of continuity connecting Jesus with the church. As we hinted earlier, on the historical side, Hoskyns's implementation of this principle was not perhaps always equally rigorous. Nevertheless, the very idea that the New Testament itself points to an integration of the two ran very much against the grain of the mainstream liberal paradigm of New Testament study, whose dominance ultimately led to the demise of the biblical theology movement.

Today one could argue that we are in some ways coming full circle in several of the major contributors to the so-called Third Quest for the historical Jesus,[46] who would argue that a plausible Jesus is one whose profile can explain the rise of the church. A number of major recent studies of New Testament Christology likewise draw attention to the fact that far from being a Hellenistic innovation decades after his death, the worship of Jesus proceeds from the heart of a Jewish monotheistic view of God (Bauckham 1998a; Hurtado 2003; Gieschen 2003). We may also note recent attempts, especially in America and in Germany, to revive a more

46. One thinks especially of works by N. T. Wright, C. Stephen Evans, Leander E. Keck, Mark Allen Powell, Richard Bauckham, and others.

methodologically aware biblical theology that is also conversant with Christian doctrine.[47]

In his stress on recognizing Christian theological contours in a historically rigorous picture of Jesus, a picture that explains not just his life but also what followed from it, Hoskyns is well worth hearing today. This is not least because for much of the later twentieth century the guild of New Testament scholarship remained so wedded to historical and analytical method that the very possibility of a return to biblical theology was "scarcely conceivable" (so C. F. Evans 1983: 71)—an impression that was widely shared in the 1970s and 1980s.

Today, however, that *continuity* of tradition that Hoskyns and Davey stressed in *The Riddle of the New Testament* is once again becoming an acceptable subject of intellectual interest and debate, not least as old critical dichotomies are crumbling. This development bears not only on our view of New Testament history, but also on the historically vital recognition that the text's theological world is in fact a space continuously populated over time by a church that for all its division, diversity, and change maintained—and maintains—a defining loyalty to the same apostolic gospel. "No phase of the apostolic age is really intelligible apart from the centrality of the death and resurrection of the Messiah": that is how Michael Ramsey summed up the basic thesis of *The Riddle of the New Testament* (in his foreword to Hoskyns and Davey 1981: xii), a thesis whose timeliness in these terms could hardly be exaggerated.

In wrestling with the relationship between good history and good theology, Hoskyns sometimes comes close to spelling out the epistemological and hermeneutical advantage of an interpreter attuned to the faith of the New Testament's implied reader. So, for

47. Perhaps the best-known representative of the return to the question of biblical theology is Childs 1992, but also and from a very different perspective Barr 1999. In Germany, key contributors are Hübner 1990; Mildenberger 1991–93; and Stuhlmacher 1992–99, 2002b. Recent multiauthor discussions include Hafemann 2002 and Hübner and Jaspert 1999. Among British New Testament scholars, Richard Bauckham, Anthony Thiselton, and Francis Watson are perhaps especially noteworthy for this combination, although none of them are straightforwardly "biblical theologians." See chapters 1–3 above.

example, in a striking departure from Lessing's hugely influential enlightenment prejudice about the relationship of history and faith, Hoskyns went so far as to claim that "the Bible is theology. It is historical theology. It can reveal its meaning only to those who regard it as the Word of God, and are able to preserve a strict confidence in the universal significance of particular historical occasions" (1960: 56).

Evangelical Catholicism

A second and related contribution of Hoskyns's work is one that may run somewhat against the grain of his own instincts, but that nevertheless seems quite clear at least with hindsight. Hoskyns's approach occupies de facto a mediating position between what today would be recognized as post–Vatican II Roman Catholic and evangelical positions, the two branches of Christian biblical scholarship that are now arguably in the ascendancy and producing some of the most vigorous new biblical research.

This needs to be stated with a measure of care and restraint, since the bandwagon of "theological interpretation" and "ecclesial reading" is in danger of becoming overpopulated with a variety of very diverse, not to say irreconcilable, approaches. And too little of what claims to pass for such theological interpretation actually provides any sort of account or rationale of the relationship between Scripture and constructive theology: Is exegesis merely illustrative, playful, or epiphenomenal mood music to accompany what is normatively determined on other grounds? Or is there some sense, however complex or attenuated, that theology *itself* is ultimately an exegetical discipline? These and other questions remain to be answered—even if the very opportunity to ask them is an improvement on former conspiracies of silence. What matters for present purposes is that Christian doctrine and the interpretation of the New Testament are no longer invariably sworn enemies, as they were in Hoskyns's day and for many a decade thereafter.

Conversely, a glance at Aberdeen and St. Andrews, or Duke and Notre Dame, shows it is no longer true that, as Wakefield still sighed in 1981, ecclesially engaged exegesis "seems somehow never to engage with the radical questions" (1981: 75). Hoskyns himself had seen the key to the Gospels in the Fourth Gospel's "steady *refusal* . . . to come to rest in any solution which conservative or radical scholars have propounded" (1947: 131, emphasis added). While in its postmodern political garb radicalness may often be in the eye of the beholder, few questions are as historically and theologically radical as the identity of Jesus and his place in Christian faith. And on this subject, a number of leading Catholic and evangelical scholars are today once again pursuing lines of inquiry comparable to those of Hoskyns's biblical theology.

In the event, postwar liberal criticism won the day, made its point, and ran its course. But while it sustains today a certain vitality in the Western academy and in high-church Protestantism, classic liberalism has clearly lost most of its living base and momentum in the churches of the West, let alone in those of the ascendant East and South. Deliberate critical detachment from hermeneutical and liturgical disciplines of faith seeking understanding can produce, almost by definition, no spiritual grandchildren. (Even liberalism's primarily adoptive children tend increasingly to take on a self-consciously postliberal or even postcritical garb, happily staking communitarian and sociolinguistic claims on orthodox doctrines and practices—and even to celebrate a "return to Scripture.")[48] Here again, Hoskyns appears surprisingly topical in his evangelical catholic impetus for a biblical scholarship that takes with wholehearted intellectual seriousness the inalienably creedal fabric of its text.

Faith and the Academy

Especially in his later years, Hoskyns increasingly asked the crucial questions about the New Testament's role in Christian theology, and about the New Testament scholar's debt to the

---

48. This is often associated with authors like Hans Frei, George Lindbeck, the later Paul Ricoeur, or even Jean-Luc Marion. For recent expositions of this trend cf. Ochs 1993 and Pecknold 2003. Note, however, the sustained theological critique of the postliberal posture in Vanhoozer 2005 (cf. the earlier and more popular treatment in McGrath 1996: 146–54).

text's theological claims and its ecclesial *Sitz im Leben*. Although ignored or ridiculed by the dominant liberalism in Cambridge and further afield, that question was made more urgent by his encounter with Barth. Hoskyns never became a Barthian; indeed, he may well have had reservations about the grandiose scholastic ambitions of the budding *Church Dogmatics*.[49] A year before he died, however, he contributed a revealing "letter from England" to a Festschrift for Barth's fiftieth birthday. Here Hoskyns poses the question most sharply: "Is a theological faculty in a university true to its subject-matter, if it never be permitted to stray beyond a purely historical description of the church in primitive and other times, or, if it be permitted to stray, to stray only into speculative theology?" (1938a: 220). Hoskyns's question of New Testament scholarship's engagement with the actual content and life of that book remains a challenge full of intellectual vitality and promise. Far from being accessible through either a mastery of secondary literature or a sociological redescription of Christian origins, Scripture's theological *res*, its subject matter and ecclesial setting, inextricably defines the New Testament's historic footprint and identity—and its implied readings. It is this object of study that *does* stare back at us through the microscope and that calls the implied interpreter to faith in the gospel of the living God.

    49. So, anecdotally, C. F. Evans 1983: 81; cf. also J. King 1984: 2, citing A. M. Ramsey. Hoskyns confided to one of his students that in his view Barth's failure was not his famous "no!" to natural theology but his lack of an adequate theology of the natural (Gutteridge 1964: 50n9).

6

LIVING MEMORY AND APOSTOLIC HISTORY

The argument of this book has now progressed to a critical point. If study of the New Testament were indeed to take useful account of the implicit readings and readers elucidated by the story of the text's own effects and reception, this in turn invites us to reconsider what a subject-appropriate historical understanding of Christian origins might look like. In these final two chapters, then, I want to suggest that a properly *historical* understanding of the New Testament and its footprint in the church requires us to take seriously the early Christian emphasis on living memory of the apostolic age. That theme will be the subject of the present chapter, while the last chapter will deal more specifically with the problem, and the significance, of early Christian memory of Jesus in his Jewish identity.

The Limits of "Archeological" History

We are faced with a tough challenge. New Testament scholars' training and ingrained professional habit leave us ill equipped to appreciate the extent to which a properly historical understanding of our text necessarily involves its footprint in its readers' faith and life.

In the nineteenth and twentieth centuries, the dominant view of the New Testament scholar's task was archeological—meticulously stripping away the layers of fictional rubble and pious debris that conceal the pristine first-century reality, which provides what we are really after. The earlier the sources, the closer we get to the truth; the later the sources, the more corrupted they have become by pious accretions and ecclesiastical impositions of conformity. But it also soon became clear that the more we deconstruct our sources, the taller our speculations become—and the more we end up unself-critically talking to ourselves about ourselves. Perhaps it is the case that the complexity of the historical onion is better understood by slicing than by separately peeling away each of the skins. As Herbert Butterfield said in the concluding sentence of his famous treatise on history: "The understanding of the past is not so easy as it is sometimes made to appear" (1931: 95).

In the desire to move past this methodological impasse to a more constructive understanding, it may initially seem tempting to follow certain postmodern trends in refusing to privilege primary over secondary sources. Should we not simply admit that historiography and the historians themselves *are* the only proper subject of the study of history (cf. the survey in R. Evans 1997: 93–102)? Events do not, after all, subsist in splendid isolation from their interpretations. And might we not, in following that line, overcome at one stroke a great many of our quandaries? Is it not the case, perhaps, that all there is in history is text and reception and that we should therefore stop the naïve silliness of worrying about truth?

Perhaps. But as Richard J. Evans forcefully shows in his acclaimed masterpiece on the study of history, the distinction between the past and discourse about the past remains fundamental to human understanding. The interpreter may be able to construct and deconstruct diverse interpretations of the past, but not the past itself: Aristotle had a point when he said that history is what

Alcibiades did and suffered (*Poetics* 2.6, 1451b11).[1] Or, to put
it in Evans's words, it remains the case that Auschwitz was not
a discourse (see 1997: 103–28, esp. 109, 124, 239).[2] The reader-
oriented fixation on contemporary subtexts, opinions, and power
plays—above all power plays—too frequently degrades the past
achievements and sufferings of real individuals in favor of narcis-
sistic inanities (cf. Evans 1997: 200–202 and Ginzburg 1999).[3]

But there may be another avenue that will prove more promising. To accept the distinction between primary and secondary
sources is not to endorse all inherited assumptions about the meaning and use of those sources. In particular, it certainly does not
require us to dismiss their entire aftermath as wholly irrelevant
to the historical subject. On this point, we surely need a fresh
point of departure.

The Promise of Effective History

As we noted in chapter 1, one idea that has been gathering pace
in recent years is the value of studying the aftermath of historical
persons, texts, and events. Swiss scholar Ulrich Luz's outstanding
contribution to New Testament scholarship is perhaps at its fin-
est in his pioneering work on the reception history of the Bible,
as shown especially in his great commentary on Matthew. While
the wonderful wealth of evidence Luz collected is in itself deeply
impressive, perhaps his most valuable contribution is in reflecting

1. Also cited in Sir Isaiah Berlin's famous essay on the concept of scientific
history (1999: 119).
2. Richard Evans also produced an expert report on behalf of the defense in
the notorious libel case Irving v. Penguin Books and Lipstadt (2000). As Philip Boobbyer 2002 demonstrates in an incisive study of Nazi and Communist historiography,
historical understanding is in the end impossible without some moral judgment and
a degree of moral realism. This is in contrast to classic older views like that of Butterfield 1931: 93.
3. These matters are taken with insufficient seriousness by K. Jenkins 1999:
95–114, who rounds on Richard Evans for failing to engage with postmodernism
in sufficient detail. Whatever hermeneutical weaknesses Evans's case manifests from
time to time, the weight of these issues is such that one cannot with Jenkins dismiss
it as nothing more than updated "Rankeanism."

on the nature of reception history and its role in biblical interpretation. One particularly powerful illustration he proposes for
the effective history of Scripture is that of the scientist analyzing
the water of a great river while sitting in a small boat that is itself
carried and driven along by that same river (Luz 1985–2002: 1.79
[ET 1989–: 1.96]; cf. also 1994: 23–38 and the earlier 1985).
This analogy presents itself as highly illuminating for the work of
biblical interpretation, not least because it places that work in its
larger ecclesial and cultural context. It nicely draws our attention
to the fact that scriptural interpretation encompasses not only what
interpreters do but what the very same process does to them. I
frequently use this illustration in my own teaching and writing.

At the same time, I have begun to wonder if it may not also have
certain limitations. Its strength appears to flag just at the point
at which we press it to reveal its analytical pay dirt. How much
can this scientist *truthfully* know about this particular river, let
alone its source? Is the relativity of all human knowledge finally
the only insight this metaphor conveys? If so, its usefulness may
be less compelling than it first appears.

Theologically, too, the analogy turns out to be problematic upon
closer scrutiny. The New Testament itself might be said to suggest
that this particular river does more than just carry the scientist's
boat as she carries out her analysis. There is a sense in which the
"river" of Scripture and Christian faith tests and analyzes the
scientist much more comprehensively than could ever be the case
vice versa (cf. Heb. 4:12). Here we may recall from the previous
chapter (p. 147) Sir Edwyn Hoskyns's comparable image of the
scientist staring down a microscope only to find rather alarmingly
that instead of the supposedly inanimate object of his inquiry
it is God peering back at him and declaring him to be a sinner.
(This is also, incidentally, an important caveat for George Tyrrell's
justly famous Narcissus metaphor of nineteenth-century historical
Jesus scholars contemplating merely their own reflections at the
bottom of a well [1909: 44]. However apt Tyrrell's cautionary
metaphor was in the wake of Schweitzer's researches, by itself it
short-circuits too easily into the conclusion that the reflection is
all one can ever hope to see.) Rightly understood as the history

of the text's effects, *Wirkungsgeschichte* speaks of how Scripture has interpreted *us*, the readers. Even where we take on board this additional consideration, however, we are still left with other problems. What, for example, is the exegetical or hermeneutical use of effective history in cases where the effects conflict with each other or even with the plain sense of the text itself? Is there a theological, ecclesiological, or political agenda that should drive our choice of one over another?

Careful engagement with Luz's massive Matthew commentary suggests that he, too, continues to struggle with unresolved issues in this department. Two contrasting examples from the final volume will suffice to illustrate the difficulty. Luz displays an exemplary sensitivity in negotiating between primary text and reception history in the Gethsemane story. Here we find that subsequent understandings were increasingly preoccupied with the existential problem of human wrestling in prayer before a silent God. In Luz's view this calls for continual reexamination in the light of close exegetical study of the text, which in fact shows a serene Jesus confident in the faithful presence of his Father (Luz 1985–2002: 4.151–53). Luz recognizes the value of new potentialities of meaning, while retaining a keen awareness of the ability of the old readings to speak afresh and shed light on the new.

By contrast with Gethsemane, the commentary's handling of Matthew's relationship with emergent normative Judaism is a rather different kettle of fish. Here a troubled *Wirkungsgeschichte* ensures that the critical knives are out, explicitly discrediting commentators like Davies and Allison who opt for a more "catholic," mediating interpretation of Matthew's place within Judaism and early Christianity.[4] We discover that Matthew's wholly unjustifiable generalizations may only be understood as "cunningly vicious historical fabrications" (*raffiniert-böswilligen historischen Fiktionen*), whose usefulness is narrowly constricted by their unique historical context (Luz 1985–2000: 4.466, 467). Luz explains the

---

4. Luz 1985–2002: 4.468 with reference to Davies and Allison 1988–97: 3.703, 723.

hermeneutical rationale for this method of *Sachkritik* only briefly
and in passing (3.397–98), but liberally applies it here (4.466) and
elsewhere (e.g., 1.94–99; 3.388–401). This question of Matthew's
relationship with Judaism will clearly be important to Luz and
most of his contemporary readers; and yet on this point no negotiation of text and effective history is offered. In the end, we can
only explicitly contradict Matthew (4.472).[5]

What accounts for this different treatment of the material? One
might be tempted to conclude that Matthew's apparent depiction
of Judaism offends some exterior canons of moral truth in ways
that the Christology of Gethsemane does not. But Luz explicitly
rejects the desire to decide between true and false interpretation
(4.470). One is left with the impression that the hermeneutical
adjudication between text and effective history is plagued by conflicting ideological commitments.[6]

Needless to say, those who live in glass houses can ill afford to
throw stones. What sort of a tool can effective history be for the
biblical scholar? Is it primarily a fascinating catalog of how we got
where we are, richly suggestive for the diversity of its hermeneutical options but in itself no more than an appendix to the task of
exegesis? And is not the "effect" of a text a kind of optical illusion,
limitless in scope and complexity and forever receding beyond our
grasp unless we impose on it some theological or ideological order?
Conversely, are not the "effects" of the text much bigger than its
conscious "reception," contrary to what is often assumed? And
most important of all: When everything is said and done, can the
history *generated* by the text shed any light whatsoever on the
history and world of meaning represented by the text itself?

Here cannot be the place to do justice to these questions. I merely
wish to offer a modest suggestion about the role *living memory* can

---

5. Ironically, Luz himself is attacked by Heikki Räisänen 2005: 120–23 for
attempting to defend Matthew's view of hell.

6. On a similar note, Luz 1985–2002: 4.471 states explicitly that Matthew *cannot*
contribute to the unity of the church in theologically and ecclesiastically articulate
ways, but *only* as a book about shared experiences. Later on the same page, however,
we learn that Matthew's "inclusive" story of Jesus demands "a *holistic* hermeneutic
in which faith and life, theology and praxis come together" (italics mine).

play specifically as an aid in the evaluation of the *first two centuries* of the New Testament's effective history. This is therefore an argument about history and memory and about how they relate to exegesis.

Truth and Memory: How We Know the Past

For good reasons, students of history are trained to privilege primary sources dating from the period under investigation. Nevertheless, we will do well to ponder for a moment what a poor track record the authors of such contemporary sources have as guides to the history of their own times. They may of course illustrate or document some of the facts, but they virtually never see the forest for the trees. This is true for everyday life as much as for events of world-changing consequence. When I first worked on this subject, I found myself in a modest library whose sole edition of the *Encyclopaedia Britannica* dated from 1940. In its hasty half-column article on Adolf Hitler, that compendium of knowledge had more to say about the man's vegetarian diet and lack of respect for the Treaty of Versailles than about his ideological views on Greater Germany or the Jews. My curiosity aroused, I quickly turned to the entry on Winston Churchill, who was then aged 66 and (until May of that year) a political has-been. Five times as long as the article on Hitler, this piece remembers him chiefly for his youthful exploits as a journalist in the Boer War, his disastrous record in charge of the British navy during World War I (e.g., Gallipoli), and a series of unremarkable budgets as Chancellor of the Exchequer before his retirement to the back benches in 1929. The End. Exit in a smog of alcohol and fat cigars.

History must be past to be knowable; and it is known first in the intersection of individual and communal memory.[7] This seems a platitude, but it holds the key to an important insight: an accurate vision of history, including that of the New Testament and its drama-

7. Some, like John Lukacs, would say that the past is all we know. Cf. Lukacs 1994: 328 with reference to C. S. Lewis and Dr. Johnson, and again in Yerxa and Giberson 2000 with reference to Kierkegaard. Cf. also his thesis about the superiority of historical to scientific knowing in Lukacs 2002. Note further Mourant 1980: 38 on Augustine's view of memory.

tis personae, requires both proximity and distance. Proximity may seem self-evidently desirable, but distance is required for historical vision and comprehension, as Carlo Ginzburg shows (2001). The trouble is that historians usually inherit distance in free abundance, but acquire what may be had of proximity only by the sweat of their brows. The best primary sources, by contrast, are invariably myopic: they enjoy proximity as their birthright, while distance remains by definition outside their grasp. This optical discrepancy tends to leave that critical equilibrium of proximity and distance precariously poised between primary and secondary writers.

Because history is about effects and consequences as much as it is about causes and conditions, an account of its impact and aftermath is indeed an integral part of all good historiography: causes and effects often help interpret each other. But here too we are inevitably hamstrung by that same balance of proximity and distance: the further the effects are removed in time from their causes, the more tenuous their connection becomes. *Wirkungsgeschichte* increasingly turns into the story of serendipitous echoes and often arbitrary canons of intertextual association, rather than a continuity of demonstrable effects. Consequences soon cease to shed appreciable light on the meaning and significance of their causes.

There is, however, a third set of voices, uniquely placed to mediate between primary and secondary sources, and between the requirements of proximity and distance. Posterity for a while includes people who retain a personal link to the persons and events concerned. That is of course an old and familiar lesson, whose illustrations reach back to antiquity.[8] And after surviving the bloodiest century since the world began, we too ought to have learned the hard way that true history includes what is remembered and not merely what happens, quite possibly in Orwellian fashion, to be recorded.[9]

8. In an important study, Hedrick 2000 takes his point of departure from *Corpus inscriptionum latinarum* 6.1783, a forty-line inscription rehabilitating the memory of one Virius Nicomachus Flavianus. In 431, thirty-five years after his death and *damnatio memoriae* as an opponent of Theodosius I, this text was reinscribed over the erasure on a statue in his honor.

9. This point is rightly stressed by Lukacs 1994: 328; cf. his précis of his own position in Yerxa and Giberson 2000. It is also one of the merits of the journal *History and Memory* to have drawn sustained attention to this dimension in relation to

My modest suggestion here is to harness the historical implications of a *Wirkungsgeschichte* on the *human* scale—the scale of personal living memory. That is to say, I propose to privilege the *earlier* over the more remote effects for a historical understanding of early Christianity's texts, persons, and events. It is becoming more widely recognized that the confluence of individual and communal memory with written sources is often the meeting ground of "good history" with what we call a "true story," offering an interpreted appropriation of the past by people who are experientially and culturally closer to the events than the historian can ever be. We should take more seriously the phenomenon that Clement of Alexandria calls "not a story but a true tradition preserved in memory" (μῦθον οὐ μῦθον, ἀλλὰ ὄντα λόγον; Eusebius, *Ecclesiastical History* 3.23.6). In antiquity, pagans and Christians alike understood that access to history depends on a conversation with the *viva vox*, the "living voice" of those who remember it—a point to which we must return below (for documentation see Alexander 1990: 224–33; Byrskog 2000: 48–65; and Bauckham 2003).

In taking remembered history seriously, we must take a particular interest both in firsthand eyewitnesses and in those who personally knew them. While the issue of memory in early Christianity has attracted a good deal of more general attention in recent years,[10] significant light has been shed on the phenomenon of named individual eyewitness testimony in the early church especially by Samuel Byrskog (2000), Richard Bauckham (2003, 2006), and recently Martin Hengel (forthcoming).

My own work in this area over a number of years leads me to believe that this phenomenon of living memory continues beyond the New Testament documents well into the second century. Indeed, it is relatively easy to show that the reality of living memory opens up

---

the history of the twentieth century. Cf. further LaCapra 1998; Bartov 1993; and the works of Saul Friedlander and Philippe Ariès.

10. See Dunn 2003 on the gospel tradition, with particular reference to Bailey 1995a and 1995b; cf. previously the writings of Birger Gerhardsson (1961 and 1986) and Rainer Riesner (1981). Verhey 2002 attempts to apply "remembering Jesus" to ethics, but without elucidating either the nature or the individuals involved in such memory.

a uniquely privileged window of up to 150 years—that is approximately the period when there were still living witnesses of the apostles or of their immediate students. This is a little longer than some scholars advocate and does not deny the validity and importance of earlier thresholds of memory; but in the case of early Christianity it seems nevertheless defensible in view of the evidence.[11]

In order to develop this idea, let me begin with an illustration. Many people can relate to this on a personal level. My grandmother was born the year after Queen Victoria's death and died in the year 2000. She had vivid recollections of a childhood in Imperial Germany before World War I and of stories about her grandparents' generation in the mid-nineteenth century. When they reach middle age, my own children are likely to retain clear memories of firsthand stories their father told them about a great-grandmother two of them once met in person, stories that will easily reach back a century and a half and more.[12] Such examples can easily be multiplied.[13]

11. Assmann 2000: 29, 37 suggests an initial threshold at 40 years and a maximum of 80 to 100 years. Murray 2001: 19, 21 argues with reference to Herodotus that oral tradition operates within a time span of 150 to 200 years (I am grateful to Jane M. F. Heath for this reference).

12. Historian John Lukacs (1994: 226) and classicist Wolfgang Schadewaldt (1985: 110) offer similar observations on the relevance and serviceability of personal memory, the latter with particular reference to a 150-year window for the development of a living oral tradition about the Gospels. Churchill (1991) composed a thought experiment on memory and history in an imaginary conversation with his father in 1947. Until very recently, it was not uncommon for elderly black Americans to remember their grandparents' stories about their own experiences as slaves in the old South. On a similar note, George Lindbeck related to me his mother's vivid stories of her grandfather's perspectives on these and other matters in the American Civil War, in which he was drafted as a recently arrived Swedish immigrant and compelled to abandon his young family in rural Minnesota (personal conversation, April 11, 2000). For an even more striking example involving Oliver Cromwell, see S. Jenkins 1999, who could truthfully claim on the eve of the year 2000: "There is a man alive today who heard a woman say: 'My husband's first wife's first husband knew that Cromwell—and liked him well.'" All this, of course, is more obviously true of ancient oriental cultures. To their long memories, moreover, one would further need to add their sustained penchant for genealogies. Descent from the prophet Mohammed is still traced by contemporary Iranian imams, as one of their nephews, a fellow undergraduate in Canada, told me in 1980.

13. Another example familiar to New Testament scholars concerns theologian Adolf Schlatter (1852–1938). At the beginning of the twenty-first century, we held a special seminar in Cambridge to celebrate his 150th anniversary (2002). One of the people in attendance was Christopher F. Evans, a former professor in Durham

To recognize "remembered history" as an important factor in our knowledge of the past is by no means to deny that such sources require careful critical scrutiny. One quickly discovers, for example, that an individual or event may give rise to diverging or contradictory strands of effective history. Multiple memories may either coalesce or disperse, and the coexistence of written and oral sources soon makes it well-nigh impossible to distinguish genuine memory from interpretation on the one hand and fiction on the other. Not all memory engenders tradition, and not all tradition is any longer related to living memory.

In order to turn living memory into a useful historical tool, therefore, it must be read both critically and *dialectically*, as between the differing views of persons or events that its sources presuppose. Where it is tied to persons or places, remembered history often continues where spontaneous reminiscence has long since ceased. Indeed, Elisabeth van Houts rightly stresses that objects and even places serve as "pegs" for memory of events and of persons (1999: 93–120). Similarly, Pierre Nora is rightly influential for drawing our attention to the fact that it is precisely in relation to such "places of memory" (*lieux de mémoire*) that recollection can be jogged as well as reassessed or corrected in light of other evidence or new experiences.[14]

This concern for personal connections with "places of memory" applies to Greek and Roman antiquity, too.[15] It finds more explicit development, however, in the memory of saints, their pupils, and their tombs. In the early church, this concerns specifically the memory of apostles like Peter or James and the places with which they were associated. Especially among Jewish Christians, the

and London now in his nineties, who shared colorful memories of attending an open evening at Adolf Schlatter's house in Tübingen as a young student in 1933. I had a similar encounter with J.-L. Leuba of Neuchâtel, another scholar in his nineties, at the University of Basel's symposium celebrating Oscar Cullmann's centenary in May 2002; he too spoke vividly of personal encounters with Schlatter.

14. See especially Nora 1984: xxxvii ("dans le mélange, c'est la mémoire qui dicte et l'histoire qui écrit"), xxxix ("la mémoire s'accroche à des lieux comme l'histoire à des événements").

15. The place of memory in the historical consciousness of Republican Rome is expertly treated in Walter 2004.

relatives of Jesus and their descendants (the so-called *desposynoi*) were also prominently remembered in the first two centuries (see Bauckham 1990 and Lambers-Petry 2003). Quite apart from the possibility of genuine living memory, many of these figures clearly did serve as "places of memory" in Nora's more wide-ranging sense.[16]

People who are separated from each other by culture or conflict frequently have irreconcilable memories of the same person or course of events. That is why a *dialectical* reading of competing stories and histories may sometimes offer us an invaluable gauge of both the inherent ambiguities and the practical impact of people's personalities, words, and deeds upon their own time.

For all its difficulties, the only good historiography remains that which knows its object from hindsight. If that applies in the case of Churchill, it is even more obviously true for a contested figure like Shakespeare[17]—or indeed for the New Testament. But during the 150-year window of living memory, tradition inhabits a narrative world that is still colored, and at least potentially subject to correction, by what is remembered. However fitfully, this reading of memory may help to impel the historical imagination toward the pursuit of truth.[18] And as we shall see in a moment, this is demonstrably true in the case of early Christianity.[19]

16. Cf. further Mendels 2004, who would include Eusebius as a "site of memory" in Nora's extended sense. Note also Eliav 2004 in relation to the tradition of the tomb of James; and, mutatis mutandis, Valdez del Alamo and Pendergast 2000 on the medieval function of tombs as fixing communal memory.

17. This point is eloquently documented by Bate 1998, to which Robert Morgan has kindly drawn my attention.

18. On the role of disciplined imagination in the writing of history, cf. G. M. Trevelyan (in Cannadine 1992: 75, quoted in R. Evans 1997: 250): "The appeal of history to us all is in the last analysis poetic. But the poetry of history does not consist of imagination roaming at large, but of imagination pursuing the fact and fastening upon it." Cf. also R. Evans 1997: 89.

19. This insight is anticipated in part by Knox 1958: 77: "The body of remembered fact and impression was throughout the first century substantial enough to prevent the wild growth of the tradition." Knox does not, however, provide any methodological account of this claim—let alone any recognition of its significance beyond the end of the first century. Dunn 2003, too, privileges "the remembered Jesus," but without offering a sustained account of memory (a term that does not feature in the index or table of contents). For a sustained methodological engagement with Dunn, see

Memories Ancient and Modern

To New Testament scholars traditionally wedded to a purely *literary*-critical paradigm, an emphasis on memory may seem to require an unpalatable and deeply problematic cocktail of chutzpah and blithe naïveté. Surely the twentieth century must have taught us the intractable vagaries of human memory, a subject that has long kept unnumbered hosts of psychologists and counseling therapists securely in clover. And even aside from well-rehearsed clinical worries about the *reliability* of human memory, what of the contentious *philosophical* debate between leading cognitive scientists about whether there is any such thing as human consciousness at all,[20] let alone any conscious memory?

Amid the bewildering profusion of Oedipal or absent-father complexes; unconscious, collective, repressed, or false, ideologically constructed, deconstructed, or "multiply drafted" memories; and all the rest of it—how could so-called memory possibly serve a useful critical function in a historical inquiry of this sort?

Thus complexified, it probably cannot. If, however, memory is taken in its plain cultural sense as the mind's retention and retrieval of past experiences (so Underwood 1997),[21] it seems more evidently open to a number of quite different approaches that hold promise for historical inquiry. Physiology or evolution-

---

Byrskog 2004 and Holmberg 2004 (with Dunn 2004 in reply); cf. my own review in Bockmuehl 2005b.

20. See especially John R. Searle's debate with Daniel C. Dennett, conveniently summarized in Searle 1997; the latter famously spells out his "multiple drafts" model of consciousness in Dennett 1991: 101–38 (all mental activity consists of "multi-track processes of interpretation and elaboration of sensory inputs," constantly under "editorial" revision [111]).

21. Cf. Dudai 2002: 157: "Retention over time of learned information . . . of experience-dependent internal representations, or of the capacity to reactivate or reconstruct such representations." To identify the memory with the self, as Augustine (*Confessions* 10.37) and others after him have done, seems an unwarranted reductionism. To defend this criticism would obviously require sustained argument, but Clement of Rome's assurance that the faithful are "engraved by God upon his memory" suggests that the one who "will wipe away every tear from their eyes" (Rev. 7:17; 21:4) is not thwarted by an impediment like Alzheimer's disease; see *1 Clement* 45.8: ἔγγραφοι ἐγένοντο ἀπὸ τοῦ θεοῦ ἐν τῷ μνημοσύνῳ αὐτοῦ (Loeb Classical Library, *pace* Lightfoot's preference for the variant reading αὐτῶν).

ary biology will shed light on the shaping of memory along with cognitive psychology, while social anthropology has produced a wealth of information about the relationship between collective and individual memories. It is that critical interrelationship, too, which helps to limit some of the well-attested vagaries of individual memory (cf. Loftus 1997, 1998; Loftus et al. 1998; Loftus and Ketcham 1994; Dodson et al. 2000). The phenomenon of "false memory" is amply documented by Elizabeth Loftus and others—a point that John Dominic Crossan attempts to exploit in support of his more skeptical assessment of Christian origins.[22] Any fondly held notions of the unimpeachable reliability of individual apostolic memory would quickly run aground on psychological case studies of this kind.

Several facts are worth noting, however. First, the casework of Loftus and her colleagues is concerned with individual memory in isolation, rather than with the critical interaction of individual and collective memory—an interaction that tends in fact to mutual correction. Many of her examples, and all of Crossan's, ironically demonstrate precisely that: contemporaries with access to relevant sources and witnesses within living memory are able to show up the errors of flawed individual memories. Second, a point not noted in Crossan's account is that Loftus's studies explicitly observe certain "metamemorial" differences between *true* memories on the one hand and *false* ones on the other: the latter tend, for example, to be characterized by a relative lack of perceptual detail (so Payne et al. 1997: 59 and Loftus 1998: 62–64) and a significantly lower rate of "recall."[23] False memories have also been shown to be more readily subject to correction or suppression in healthy adults (Kensinger and Schacter 1999).

Such insights suggest that memory's role in religion, too, is open to diverse modes of inquiry.[24] Within biblical studies in par-

---

22. Cf. Crossan 1998: 59–68, in explicit controversy with his critics, including N. T. Wright and Raymond E. Brown (49–58) and James D. G. Dunn (68).

23. Loftus 1998 found a rate of 25 percent for "planted" childhood memories versus 70 percent for real ones.

24. See C. Elliott 1995, who employs Jungian, Freudian, and Kleinian analysis in arriving at an ideologically deconstructive treatment of the place of memory in the

ticular, the transmission of memory has long been of interest in the ancient Jewish and early Christian contexts, especially in the Jesus tradition (see n. 26 below). Both the cultural and ideological analysis of oral history[25] and the role of memory in the processes of tradition have given rise to a wealth of literature. Two points, however, are worth noting. First, much of the work in biblical studies has concentrated on the *fact* and the *mode* of the human memory's role specifically in the gospel tradition. After form criticism had long stressed an anonymous and largely uncontrolled transmission process for the individual units of gospel sayings, more recently many writers have drawn attention to more formal aspects in the Jesus tradition.[26] In particular, Samuel

Gospels and in the church. At the same time, memory still finds little or no discussion in many textbooks of the psychology of religion; so Wulff 1997; Watts and Williams 1988; and Wall 1995. It is also remarkably absent from many large-scale theological reference works; thus the forty-volume *Theologische Realenzyklopädie* omits issues of memory (e.g., "Erinnerung" and "Gedächtnis") from its approximately two thousand entries; even Gassmann 1998 deals only with "reception" as a hermeneutical principle in the early church. Volume 3 of the fourth edition of *Religion in Geschichte und Gegenwart*, by contrast, now has three apposite if brief articles on "Gedächtnis" (Assmann on memory in the study of religion, Schröter in Scripture, Figal in philosophy).

25. On the general phenomenon of orality in the New Testament and its world, see Achtemeier 1990. Ideological deconstructions of the tension between early Christian literature and orality are developed by Kelber 1983 and Vouga 1997. Cf. further Graham 1987: 117–54; Müller 1997; and Davis 1999. Classic textbooks of oral history include Vansina 1965, 1985; P. Thompson 1988; and Tonkin 1992 (note, however, the cautious evaluation of Vansina in Fentress and Wickham 1992, drawing inter alia on de Heusch 1982). Another well-known pioneer of the field was Lord 1960. Aside from Vansina's expertise in African and Lord's in traditional Serbo-Croat anthropology, other fertile areas of study include feminist oral history (Gluck and Patai 1991; Roberts 1984, 1995) and the place of memory under totalitarian regimes (Passerini 1992). There would still seem to be scope for a further assessment of the relevance of this work for the area of biblical studies; note also Assmann 1982 and 2000 and Halbwachs 1941 (ET 1992).

26. On memory and tradition in the Old Testament, see Childs 1962 and Schottroff 1964; cf. the earlier work of Gunkel (ET 1987). For the New Testament, such study was advanced with reference to Jewish tradition especially by Gerhardsson 1961, 1986; Riesner 1981: 450–53; and Byrskog 2000 (with specific reference to the character of eyewitness). Bailey 1995a and 1995b are sometimes adduced in this connection (Dunn 2001, 2003, and Wright 1996: 133–37) as documenting continuous Middle Eastern patterns of informally controlled oral history. Bailey's evidence, however, is itself too informal and uncontrolled to support the burden of proof that Dunn and Wright expect it to bear. For a critique of Bailey (and Byrskog), cf.

Byrskog, Richard Bauckham, and others place considerable emphasis on the nature of eyewitness testimony, while James Dunn
speaks of the "remembered impact" of Jesus of Nazareth himself
upon the oral performance tradition.[27] At the same time, while this
material is highly valuable and germane to the perspective I wish
to advance here, it tends as a matter of fact to concentrate on the
genesis specifically of the Gospels. For the period here in view,
the emphasis thus far has typically been less on the significance
of identifiable living memory for the early church's development
of Christian faith and history.

The second point follows as a natural corollary—and it is one
to which Samuel Byrskog, for instance, gives significant attention. In understanding the place of a personal recollection of the
apostles in the early church, we will obviously do well to avoid
importing anachronistic modern understandings of memory. We
must concentrate on how the early Christian assertions function
within their own world, rather than how they might appear to
postmoderns more concerned with conflicts about power and its
subversion in favor of special interests.

However uncomfortable it may be to contemporary cultural
sentiment, recent scholarship again demonstrates the extent to
which the ancients regarded individual leaders as vital guarantors
of collective memory and tradition. Whether for Jews, Christians,
or pagans, in the absence of centralized records or historical ar-
chives it was oral testimony, received from firsthand witnesses, that
kept the formative past alive and enabled the mutual validation
of personal and collective memory.

In this connection we may recall the pioneering study of social
memory and topography in the Gospels by French sociologist
Maurice Halbwachs, published during the Second World War.[28]

also Head 2001: 278n14, citing T. Weeden. Most recently, Bauckham 2003, 2006,
and Hengel (forthcoming) have engaged in important further work on eyewitness
testimony in the Gospels.

   27. Dunn 2003 and 2005, with responses to criticisms offered in Dunn 2004 (vis-
à-vis Holmberg and Byrskog) and Dunn (forthcoming) (vis-à-vis oral history).

   28. Halbwachs 1941, especially as refined by B. Schwartz 1982 (a refinement
also acknowledged by L. A. Coser in Halbwachs 1992: 26, 30).

In this work, which long remained virtually unknown in New
Testament scholarship, Halbwachs points out,

> The memory of groups contains many truths, notions, ideas, and
> general presupposition; the memory of religious groups preserves
> the recollection of dogmatic truths that were revealed to them in the
> beginning and that successive generations of believers and clergy-
> men formulated. But if a truth is to be settled in the memory of a
> group it needs to be presented in the concrete form of an event, of
> a personality [d'une figure personelle], or of a locality. (Halbwachs
> 1941: 158 [ET 1992: 200])[29]

In practice, Halbwachs's implementation of this insight was criticized for his virtual elimination of real personal memory and
indeed of history itself;[30] but his important stimulus for the relationship between individual and social memory remains well
worth acknowledging.

For the early Christians, the role of social memory was explicitly
strengthened both by the apostles' specific dominical mandate and
by the church's resolute commemoration of its martyrs, a custom
inherited from Judaism.[31] It is no surprise, then, that recollections of
the apostolic generation played a vital role in this connection.[32]

29. On Halbwachs and his near-contemporary Philippe Ariès, who also explored
the relationship between history and collective memory, see Hutton 1992, 1993. Cf.
further Barash 1997.

30. So, e.g., Gedi and Elam 1996: esp. 40, 46. Ancient dimensions of collective
memory are also explored in Baroin 1998: 71; Theiler 1966; and Stemberger 1996:
8–14, 37–44. Cf. more generally Assmann 1982: 196–228 on the cultural dimension
as an additional feature of memory (also Assmann 2000). See further Le Goff 1992;
Jeffrey and Edwall 1994; and others on the interrelation of memory and history; and
note the important work of Nora 1984 (partial ET 1996) on the idea of "places of
memory" (lieux de mémoire).

31. See already Martyrdom of Polycarp 18.3 (second century). On the Jewish
antecedents of the veneration of saints and martyrs, see Horbury 1998a. With reference
to the Maccabean martyrs in particular, the ancient Christians continued their commemoration on August 1 (a practice continued to this day in the East). Cf. further the
classic study by P. Brown 1981 on the role later played by saints, and by Frank 2000
on ascetics. On a somewhat different note, it is interesting to compare the application
of this principle to Latin American liberation theology in Hoornaert 1989: 1–10.

32. On the view of memory among the ancients, see further Coleman 1992: esp.
1–62. Cf. also Small 1997, although her account leaves a less disciplined impression of

The Proof of the Pudding

But is all this relevant to New Testament interpretation, or is it just another lot of theoretical scaffolding? The proof of the pudding is invariably in the eating. The available illustrations of my point are necessarily eclectic, as we shall see below. Working backward, we might begin in the late second century with Bishop Irenaeus of Lyons (ca. 130–200), the last identifiable individual known to us who could truthfully claim personal acquaintance with an eyewitness and associate of the apostles (in this case Polycarp, a disciple of John).[33]

Before turning to a few texts for illustration, we may note in passing a related and somewhat unexpected corollary of attending to effective history on the human scale of memory. This is the emergence of a generational periodization of early Christian memory, reminiscent in some ways of the generational scheme encountered in rabbinic studies. For present purposes, we are chiefly interested in three "generations": (1) sources dating roughly from the lifetime of the apostles (ca. 1–70); (2) younger contemporaries like Polycarp, who personally remembered either the apostles or their close associates (ca. 70–130); and (3) people like Irenaeus, who in turn were taught by these students (ca. 130–200).

Needless to say, antiquity's average life expectancy of under thirty-five years would in practice make this window of three generations of living memory a good deal shorter for most individuals. But two mitigating factors must be born in mind. First, and despite the unimaginable levels of infectious disease, infant mortality, and childbirth mortality, it remains the case that among people who were still alive at the age of thirty-five, a good many, including at least *some* identifiable early Christians, did indeed live to old age (for assessments of old age in antiquity, see Brandt 2002 and Minois 1989). Recent studies suggest that while only 20–25 percent of the population of Imperial Rome reached middle

---

ancient memory than in fact seems likely to have been the case (cf. Horsfall 1998). Late antique and medieval views are treated in Coleman 1992 and Carruthers 1990.

33. Irenaeus, *Against Heresies* 3.3.4; *Letter to Florinus* (in Eusebius, *Ecclesiastical History* 5.20.6); cf. Eusebius, *Ecclesiastical History* 5.5.8.

age, about 5 percent of the population at any one time was aged over sixty (Brandt 2002: 159, 159n433, 212, citing earlier work by R. S. Bagnall, B. W. Frier, and W. Scheidel). What is more, famous and influential individuals and their disciples are almost by definition likely to be personally remembered by a larger number of people, some of whom would presumably live to the sort of old age reached by a Polycarp or an Irenaeus.

All this, then, serves to confirm that the three proposed generations are not merely a convenient fiction. Around 130, the last eyewitnesses of the apostles may be presumed to be dead or extremely elderly; but there would be many Christians who personally knew these witnesses, their personalities, stories, and traditions. By 200, the last of these spiritual "grandchildren" would themselves be dying out, and with them the last traces of personal living memory. After 200, the chain of tradition might be expected to take on a different shape[34]—indeed, it is highly revealing to note the loss of credibility that nonliterary traditions seem to suffer in pagan attacks on Christianity in the third century.[35]

In practice, of course, the chronology involved in such a model needs to operate on rather more flexible, indeed quite relative, time frames.[36] We are dealing with the interlinked human memory of single life spans. People living in the same decade may theoretically belong to different generations of memory; conversely, in many cases the assignation of a source to a particular generation can rely only on implicit evidence. Especially third-generation memory must be read with a great deal of caution. Thus, a recent study of

34. There is a big difference between the memory of survivors and that of their children, and a further appreciable difference between that and the ossified, ritualized Ulster Protestant's commemoration of the Battle of the Boyne or, still more extreme, Serbia's mythology of its inalienable "heartland" in Kosovo.

35. Porphyry's critique of Peter is a good example of this. His only evidence not based on Scripture seems to be the widespread tradition of Peter's crucifixion (unless one includes the designation of him as the disciples' "leader" [κορυφαῖος]—a term also used in some second-century Christian sources).

36. Even the extent of the first generation is difficult to pin down: a number of early Christian sources insist that some of the apostolic generation survived to the time of Trajan (Irenaeus, *Against Heresies* 2.22.4; 3.3.4; Epiphanius, *Refutation of All Heresies* 30.24.6; Jerome, *Lives of Illustrious Men* 9; *Against Jovinianus* 1.26; cf. John 21:22–24).

the grandchildren of Nazi-era Germans illustrates the extent to which even third-generation personal memory, especially of the informal and uncontrolled sort, may depart quite dramatically from its source whenever apologetic or other ulterior motives are at stake.[37] In the early Christian context, too, the available witnesses often reflect a mixture of memory, tradition, and interpretation of apostolic writings. Needless to say, there may be limited merit in recollections that show no signs of dependence on anything other than extant written sources.

The Early Church's Memory of the Apostles

All this suggests an attractive and methodologically accessible grouping of the postapostolic material. What matters finally, of course, is that this method is not simply imposed as a counsel of convenience, but actually arises out of an explicit concern in the ancient Christian sources themselves. Even if we leave aside the stories relating various second-century figures to the apostle John, the tradition repeatedly draws attention to those who belong to a chain of memory, from Mark as Peter's assistant to Irenaeus of Lyons, who claimed in his youth to have heard Polycarp, the companion of the apostles. Similar appeal was made in the later second century by Polycrates, the bishop of Ephesus and a leading quartodeciman spokesman, to personal local memory of apostolic leaders who died in Asia (Eusebius specifically cites John the Elder and Philip the Apostle as well as Polycarp).[38] And according to Hegesippus and Julius Africanus (ca. 180–250), the second century kept alive an early memory of the relatives of Jesus (known as the *desposynoi*) who came from Nazareth and Cochaba as

---

37. Welzer et al. 2002: 44–80. Note the chilling conclusion: "Die Vergangenheit der vernichteten jüdischen Deutschen kommt in nichtjüdischen deutschen Familien lediglich als Geschichte ihres Verschwindens vor, nicht einmal als Geschichte der Toten, geschweige denn als lebendige Geschichte." [In non-Jewish German families, the annihilated Jewish Germans' past features only as a history of their disappearance—not even as a history of the dead, let alone as living history.]

38. Eusebius preserves two excerpts from Polycrates' letter to Pope Victor, written ca. 190 (*Ecclesiastical History* 5.24.2–8; 3.31.3).

influential traveling missionaries and leaders in the churches of Jerusalem and the holy land.[39] Among the Gnostics, too, Basilides' supposed teacher Glaucias was asserted to have been, like Mark, an "interpreter" of Peter, just as Valentinus was said to have been taught by Theudas, the hearer of Paul (Clement of Alexandria, *Miscellanies* 7.17).[40] A brief glance at the form and function of these traditions of living memory suggests that they often served a legitimating function, sometimes vis-à-vis explicit opponents. Agendas, however, need not render the underlying claims invalid; indeed they may well underscore the motivation to keep memories alive. What strikes one about the second-century Christian assertions of memory is often their high degree of specificity and their claims of a living association with apostolic founder figures or their students—and thus the extent to which they connect organically and personally with the concerns of the very beginnings of Christian faith.

Remembrance (*anamnēsis*; Luke 22:19; 1 Cor. 11:24–25) of *Jesus* was of course at the heart of corporate Christian worship from the start. And the theological importance of memory first arose in the context of the Old Testament's foundational command to "remember and do not forget" (Deut. 9:7) the history of the deliverance of God's people.[41] Still, the story of Christian origins is the more remarkable for attaching its founding memory not only to a saving event but also, explicitly, to a saving *person*:

39. See Julius Africanus's letter to Aristides in Eusebius, *Ecclesiastical History* 1.7.14; and Hegesippus in ibid., 3.11; 3.19.1–20.6. Relatives of Jesus as traveling missionaries are already mentioned in 1 Cor 9:5; this tradition may ultimately account also for the inclusion in the canon of the letters of James and Jude. See most fully Bauckham 1990.

40. Clement's sources on Basilides generally appear to be the most reliable, and this particular tradition seems at least possible; cf. Löhr 1996: 27n92, chap. 3. By contrast, the parallel claim that Basilides received secret dominical revelations from Matthias (Hippolytus, *Refutation of All Heresies* 7.20.1) has rather less historical plausibility; see Löhr 1996: 26–29.

41. Note Deut. 5:15: "You shall remember that you were a slave in the land of Egypt, and the LORD your God brought you out from there with a mighty hand and an outstretched arm." Cf. 7:18; 8:2, 18; 9:7; 11:2; 15:15; 16:3, 12; 24:18, 22. Cf. further Starobinski-Safran 1988.

"Do this in memory *of me* [εἰς τὴν ἐμὴν ἀνάμνησιν]" (Luke 22:19; 1 Cor. 11:24–25).[42] Such original remembering is, at the same time, closely interwoven with memory of the apostles themselves. The word of Jesus continues in the disciples through their recollection of him, with which they are repeatedly charged.[43] For the Fourth Gospel, despite its lack of a final Passover meal and words of institution, none other than the Holy Spirit serves as the catalyst of apostolic memory (John 14:26). As Peter Stuhlmacher shows, this "anamnetic" role of the Spirit takes shape precisely in a spiritually articulate remembering of the history of Jesus as the Logos (2004; cf. 2002a). And at the same time, while the disciples' faith in Jesus draws on memory of him (2:17, 22; 12:16; 15:20; 16:4), the Beloved Disciple himself is remembered above all as the guarantor of the truth of the gospel story, indeed the one on whose eyewitness the story's integrity depends (15:27; 19:35; 21:24; 1 John 1:1–4).[44]

For the second generation, in other words, memory of Jesus is accessible via the living memory of the apostles. In this sense the later New Testament's repeated instruction to call to mind

42. On the importance of *anamnēsis* in the New Testament, see further the seminal study of Dahl 1948; cf. Michel 1967. Basset 1988: 101–2 points out that the motif of remembrance explicitly surfaces on half a dozen occasions in the passion narrative, not counting the usual Greek designation of a tomb as μνῆμα (Mark 15:46; Luke 23:53) or μνημεῖον (Matt. 27:52, 53, 60; John 19:41): (1) the anointing at Bethany "in memory of her" (Mark 14:9 ‖ Matt. 26:13; cf. John 12:7–8); (2) the Last Supper itself (Luke 22:19; 1 Cor. 11:24–25); (3) Peter remembering after his denial (Mark 14:72 ‖ Matt. 26:75 ‖ Luke 22:61); (4) the crucified criminal's appeal to "remember me" (Luke 23:42); (5) the authorities recalling Jesus's prediction of his resurrection (Matt. 27:63); and (6) the memory of words of Jesus and of Scripture in Luke's resurrection account (Luke 24:6, 8, 25–27). With regard to Mark 14:9 and parallels, the widely celebrated feminist work of Schüssler Fiorenza 1983 startlingly fails to make more than a single casual reference (xiii) to the text from which its title derives. For a provocative (and in its own terms no less feminist) critique of the influential paradigm that Schüssler Fiorenza helped to construct, see Corley 2002.

43. See Mark 14:72 ‖ Matt. 26:75 ‖ Luke 22:61; also 24:6, 8; John 15:20; Acts 20:35; 2 Tim. 2:8. Cf. Michel 1967: 677, 682. Kirchner 1991: 290 notes that the same formula in *Apocalypse of James* is apparently reappropriated for anticatholic ends, viz., to downplay traditions of the earthly Jesus in favor of revealed sayings of the exalted Lord—an exception that could be said to prove the rule. Needless to say, the "orthodox" use of apostolic memory may at times serve an equally polemical purpose.

44. Bauckham 2003: 58 rightly notes this implication of John 15:27.

the apostles aims to provide a living bond of fellowship with the witnesses of the original events, both in their absence (1 Cor. 4:17; 11:2; 1 Thess. 2:9; 2 Thess. 2:5; Col. 4:18; see also Phil. 1:30; 2:17) and, in due course, after their deaths. A good example of this sort of posthumous and quasitestamentary appeal occurs in 2 Peter 1:12–19 (cf. also 2 Pet. 3:1–2, 15–16; Heb. 13:7).[45] In the face of his approaching death, the apostle expresses his desire to "keep on reminding you" (ἀεὶ ὑμᾶς ὑπομιμνῄσκειν) of the founding truths of the gospel, of which the apostles are eyewitnesses (ἐπόπται); his parting wish is, "as long as I am in this body, to refresh your memory [διεγείρειν ὑμᾶς ἐν ὑπομνήσει]," in order that "after my departure you may be able at any time to recall these things [τὴν τούτων μνήμην ποιεῖσθαι]." Even if we accept the conventional date of 2 Peter (around the beginning of the second century), pseudonymity by no means renders such an appeal to remembrance wholly fictitious. Indeed, its testamentary genre lends the letter's appeal to Petrine memory a special sincerity and gravitas. The writer, who claims a close implicit Petrine link and authority, clearly intends to keep alive a genuine memory of the apostolic "we" (1:16–18), as well as of "your apostles" (3:2). And even though the apostolic "fathers" may now have suffered martyrdom and "fallen asleep" (3:4, 15–16), the date and emphatically Petrine prescript of the letter leave the author's firsthand acquaintance with the apostle and his circle entirely plausible.[46]

Regardless of the merits of this particular case, the chain of living memory demonstrably continues for decades after the composition of 2 Peter. Irenaeus recalls his experiences at the feet of his teacher Polycarp, whose recollections made him the bearer and transmitter of the authentic tradition of the apostles. This in

45. For the testamentary nature of 2 Peter, see Bauckham 1983: 131–35, 158–62; and J. Elliott 1992: 283.

46. Contrast bald and unargued assertions like that of Boring 1996: 403: "This means that not only did the author not witness the saving events of the first generation himself, *he no longer knows anyone who did*" (emphasis added). It is intriguing, too, to note the difference in this respect between 2 Peter and the earlier Pastoral Epistles: the latter show as yet no comparably distanced, second-generation injunction to "remember the apostle."

turn allowed his pupil to speak of it with confidence in his famous
rebuke of the gnostic Florinus:

> I remember [διαμνημονεύω] the events of those days more clearly
> than those which happened recently, for what we learn as children
> grows up with the soul and is united to it, so that I can speak even
> of the place in which the blessed Polycarp sat and disputed, how
> he came in and went out, the character of his life, the appearance
> of his body, the discourses which he made to the people, how he
> used to report [ἀπήγγελλεν] his intercourse with John and with the
> others who had seen the Lord, how he remembered [ἀπεμνημόνευεν]
> their words, and what were the things concerning the Lord which
> he had heard from them, and about their miracles, and about their
> teaching, and how Polycarp had received them from the eyewitnesses
> of the Word of Life [or "eyewitnesses of the Word's life": παρὰ τῶν
> αὐτοπτῶν τῆς ζωῆς τοῦ λόγου παρειληφώς], and reported [ἀπήγγελλεν]
> all things in agreement with the Scriptures [πάντα σύμφωνα ταῖς
> γραφαῖς]. I listened eagerly even then to these things through the
> mercy of God which was given me, and made notes of them, not on
> paper but in my heart [ὑπομνηματιζόμενος αὐτὰ οὐκ ἐν χάρτῃ, ἀλλ' ἐν
> τῇ ἐμῇ καρδίᾳ], and ever by the grace of God do I truly meditate on
> them [ἀεί . . . γνησίως αὐτὰ ἀναμαρυκῶμαι]; and I can bear witness
> before God that if that blessed and apostolic presbyter had heard
> anything of this kind he would have cried out, and shut his ears,
> and said according to his custom, "O good God, for what a time
> have you preserved me that I should endure this?" He would have
> fled from the very place where he was sitting or standing, when he
> heard such words. (*Letter to Florinus*, in Eusebius, *Ecclesiastical
> History* 5.20.5–7 [adapted from Loeb Classical Library])

As in his great work against the heretics, Irenaeus affirms a
harmony of Scripture and its tradition of interpretation, which
the church has inherited from the apostles. And this tradition for
him is no mere ideological figment of a "collective memory," but
it is vouchsafed by an unbroken and identifiable chain of *personal
recollection* reaching back to the apostles themselves (*Against Heresies* 3.1–5).[47] That this appeal is no freak exception can also be

---

47. For the interdependence of ecclesiology and Scripture in this passage, see
Löhr 1997: 221, citing Le Boulluec 1996 and Benoît 1960.

seen from his comments about Clement of Rome, whose firsthand memory of the apostles Irenaeus regards as of key importance in the interpretation of their writings.[48] Justin Martyr, too, refers more than a dozen times to the Gospels as "memoirs" of the apostles (τὰ ἀπομνημονεύματα τῶν ἀποστόλων) (*Dialogue with Trypho* 100.4; 101.3; 102.5; 103.6, 8; 104.1; 105.1, 5, 6; 106.1, 3h, 4; 107.1; cf. *First Apology* 33.5; 66.3; 67.3). It is unclear how much personal memory Justin assumes to have been transmitted in these sources or even to what extent this term also serves as a stylized and possibly apologetic appeal to a philosophical commonplace that had been familiar ever since Xenophon published his own *apomnēmoneumata* of Socrates.[49] Nevertheless, Justin's actual use of the term, both in addressing pagans and in dialogue with Trypho the Jew, does imply rather more than a stereotyped convention of reverence for a great sage: he regards the Gospels as recording specifically apostolic accounts of Jesus within the period of living memory.[50]

Papias of Hierapolis has been much discussed for his notoriously enigmatic preference of the *viva vox* of oral apostolic tradition over merely written sources. As Winrich Löhr shows against in-

48. *Against Heresies* 3.3.3: ὁ καὶ ἑωρακὼς τοὺς μακαρίους ἀποστόλους καὶ συμβεβληκὼς αὐτοῖς, καὶ ἔτι ἔναυλον τὸ κήρυγμα τῶν ἀποστόλων καὶ τὴν παράδοσιν πρὸ ὀφθαλμῶν ἔχων, οὐ μόνος· ἔτι γὰρ πολλοὶ ὑπελείποντο τότε ὑπὸ τῶν ἀποστόλων δεδιδαγμένοι (Rousseau and Doutreleau 2002: 2:34). ["(Clement,) who had both seen the blessed apostles and associated with them, and had the teaching of the apostles still in his ears and the tradition before his eyes. And he was not alone: for at that time many who had been taught by the apostles were still alive."]

49. Abramowski 1990: 334 suspects a specifically antignostic bias. Justin cites Xenophon in *Second Apology* 11.

50. Cf. Barnard 1967: 56–60; Hyldahl 1960: 79–80; and Dungan 1999: 30–33, who notes an element of appeal to "eyewitness immediacy" and suspects a possible link with Papias. Justin notes specifically that these "memoirs" were drawn up by Jesus's own apostles and those who followed them (*Dialogue with Trypho* 103.8). In *First Apology* 33.5 the apostolic teachers whom Christians have believed are "they who recorded all that concerns our Savior Jesus Christ" (ὡς οἱ ἀπομνημονεύσαντες πάντα τὰ περὶ τοῦ σωτῆρος ἡμῶν Ἰησοῦ Χριστοῦ ἐδίδαξαν, οἷς ἐπιστεύσαμεν). Second-century Palestinian Christian Hegesippus, too, wrote five books of "memoirs" (ὑπομνήματα), concerned primarily with the early history of the church in Jerusalem, mentioned in Eusebius, *Ecclesiastical History* 2.23.3; cf. further Abramowski 1990: 334, following Hyldahl 1960.

terpreters like Hans von Campenhausen, however, this preference is not a vote for uncontrolled proliferation of oral tradition so much as a quite specific and polemical assertion of the superior *authenticity* of Papias's own exposition of the apostolic gospel of Christ.[51] What matters for present purposes is that Papias's famous text actually brings to eloquent expression the importance of a personal memory of the apostles in understanding the meaning of Christian origins:

> And I shall not hesitate to append to the interpretations all that I ever learnt well from the presbyters and recalled well [καλῶς ἔμαθον καὶ καλῶς ἐμνημόνευσα], for of their truth I am confident. . . . If ever anyone came who had followed the presbyters, I used to inquire into the words of the presbyters, what Andrew or Peter or Philip or Thomas or James or John or Matthew, or any other of the Lord's disciples, had said [εἶπεν], and what Aristion and the presbyter John, the Lord's disciples, are saying [λέγουσιν]. For I did not suppose that information from books would help me so much as that which comes from a living and surviving voice [τὰ παρὰ ζώσης φωνῆς καὶ μενούσης]. (Eusebius, *Ecclesiastical History* 3.39.3–4 [adapted from Loeb Classical Library])

Although Papias's point of view was in time necessarily tempered by the antiheretical imperative of a finite and written canon, the stress on living memory and its integration into a chain of tradition remained of lasting importance. Indeed, it is highly significant to observe the extent to which even Irenaeus can still justify his condemnation of Valentinian Gnosticism on the grounds that it is repugnant to the living memory of the apostolic teaching as expounded in keeping with Scripture. Earlier in the century, the

51. In other words, Papias's claim seems in fact to reinforce the emerging authority of some texts vis-à-vis others. See Löhr 1997: 212–15 and Baum 1998. The significance of Papias's attention to memory was previously recognized by Knox 1958: 70–71, who compares this with instructions to "remember the words of the Lord Jesus how he said . . ." in passages like Acts 20:35; *1 Clement* 13.1; and Polycarp, *To the Philippians* 2.3. Most recently Norelli 2005: 253–56 more reservedly downplays the connotation of memory that, although admittedly present, is in his view here (as at times in Justin; cf. Aragione 2004) less prominent than the notion of recall for the purpose of "recording" or "giving an account" (even "redacting").

apologist Quadratus insisted that some of those healed or raised by Jesus survived "until our own days" (in Eusebius, *Ecclesiastical History* 4.3.2).[52] By their stress on surviving apostolic memory, deliberate in intention and rhetoric (if not always in delivery), the mainstream writers of the early church draw on a well-known Greco-Roman appreciation of eyewitness history (see Alexander 1990; Bauckham 2003; Byrskog 2000), while also illustrating the indispensable realism of an incarnational faith.

Memory and History

This remarkable stress on memory must be understood vis-à-vis pagan (and some heretical) detractors who held that, even at their best, theological myths reveal nothing more than timeless metaphysical verities—things that "never happened, but always are."[53] Christians, by contrast, believed in the vital urgency of memory, of rehearsing the story whose saving power in history is forfeited by those who forget (cf. Dumas 1996: 44–46). They were convinced that amnesia of the apostles and their story abandons the only account of the deliverance of this present world. As André Dumas puts it, to desert this memory would be to desert the history of the salvation accomplished among us (1996: 48: "Si on quitte cette mémoire, on quitte l'histoire du salut au milieu des hommes"). Faithful memory, by contrast, encountered that history's human protagonists, the saints both great and small, as living and present fellow pilgrims.

What does this mean for our reading of the New Testament? Important events often give rise to an effective history whose scope is impossibly vast and complex. Who could presume to recount the *Wirkungsgeschichte* of Churchill's return late in life from the political wilderness to replace Chamberlain as prime minister one

52. A similar tradition was apparently attributed to Papias by Philip Sidetes (see Norelli 2005: 383 and frag. 10).
53. Thus Sallustius, the friend of Emperor Julian the Apostate (361–63), in his anti-Christian manual for neoplatonic paganism; *On the Gods and the World* 4. Cf. p. 69n61 above.

Monday in May 1940?[54] It is probably no exaggeration to assert
that Europe continues to owe its freedom to that event, which is
vividly remembered by people alive today. Needless to say, the
same applies a fortiori to the effective history of the New Testament and of its principal actors: even the truly magnum opus of
Luz on Matthew, for example, can do little more than to offer
an eclectic glimpse of this richly layered heritage. Nevertheless,
it remains worth pondering that Christian faith traces a history
of incalculable consequence to the memory of one man's act of
obedience—an act whose eyewitnesses were themselves long remembered in the early church.

Jean-Paul Sartre once said that whether the past lives or dies
depends on the here and now (cited in Dumas 1996: 49; cf. Sartre
1956: 110–12); and many of our self-consciously postmodern
contemporaries would agree with him. So would many ancients.
Jews and catholic Christians, however, have invariably affirmed
exactly the opposite: whether there is life in the present depends
wholly on the remembrance of God's saving acts—and hope in
his promises. Until the end of the second century, that Christian
point of view was rooted in part in a living memory of the original
actors in the saving story of Jesus of Nazareth—those whom Irenaeus called the eyewitnesses of the Word of Life. And in its day,
this living memory in turn accompanied and guided the writing
and reading of the apostolic word—serving as a vital historical
index of the potential breadth, and the hermeneutical limits, of
authentic apostolic faith.

54. After Chamberlain resigned over the German invasion of the Low Countries
on May 10, Churchill first addressed Parliament as prime minister on May 13 with
his famous "blood, toil, sweat, and tears" speech. At the end of the century, the *Encyclopaedia Britannica* would declare that "the whole of Churchill's previous career
had been a preparation for wartime leadership" (Nicholas 1997: 373).

7

SEEING THE SON OF DAVID

We have left the most decisive subject to the end. In re-envisaging a common conversation about the New Testament, how then shall we speak about Jesus of Nazareth? It has been several centuries since systematic theologians and exegetes were last able to look each other in the eye and agree that the Jesus they encountered on the pages of the New Testament was the person they confessed in the creed. Gone too are the days when historical critics had for the most part a common mind on methods and criteria of interpretation that might lead the conscientious exegete to uncover Jesus of Nazareth—whether as a liberal teacher of the fatherhood of God and the brotherhood of man, as a failed apocalyptic prophet, as a radical taboo-toppler and law-transcender, or as the inclusive and unjudging sage. What might it mean to proceed to a study of Jesus as the New Testament's central subject in a way that takes seriously the text's implied readings and its early reception history as a deposit of apostolic memory? In this concluding chapter, I wish to explore the historical and theological implications of one particular insight on which virtually all contemporary approaches agree: Jesus of Nazareth was a Jew.

The Israelite identity of Jesus Christ—a seemingly platitudinous commonplace. How much can it really matter? But there's the rub: How much *does* it matter? Does the Jewishness of Jesus make any fundamental difference in seeking to get the measure of the man, whether our interest be Christian, Jewish, or for that matter merely historical? The short answer is: it makes all the difference in the world. That is the contention of this final chapter, and I hope to demonstrate its pertinence for revitalizing subject-appropriate New Testament study.

Access to the topic is obstructed by barricades of confessional history and scholarly habit and increasingly even by basic disagreements about the very nature of good evidence and sound argument in biblical scholarship.[1] We will begin by defining some terms and then drawing a map of how Jesus's Jewish identity tends to be understood in current debate.

Some Prickly Prolegomena

Identity?

The meaning of the fashionable term *identity* may seem obvious to popular culture in the late- or postmodern West. Philosophical and theological clarity on this matter is, however, rather more elusive: we may agree that it involves intentional agency in the light of historical antecedents and social consequences (Rorty 1976: 15), but is that enough? Our need for a definition seems underscored by the vagueness of common usage, where someone's identity can comprise a bewildering range of qualities derived from the expression of habits and preferences of culture or lifestyle—vegetarian, blonde bombshell, eco-warrior, neocon-

---

1. A point that is increasingly driving even sympathetic observers of the discipline to distraction; see recently Williams 2003: 218—with explicit, if opaque, reference to the Jesus Seminar. Cf. also chapter 1 above.

servative, night owl, musician, Muslim convert, transgendered, or what have you.

What is intriguing is the extent to which such seemingly subsidiary and often volitional or impermanent qualities have in large areas of society fused with an almost metaphysical ontology of identity. Contemporaries who take this (essentialist) view of identity will frequently set out to "find themselves"; they may base moral or lifestyle decisions ranging from the trivial to the life-changing on the earnest conviction that "this is who (or how) I am." They may even invoke religion, employing a questionable doctrine of creation to lend gravitas to a matrix of cultural or relational preferences and habits, basing this on "how God has made me."

Leaving aside the problem of whether such an essentialist anthropology can ever be compatible with a Christian view of creation, vocation, and redemption, the examples cited suggest that popular notions of identity may not be self-evidently useful in establishing the meaning of that word for a theological inquiry concerned with Jesus.

On browsing a number of dictionary definitions, the one that seems most appropriate here concerns distinguishing characteristics that express individuality or identification. Paul Ricoeur writes eloquently about narrative identity as a function of permanence over time, established by self-constancy (being true to one's word) and by perseverance of character (the acquired habits and identifications that constitute "the 'what' of the 'who'") (Ricoeur 1992: 113–39, esp. 118–23).[2] This clarification, I take it, may be acceptable to proceed for present purposes.

Jesus's Identity?

In the case of Jesus, however, it is impossible to speak Christianly of his individuality without at the same time speaking of his metaphysical essence. His is a self-constancy and perseverance of character, in other words, that attests his permanence both in

2. I am grateful to C. Kavin Rowe for drawing my attention to this argument.

time and beyond time. The New Testament insists that in Jesus of Nazareth God's own identity came to full expression—and that in bloody historical concreteness, σωματικῶς.

But nor is this all. In other cases we might claim to find God powerfully revealed in a saintly life, in festive worship, or in meditation on Scripture—or for that matter in a Sienese hillside or a Boccherini cello concerto. But in none of these cases could we say that the saint herself *is* God, or that sunset vespers at Sant' Antimo reveal *all* that can be known of God.

Precisely that reverse assertion, however, is what the New Testament uniquely affirms of Jesus. His self-constancy and perseverance of character, in other words, are consistently construed in relational terms as between the Son and the Father. "God was in Christ" (2 Cor. 5:19); but also: Jesus is the identity of God. What you see is what you get: indeed, what you see here is all you could possibly get. For the Fourth Evangelist and others this is crystal clear. To see Jesus is to see the Father of Jesus (John 14:9), Abraham's and Isaiah's thrice-holy Lord made flesh (John 8:56–58; 12:41), the unique Son who alone bears the ineffable name (Phil. 2:9; Eph. 1:21; John 17:11–12): "the Messiah who is over all, God blessed forever" (Rom. 9:5) who sits on the heavenly throne, at God's right hand (Mark 14:62; Rom. 8:34; Eph. 1:20–23; Heb. 12:2; Rev. 7:17) and to whom is due the worship of all creation (Phil. 2:10–11; Heb. 1:6; Rev. 5:12–14; 22:3). In keeping with that conviction, several authors go so far as to claim that *only* here can God be seen: *no one* comes to the Father except through Jesus (John 14:6; Acts 4:12).

The New Testament tends to state such convictions constructively and somewhat delicately, more as an article of eschatological confession and confidence in the Lord's Chosen One than as a disciplinary instrument for the eternal elimination of the unconfessing many. To be sure, the church did go on before long to conclude that this placed Jesus and the church fundamentally at loggerheads with all those outside it. No salvation outside the church, preferably the Roman church—*nulla salus*: not for pagan infidels and a fortiori not for Jews. Judaism for its part returned the compliment; and at some time during their complex and often unhappy relations between the times of Bar Kokhba and Justinian, Jews and Christians came to agree on the tragic conclusion that one could not both follow Jesus and practice Judaism.[3] It was a conclusion, to be sure, which on the Christian side sometimes found succor in quasi-Marcionite readings of Paul, but tragic nonetheless, in that it generated a Jesus who had for both Jews and Christians ceased to be recognizable as the Messiah of Israel. The Christian identity of Jesus (as Christ and Son of God) ruled out any possibility of a Jewish identity (as first-century Galilean *tsaddiq*). This in turn is a conviction that necessitates our third prolegomenon.

Jesus's Jewish Identity? A Historic Oxymoron

As the ancients concluded, to assert the Jewishness of Jesus is a dangerous nonsense; it substitutes semantic games for a truthful account of either Judaism or Christianity. Though Jewish and possibly even observant in appearance, Jesus had in fact put an end to Jewish life based on the Torah by revealing the new dispensation that would henceforth displace it. Thus the first Gentile bishop of Antioch, born less than a generation after Jesus's death, bluntly affirms that "it is monstrous to talk of Jesus Christ and to practice Judaism" (Ignatius, *To the Magnesians* 10.3; cf. 8.1–2).[4] One could argue that opposition to gnostic and Marcionite views partly attenuated this position in later second-century writers like Justin, Irenaeus, or Tertullian, although their polemics never quite extended to a positive appreciation of Jesus *qua* Jew. Nevertheless, Eusebius of Caesarea articulately confirms what was by his time a familiar view—Jesus had come quite simply to replace Judaism with Christianity:

3. The tenuous complexity of this history is mapped with acute perception in Boyarin 2004; cf. also Lieu 1996, 2002, 2004; and S. Schwartz 2001.

4. Ignatius concedes, however, that the Christianity of the circumcised may be a lesser evil than the Judaism of the uncircumcised (*To the Philadelphians* 6.1–2); and he emphatically claims Jesus "our God" as Son of David, born of Mary according to the Scriptures (*To the Ephesians* 18). For the possibility that Ignatius was the first Gentile bishop of Antioch, see my arguments in Bockmuehl 2003c: 142.

194 SEEING THE WORD

Christ spent his life, and the teaching of the new covenant was carried to all nations. Then immediately the Romans laid siege to the city of Jerusalem and destroyed it along with the temple there. At once the whole ordinance of Moses was abolished along with everything relating to the old covenant. The curse was transferred to those who continued to keep the Mosaic law after its time had passed, and thereby became lawbreakers.[5] Now at this same time the perfect law of the new Teaching was introduced in its place. (*Demonstration of the Gospel* 1.6.39, my translation)

ὁ Χριστὸς ἐπεδήμει τῷ βίῳ καὶ τῆς καινῆς διαθήκης προεβάλλετο πᾶσι τοῖς ἔθνεσι διδασκαλία, παραχρῆμά τε ῾Ρωμαῖοι τὴν πόλιν ἑλόντες πολιορκίᾳ καθεῖλον [τὰ ῾Ιεροσόλυμα] καὶ τὸν αὐτόθι νεών· λέλυτό τε αὐτίκα πᾶσα ἡ Μωσέως διάταξις, καὶ τὰ τῆς παλαιᾶς περιήρητο διαθήκης, τά τε τῆς ἀρᾶς μετήει τοὺς παρὰ καιρὸν τὰ Μωσέως πράττειν, παρανομοῦντας εἰς αὐτά, βιαζομένους· ἀντεισήγετο δὲ ὁμοῦ καὶ κατὰ τὸ αὐτὸ τῆς νέας καὶ ἐντελοῦς διδασκαλίας τὰ νόμιμα.

In the same vein, Eusebius and others found it suitable that architecturally the Christian Jerusalem of Constantine, centered on the Holy Sepulcher of Jesus, was now replacing the ruins of Judaism once and for all.[6]

Ever since antiquity, theologians have tended to privilege universalizing abstractions about Jesus's person and teaching over the Jewish particularities of his dress, his diet, and his disputes with fellow Jews. One could debate why this has been so, or indeed whether it may be a necessary consequence of the New Testament's own universalizing witness. That it occurred is an uncontroversial matter of historical record—as is the fact that the wedge driven between Jesus and Judaism by Jews and Christians alike has, from antiquity to the period of living memory, wrought consequences of incalculable horror.

5. Similar arguments about Torah observance as "lawbreaking" are present in other patristic authors.
6. See Eusebius's *Life of Constantine* 3.33. To Cyril of Jerusalem preaching at the Holy Sepulcher in the fourth century, the ruins of the temple "opposite us" (ἀντικρὺς ἡμῶν) showed "the sin of the transgressors" (*Catechetical Lectures* 10.11; cf. Origen, *Against Celsus* 4.22). The antichrist would come and attempt "to take his seat in the temple" (2 Thess. 2:4) once the site had been flattened completely, whether by decay or demolition, leaving "no stone upon another" (Cyril, *Catechetical Lectures* 15.15). That Julian the Apostate's rebuilding project of the year 363 failed in unusual circumstances was seen by many as confirmation of the divine judgment; see Parmentier 1996: 150–53. Amitzur argues that quasi-Solomonic architecture and ideology explicitly underlie Justinian's sixth-century Nea church.

All this leaves us in an awkward position when trying to address the Jewishness of the person and aims of Jesus. From antiquity until the twentieth century, the notion of Jesus's Jewish identity was almost universally acknowledged by both Jews and Christians to be an oxymoron—somewhat like the question of whether the Lubavitcher Rebbe would have liked his cheeseburgers cooked medium rare.

This dichotomous heritage is by no means straightforwardly anti-Semitic, although scholarly discussion in the last twenty-five years has sometimes chosen to caricature it in that fashion. To some extent it is deeply bound up with the early church's quest for self-definition and for a Christian identity. Be that as it may, as far as the person and identity of Jesus are concerned, opposition to Judaism, to Christianity, and perhaps above all to Jewish Christianity have all played a part in reinforcing that classic denial of a Jewish Jesus. There may also be something in it of a certain genetic predisposition among interpreters of Paul, a revisionist and iconoclastic trait that, as Harnack thought, reached from Marcion (via Origen and Augustine?) to Luther and culminated in the assured results of nineteenth-century German *Wissenschaft*.[7]

Another issue is worth pondering in this connection. In the 1990s a great deal of North American media publicity swirled around the image of a liberal-minded, egalitarian social reformer conversant with populist philosophical aphorisms rather than religious dogma or observance. The self-styled Jesus Seminar, widely known for its sometimes sensationalist pronouncements on a Jesus construed from the hypothetical source Q and the so-called *Gospel of Thomas*,[8] gave rise to a surprisingly influential

7. At age nineteen, Harnack first programmatically spelled out his view in the major 1870 prize essay for Dorpat University's theology faculty, only recently rediscovered (Harnack 2003), which laid the foundation for his better-known later monograph on Marcion (1924). For Harnack's convictions about the need for hermeneutical "violence" and "iconoclasm," see his 1885 correspondence with Friedrich Loofs (quoted in Zahn-Harnack 1936: 102–3). The import of this intellectual heritage is rightly recognized in (then) Cardinal Joseph Ratzinger's preface to Pontifical Biblical Commission 2002 (on which see Bockmuehl 2003a).

8. Whether the document now known as the *Gospel of Thomas* was so titled in antiquity is uncertain. Only the Coptic manuscript contains the description or title

group of authors, including John Dominic Crossan, Robert W. Funk, Burton L. Mack, and (from a more pastoral angle) Marcus J. Borg. Although these writers never explicitly deny Jesus's Jewishness (and generally take vociferous exception to the charge that they do), they do in fact develop a Jesus largely neutered and declawed as to Jewish religious specifics.[9]

The resulting metamorphosis has proved astonishingly popular among a generation of aging flower children: here is a less judgmental, more inclusive peasant philosopher of timeless universal wisdom and countercultural charisma. Jesus's teacher, John the Baptist, was an eschatological prophet of judgment and repentance, and some of these concerns were shared by Jesus's followers; but Jesus himself remained wholly untainted by apocalyptic fancies of this sort. We discover that such Jewish moral or eschatological themes as have found their way into the Q construct against

---

"The Gospel according to Thomas," but places it at the end (Layton 1987: 380 note a). No manuscript has a superscript analogous to those of the canonical Gospels, and no ancient writer unambiguously identifies our text as a "gospel." Hippolytus, who comes closest to doing so, cites a Naassene work inscribed "the Gospel according to Thomas" (*Refutation of All Heresies* 5.7.20), but it strains credulity to see in his quotation "incontrovertible" evidence (so Cameron 1992: 535) of the *Gospel of Thomas* 4 (cf. POxy 654.21–27). Just two words are paralleled, and only one is identical:

Hippolytus	*Gospel of Thomas 4*
One who seeks me will find me in children from seven years old. For there I become manifest, having been concealed in the fourteenth eon.	The person old in days will not hesitate to ask a child aged seven days about the place of life; and that person will live. For there are many first who shall be last, and they shall become a single one.

Beyond this, a "gospel"—often an infancy gospel—of the same name was indeed known to patristic writers (as indubitably heterodox and recent); as a result, identifications like those of Origen (τὸ κατὰ Θωμᾶν εὐαγγέλιον, *Homilies on Luke* 1 [Die griechischen christlichen Schriftsteller 49.5.9]) or Eusebius (*Ecclesiastical History* 3.25.6) are impossible to identify with confidence. In view of much scholarly misuse of the term *gospel*, it is worth recalling that an analogous point, occasionally noted by critics of the Q-Thomas school of thought, applies much more clearly in the case of Q. Attested by no ancient writers, it was certainly never called a "gospel" (*pace* Mack 1993; Crossan 1998; Horsley 2003; and many others) until the closing years of the twentieth century.

9. Instead of this feline metaphor, Pearson 1995: 334 prefers the culturally appropriate but perhaps excessively melodramatic one of "forcible epispasm." Pearson 2004 explores similarly problematic claims about a Galilean "Q community."

the odds[10] are invariably the effect of a later Judaizing editorial veneer—a distortion of the gentle mystic's original intentions in the direction of an Israel-centered messianism preoccupied with an eschatological kingdom of God.[11]

What is perhaps most striking about this "new vision," as Borg 1987 calls it, is less its newness than the family resemblance it bears to its critical predecessors. Here, the nineteenth-century ethical-liberal idealism of Albrecht Ritschl, Adolf von Harnack, and others seems to have been echoed and transformed into the Jesus Seminar's ahistorical spirituality and mellifluously bland (or, on the other hand, neo-Marxian) moralism.[12]

Similarly, the de facto de-Judaizing of Jesus's aims and teaching is reminiscent of the so-called New Quest for the historical

10. At a time of growing scholarly doubts about the very existence of Q, it may be permissible to point out the circularity of many of the arguments around "Q Christianity": by ruling out all that the Petrine tradition knew about Mark, and all that either Matthew in Syria or Luke in Rome knew independently of the other, one arrives unsurprisingly at a disembodied, storyless Jesus who looks very unlike what is found in any actually extant first-century gospels or any known second-century expositions of those same gospels.

11. Allison 1998 offers one of the most trenchant critiques of the Jesus Seminar's quasiarcheological gadgetry to extract a noneschatological Jesus. For him, authentic and redactional material is in fact found intermingled not merely in the supposedly earliest layers, but throughout the tradition: "We cannot separate chemical compounds with a knife. Nor can we tell at the end of a river what came from the fountainhead and what from later tributaries" (33).

12. "Jesus," wrote Harnack 1957: 122–23, "opens up to us the prospect of a union among men, which is held together not by any legal ordinance, but by the rule of love"—a glorious egalitarian ideal that "ought to float before our eyes as the goal and guiding star of our historical development" (also quoted in Novak 1989: 75). On the close relationship between Harnack and Ritschl, see Zahn-Harnack 1936: 92–95. I am grateful to my former colleague Winrich Löhr for pointing out that Harnack was not a "moralist" in the same sense as Ritschl; indeed, he explicitly excluded moralism on the strongest terms (e.g., Harnack 1924: 225) and denied that Christianity, which he understood in idealized but radical terms of divine salvation and an ethic of love, could be reduced to a bourgeois notion of progress (cf. 1924: 18; 1957: 90). Philip Jenkins, one of the more bracing of recent commentators on the contemporary Jesus industry, excoriates the Jesus Seminar's tendency to repackage as "new" noncanonical sources that critical scholarship has long since known and found unreliable. He quotes Chesterton 1955: 222, writing as long ago as the 1920s: "Those who maintain that Christianity was not a church but a moral movement of idealists have been forced to push the period of its perversion or disappearance farther and farther back" (Jenkins 2001: 123).

Jesus in the 1950s and 1960s, whose protagonists held as one of their most treasured methodological commitments the so-called criterion of dissimilarity: assurance of the authentic Jesus could be found above all at those points where he departed most clearly from contemporary Palestinian Judaism. While double dissimilarity from both Judaism and the later church may indeed serve a modest purpose as a criterion of irreducible minimalism, it is hardly serviceable to shed much coherent light on a Jewish Jesus.[13]

An eerie twist on that same predisposition appeared some decades earlier in the writings of Grundmann and fellow ideologues among the "German Christians," who argued that the authentic (quasi-Aryan) gospel of Jesus had in its canonical form become editorially tainted and even falsified in a Judaizing direction. Indeed, one could not view Jesus's own racial identity or ancestry straightforwardly as that of a Palestinian Jew, since Galilee was home to a multitude of different racial groups.[14] Grundmann and his colleagues even produced a *Volkstestament* that became a huge media success, consisting of the supposedly oldest, de-Judaized sayings of the Jesus tradition and stripped of stories and sayings falsely attributed to him (see Jerke 1994 on Anonymous 1940). Indeed, as Grundmann argued in reliance on Rudolf Bultmann, "salvation is from the Jews" (John 4:22) is contextually impossible and represents a later gloss introduced by an "apocalyptic" redactor from circles close to the author of Revelation (Grundmann 1938: 5–6). This scholarly insight, he argued, should be popularized as the basis for a new culturally appropriate Christianity that could free itself from the church's traditional (and in his view really "talmudic") preoccupation with the authority of what is "written" in the Bible (1938: 8).

13. Cf. also Osborn 1990: 218–21 on Rudolf Bultmann, Norman Perrin, and others in this period. For a thorough discussion and critique of the now largely discredited criterion of dissimilarity, see the important work of Theissen and Winter 2002, who advocate in its place a "criterion of plausibility" (cf. already the questions raised by Hooker 1971 and 1972; also Wright 1996: 89–121). The "new proposals" of Porter 2000: 126–237 (Greek language, "textual variance," and "discourse features") seem less promising, although offering some useful criticisms of earlier criteria (63–123).

14. For this discussion see Heschel 1994; Head 2004; and Kleine 2002: 10 citing Grundmann 1938 and 1940. Cf. further Meeks 2004 on Gerhard Kittel's exegesis.

Lest these findings be too swiftly dismissed as an ideological extreme and wholly irrelevant to contemporary de-Judaizing of Jesus and Galilee, we will do well to ponder the Grundmann team's not unreasonable postwar claim that their Jesus scholarship and its conclusions had in fact been *in the international mainstream* (see Head 2004: 85–86, 85n118, citing Heschel 1994: 600 and 1999: 81–82). By replacing "racial" with "religious" or "philosophical" (and "Aryan" with "postmodern"), it is tempting to uncover here a prescient, if rather more explicit, variation on the Jesus Seminar's major presuppositions. One thinks of its "red letter" editions purged of Jewish apocalyptic motifs (beginning with Funk et al. 1988; Funk and Smith 1991) and of its missionary drive to popularize its scholarly findings as the basis for a more authentic, more contemporary Christianity than is on offer from the traditional church with its Jewish Jesus and its Bible of two Testaments. This is of course a caricature, but like all good caricatures it captures an important characteristic. It matters for the cultural and political agenda of the Jesus Seminar's main protagonists that Jesus was not an observant Jew but a "secular sage" (so Funk 1993: 287, also quoted in Pearson 1995: 337–38).[15]

And so we seem to arrive at the logical conclusion of a process that has been a hallmark of post-Enlightenment scholarship[16] and that arguably has deep roots even in patristic thought. We are therefore inevitably caught between the horns of a dilemma: even allowing that it is historically plausible, can a Christian point of view affirm the essential Jewish particularity of Jesus's identity without thereby denying a part of its own heritage? The answer

---

15. For a learned and thoughtful reflection on the secularizing of Jesus in some recent Western scholarship, note Allison 2000.

16. Dale C. Allison kindly points out to me that similar tendencies were already evident among some of the early-eighteenth-century English Deists, including Shelley and Thomas Morgan. Even today, however, this evacuation of Jesus's Jewishness is by no means restricted to one particular school of thought. The following assessment of Merkel 1984: 144 is characteristic of a broad stream of twentieth-century exegetical opinion: "All ideals, however great or sacred they may be, must be subordinated to love for one's neighbour. With this precept Jesus placed himself outside all parties and groups of his time. Once we become aware of how often Jesus burst through the bounds of conventional thought and behaviour, we must regard a conflict between him and the representatives of the traditional order as unavoidable."

to that question might conceivably require theology to undergo
a degree of intellectual "gene therapy"—a task that has begun to
be noted and addressed in recent discussions of church and Israel,
but that transcends the scope of this book.[17]

The Historical Quest's Brittle Cliché of Jesus the Jew

Historically, as we have seen, the idea of "Jesus the Jew" has
been an oxymoron. Within the world of Jesus scholarship, however, it had become something of a platitude by the end of the
twentieth century—so much so that few brows could now be
wrinkled by books like *Jesus the Jew* (Vermes 1983) or *Jesus and
Judaism* (Sanders 1985), which in their day caused storms of excitement and debate. For all the vigorous debate and continuing
disagreement about many critical issues, at the beginning of the
twenty-first century a high percentage of New Testament scholars
in North America and a clear majority in Britain and the European
continent agree on the fundamentally Palestinian Jewish religious
framework of the aims and teaching of Jesus[18]—a framework
about which recent textual and archeological discoveries have
enabled us to know more than perhaps any other generation of
Christians since the second century.

Whether one accepts the problematic identification of the current
wave of scholarship as a Third Quest (after the nineteenth-century
lives of Jesus and the mid-twentieth-century form-critical hunt for
authentic logia),[19] it seems reasonable to suggest, as a major con-

17. See the circumspect discussion of this subject in writers like Soulen 1996; B.
Marshall 2001; and Jenson 2003b, as well as the provocative ecclesiological proposals of Kinzer 2005.

18. Meier 1999: 485 rightly concludes that "apart from the Jesus Seminar, most
participants in the third quest . . . have helped make 'Jesus the Jew' more than just a
fashionable academic slogan." A smaller but growing number, including the present
writer, would moreover argue strongly that these aims were formulated and imple-
mented, both during and after Jesus's lifetime, in a deliberate context of national
renewal, religious observance, and halakic awareness, however controversial this
stance may have proved in the eyes of some Jewish contemporaries.

19. The terminology has widely caught on after being famously introduced by
N. T. Wright in Neill and Wright 1988: 379–403 and being incorporated into the title

tributor recently did, that the recovery of Jesus's thoroughly Jewish religious context is perhaps the single most important result of the recent flood of research (so explicitly Meier 1999: 486). Four interlinked factors contributed to this intriguing twentieth-century shift in the understanding of Jesus. First, the seeds were sown in a notable revival of Christian interest in Jewish studies in the late nineteenth and early twentieth centuries. Hints of this emerge in Julius Wellhausen's famously overstated cliché that Jesus was not a Christian but a Jew ("Jesus war kein Christ, sondern Jude"; 1905: 113). Building on the work of writers like Johannes Weiss and Albert Schweitzer, with their stress on the Jewish eschatological dimension of Jesus's talk about the kingdom of God, after World War I a small number of distinguished scholars advanced the study of Christianity's Jewish origins in significant ways.[20] For perhaps the first time since antiquity (with the possible exception of John Lightfoot and British Philo-Semitism; see Katz 1982 and Schertz 1977), Christian scholars came to take seriously the Jewish literature of the Second Temple and rabbinic periods in its own right and to study it as necessary background for an understanding of Christian origins.

---

of an influential survey (Witherington 1995). Given the disparate presuppositions, aims, methods, and conclusions involved, however, the notion of a coherently identifiable Third Quest was perhaps never particularly persuasive; and the underlying periodization (First Quest, no quest, New Quest, Third Quest) is itself facile and problematic. As Weaver 1999 and others rightly point out, the notion that the first half of the twentieth century was the period of "non-quest" (so Neill and Wright 1988: 380) is easily debunked and a patent injustice to the work of major scholars, including Gustav Dalman, Joachim Jeremias, Joseph Klausner, C. H. Dodd, A. M. Hunter, and Thomas W. Manson (not to mention the more sinister but influential Nazi scholarship discussed above), most of whom are virtually ignored by Wright and Witherington. Conversely, the demarcation between the methods, aims, and conclusions of the New Quest and those of the Q-Thomas scholarship championed by scholars of Harvard, Claremont, and the Jesus Seminar is far from obvious. Indeed, it seems far more plausible to see in the latter a virtually unbroken continuity with the former, a continuity personified in several leading lights who have featured in both (including James M. Robinson and Robert W. Funk). For a similar critique cf. further Marsh 1997; Allison 2000; and Porter 2000: 56.

20. They included Adolf Schlatter, Hermann L. Strack, Paul Billerbeck, George Foot Moore, Samuel Krauss, F. C. Burkitt, C. G. Montefiore, and Joseph Klausner, among others.

A second important, if self-explanatory, factor was the geno-
cide of World War II followed by the establishment of the State
of Israel. This was in significant respects a deliberately secular
development. Many religious Zionists, however, often with the
explicit support of sympathizing evangelical Christians, have consistently interpreted the origin and history of the State of Israel in
biblical and eschatological terms.[21] Although anticipated in various
forms and for various reasons,[22] after the 1940s a sympathetic
view of Judaism and Jewish history entered mainstream Christian
consciousness to an unprecedented degree.

Third, the prewar blossoming of Jewish studies received a major
boost from the discovery in 1947 of the Dead Sea Scrolls, which
gave further impetus to a boom in scholarship on Judaism and
Christian origins. By the 1980s and early 1990s this excitement had
reached a fever pitch, spawning a flood of specialist literature and
even a series of dedicated new teaching positions in Qumranology.
While the tension and glamor as well as the conspiracy theories
have now given way to sober historical study, it remains the case
that Qumran has revolutionized our understanding of the social
and religious setting in which Jesus preached. Several aspects of the
gospel tradition that hitherto seemed opaque or *sui generis* have
begun to shine more clearly in historical technicolor.[23] This vast
increase in our sources for first-century Judaism has gone hand
in hand with an often equally impressive, if less widely heralded,
deepening of critical study of previously known ancient Jewish
sources from the Second Temple and rabbinic periods.

Linking all of these factors together, finally, has been a development at the front line of church (and to a lesser extent synagogue)
life. With occasional exceptions, the Christian churches have on the

21. Note, at the same time, recent inner-evangelical questioning of uncritical
support for the State of Israel, including Weber 2004 and (more controversially)
Burge 2003.

22. It is worth recalling the significant charitable and missionary activities of
Gentile and Jewish Christians among early Jewish settlers in Palestine as early as the
mid-nineteenth century.

23. Examples include the text and prophetic interpretation of the Old Testament,
John the Baptist, and various teachings on marriage and divorce, the temple, worship,
baptism, Israel, religious dissent, and community of goods.

whole been remarkably welcoming of this more Jewish understanding of Jesus, no doubt encouraged in part by a significant increase in Christian-Jewish dialogue in the postwar period. Perhaps the single most visible initiative in this respect came during the papacy of John Paul II, culminating in his visit to the holy land and prayer at Jerusalem's Western Wall in the Jubilee Year 2000.[24] Initiatives from the Jewish side have been less prominent (if no less interesting), have tended to emanate from individuals rather than groups, and have sometimes incurred fierce resistance from within Jewish circles. It is perhaps also the case that recent corporate statements like *Dabru Emet* (Novak et al. 2000) or books like *Christianity in Jewish Terms* (Frymer-Kensky et al. 2000) curiously manage to address Christianity without saying much about Christ. But the fact that they exist at all reinforces the sense that the identity of the Jesus whom Christians follow is of pertinence to Jews and Christians alike.

These developments and others have contributed to what is today a clear, though admittedly not unopposed, consensus: at the historical level Jesus of Nazareth is most appropriately understood in the cultural and religious setting of first-century Judaism in the land of Israel.

That consensus on the Jewish Jesus, however, remains fragile and under constant challenge: even those who share it cannot agree on what it means or entails—in part because Judaism itself found bewilderingly diverse expressions in first-century Palestine. The different interpretative options invariably carry significant ideological freight and legitimate a striking variety of ulterior motives or subtexts.[25] New Testament scholars, even if they talk the talk of a Jewish Jesus, do not always walk the walk—either hijacking narrowly particular phenomena for ideological ends or more commonly continuing in blithe neglect of actual particularities in order to highlight their conveniently relativizing diversity. Challenges arise not only from historical skeptics and the protagonists of the Jesus Seminar, but also from the proverbial

---

24. Another noteworthy statement from this pope's period of office is Pontifical Biblical Commission 2002.

25. A point rightly stressed by Arnal 2005 and other contributors to Kloppenborg and Marshall 2005.

force of old scholarly habits. It remains the case that more than a few New Testament scholars lack a firsthand familiarity with the relevant Jewish sources and their setting, even in translation. For all the advances in the social history and anthropology of early Christianity, one still finds in many theologically alert Gospel studies remarkably little concrete awareness of the nature of the land, social geography, institutions, history, orality, or memory. And even in the age of discount airfares, one can still encounter authors of "historical" Gospel commentaries who never bothered to set foot in the land in which the events took place.

Whether for conventional or confessional reasons, many continue to favor the notion of Jesus's opposition not perhaps to Judaism *tout court*, but certainly to the teaching of any and all Jewish individuals and groups actually known to us. This applies especially in the case of law, where a majority still assume that at least in a handful of programmatic words and actions Jesus deliberately "broke" or "annulled" the Torah and thereby did place himself consciously over against Judaism.[26] Quite how one should envisage this kind of comprehensive dissent from all possible Jewish options is often opaque, especially if one bears in mind a religious context as complex as that of Galilee and Judea before AD 70. What is clear is that conservatives are often just as keen on this theme of Jesus's superiority or separation from contemporary religious Judaism as ostensibly more liberal interpreters. Making Jesus more of a Jew may seem to have the effect of making him less of a Christian—or at any rate less of a Western Enlightenment Protestant.

There is at present no such thing as an agreed benchmark of Jesus scholarship, and the map sketched above will not be to every reader's liking. Nevertheless, it seems relatively uncontroversial to discern a certain agreement, however tacit and fragile, on the *fact* and the *importance* of Jesus's Jewishness for his identity.

Quite what this might mean, however, either for history or for faith, is a question on which we remain very far from a consensus.

---

26. Classic examples of such misreading, represented even in major Third Quest scholars like E. P. Sanders, include the Matthean antitheses (Matt. 5:21–48) and above all the instruction to "let the dead bury their dead" in Matt. 8:22 ‖ Luke 9:60, on which see my remarks in Bockmuehl 2000b: 24–46.

The remainder of this chapter will attempt to offer a thumbnail sketch of Jesus of Nazareth's Judaism and conclude by asking what difference this might make for a Christian theological understanding of his identity.

Eschatology and Identity: The Case of Jesus "Called the Christ"

How much of real substance can New Testament scholarship of the early twenty-first century reasonably bring to a discussion of Jesus's Jewish identity? Clearly the answers, once again, are many and conflicting; skepticism is cheap, and jaded vacillation, as ever, rules the academic roost. If the question before us is to prove theologically worthwhile, therefore, we may need to suspend the professional's instinctive posture of ambidextrous self-preservation and push the boat out a little farther in order to let the nets down a little deeper than one might ordinarily choose to do in a purely academic forum.[27]

What follows is necessarily a reconstruction. It may emerge from a decade and a half of research and writing in the area, but it remains a reconstruction. As such, it is at best of ephemeral value to theology; as such, too, it has weaknesses, many of which mirror my own and those of my environment of work and worship. Nevertheless, as John Dominic Crossan declaims in a famous half-truth to conclude his own very differently construed argument, "If you cannot believe in something produced by reconstruction, you may have nothing left to believe in" (1991: 426). The point may be put in more theological terms: as long as salvation matters to history (and vice versa),[28] then to seek to understand them both becomes a theologian's obligation.

27. Perhaps the advice of Hillel, Jesus's famous older contemporary, applies to scholars too: he urged his followers to "dare to be a man [or a *Mensch*] in a place where no one else is" (*bammaqom she'eyn 'anashim, hishtaddel lihyot 'ish*; Mishnah, tractate *Abot* 2.6).

28. Cf. on this relationship most recently the pensive remarks of Hengel 2003b, a doyen of New Testament historians.

Regardless of whether any particular historical reconstruction stands or falls, one point remains indispensable to any viably Christian interpretation of the identity of Jesus. Against obscurantist dogma of both the skeptical and the fideistic kind, even the most theological of New Testament authors insist that the fundamental trustworthiness of Gospel testimony is a sine qua non of the entire Christian enterprise. Contra certain postliberal views sometimes (rightly or wrongly) associated with Hans Frei (most influentially 1975; cf. also p. 159n48 above), for the early Christian church the identity of Jesus is *not* accessible simply in "stories" about him that may or may not have a bearing on history. It is the *referential truth* of that apostolic testimony that undergirds the very possibility of faith (John 19:35; 21:25); indeed, "if Christ has not been raised, your faith is futile and you are still in your sins" (1 Cor. 15:17 NRSV). And what is "doubting" (ἄπιστος, "faithless") about the Fourth Gospel's Thomas is not his desire for facts but his emphatic refusal to trust the apostolic testimony: unless he personally sees and touches the evidence, he *"will not* believe" (John 20:25, 27, 29). Unless at some basic level we are prepared to receive, trust, and inhabit a given communal embodiment of memory and witness, we can know nothing at all. The solipsism of *cogito ergo sum* is logically compelling only in the madhouse.

While a good many historians may contest Jesus's birth in Bethlehem of Judea with its Davidic connotations, everyone agrees that his main formation and early ministry are set in a wholly Galilean context during the reign of the Emperor Tiberius (AD 14–37) and his puppet king Herod Antipas (4 BC–AD 39), son of Herod the Great (37–4 BC). At the same time, Jesus evidently had some followers in Judea, where his ministry concluded during a Passover pilgrimage to Jerusalem that began with a controversial demonstration in the Jewish temple and ended on a Roman cross.

Contrary to the assertions of some, including scholars associated with the Jesus Seminar, recent literary and archeological research shows early-first-century Galilee to have been thoroughly Jewish in population, in worldview, and to a surprising extent in praxis (see Chancey 2002, 2005; C. A. Evans 2001; Freyne 1998, 2004). Although showing significant Phoenician and Hellenistic influence until the third century BC, in the aftermath of Maccabean expansion and resettlement Galilee remained at most very superficially Hellenized. And while thriving Hellenistic cities surrounded Galilee in Syria, on the coast, and in the Decapolis, the attempt to interpret Jesus as a philosopher in Cynic vein founders inter alia on his apparent avoidance of such cities[29] and the complete absence of evidence for identifiable Cynics or their ideas within first-century Galilee. This point, stressed in study after study by archeologists and historians, is rarely acknowledged by advocates of the Cynic view, who tend to base their arguments on generalizing extrapolations from a cultural anthropology of generic "Mediterranean peasants."[30] (Indeed it has taken key players in the Jesus Seminar a long time to consider the distinguished body of scholarship that questions their assumptions. This is particularly true of crucial questions like the early date and literary independence of the so-called *Gospel of Thomas*, on which this school of thought sets great store.)[31] In terms of ideas, the links between Jesus and the Cynic or Stoic philosophers are no closer than those between Qumran and the Zoroastrians. Every era has its "big ideas" that, far from being the property of any one group, may appeal instead to people across a wide range of competing but mutually fertilizing worldviews.

29. None of those cities nearest to Galilee feature in the Gospel tradition (though cf. John 6:23), and even "Tyre and Sidon" appear to denote a geographic area to the exclusion of the actual cities (Mark 7:24, 31 ‖ Matt. 15:21 and Matt. 11:21 ‖ Luke 10:13).

30. This somewhat arm-waving "pan-anthropological" perspective, characteristic of John Dominic Crossan's approach, is in fact remarkably widespread in New Testament studies and owes much to the influence of Bruce J. Malina and others (Malina 2001, on which cf. Bockmuehl 2002). Crossan himself appears ironically to acknowledge this methodological vagueness and to soft-pedal earlier claims: "If Cynicism had never existed, nothing would change" in his reconstruction of Jesus (1998: 334). Jesus the Cynic no longer features in Crossan and Reed 2001.

31. The dependence of significant parts of the *Gospel of Thomas* on *redactional elements* in the Synoptic Gospels is carefully demonstrated by Tuckett 1988, 1998; cf. also 1999: 265 specifically on Crossan's methodology vis-à-vis the *Gospel of Thomas* and other, often hypothetical sources. More recently still, Perrin 2002 argues that the *Gospel of Thomas* may in fact depend on the *Diatessaron*; this is a case that, despite weaknesses in method and implementation, merits fuller consideration—at least inasmuch as it may suggest something of the context and milieu in which the *Gospel of Thomas* originated.

Jesus's development and praxis as a religious Jew are amply reflected in the Gospel narratives. Following on from the genealogies and birth narratives, these features include his apprenticeship under John the Baptist; his inaugural message about the impending kingdom of Israel's God; his enactment of divine forgiveness and call to repentance; his exorcism of unclean spirits, including the Roman "Legion" personified;[32] his calling of twelve disciples to evangelize and ultimately to judge the twelve tribes of Israel; his general avoidance of Gentiles, at least to the extent that the two apparent exceptions in the Gospels attract special attention (see Mark 7:24–30 ‖ Matt. 15:21–28 and Matt. 8:5–13 ‖ Luke 7:1–10);[33] his classic teachings and miracles steeped in scriptural typologies of the Israelite prophetic tradition; his disputes with contemporaries about the right interpretation of Torah, disputes that arise out of a largely shared hermeneutical framework and in which more than once he takes views that are also cited or even endorsed in subsequent rabbinic halakah; and his climactic Passover pilgrimage to Jerusalem, complete with an enactment of a messianic entry into the city and passionate concern about the corruption of the temple, the place of God's dwelling, which to him meant the universal house of prayer. Others called him rabbi, teacher, prophet, or Messiah; like the later rabbis he in turn called his followers "disciples" (μαθηταί, talmidim) and made at least some of them his empowered "emissaries" (ἀπόστολοι, shelukhim). The Jesus of the Synoptic tradition approved of tithing, endorsed sacrifice and voluntary gifts to the temple, even paid the controversial temple tax (however grudgingly), said grace before meals, and wore tassels on his clothes. "His" prayer is quintessentially

32. Cf. Horsley 2001: 145–47 (along with the bracing critique of Engberg-Pedersen 2003: 245).

33. The dialectical approach to this issue in Jeremias 1967 still offers a useful orientation, despite a continuing and sometimes uncomprehending chorus of critics; note especially his discussion (46–51) of the place in Jesus's teachings of Elijah's dealings with the widow of Zarephath and of Elisha's with Naaman, as well as of the Gentiles of Nineveh, Sheba, Tyre and Sidon, and Sodom and Gomorrah sharing in the resurrection. Despite his frivolously dismissive critique of Jeremias, S. McKnight 1999: 82n47 is right to see the later Gentile mission as an outworking of Jesus's concern for Israel.

Jewish and particularly close in form to the ancient Kaddish prayer of the synagogue.[34]

The very nature of his repeated disputes about matters like vows, food and corpse impurity, divorce, the Sabbath, and the temple presupposes Jesus's affirmation of the Torah's authority. At issue are the hermeneutical priorities within Scripture, as well as between Scripture and subsequent innovation, some of which he rejected (e.g., in the area of secondary purity). Jesus appears consistently to stand in dialogue, and often in agreement, with known halakic positions within Pharisaic Judaism or at Qumran.[35] In this connection he sometimes restricts or forbids what the Torah permits, but never permits what it clearly forbids (so the catchy summary of Hooker 2000: 125).

During a Passover (or Passover-like) meal on the eve of his crucifixion, Jesus brought all these concerns to a sharp focus by taking what appears to be a Nazirite vow (which commits a lay Israelite to priestly holiness, usually for a finite period) in anticipation of the coming kingdom (Mark 14:25 ‖ Matt. 26:28). Even his execution on a classically Roman gibbet listed as his crime the only version of his Jewish messianic claim that Roman executioners could understand: *Rex Iudaeorum*. And however unexpected the events may have seemed even to his own disciples, the claim of Jesus's bodily resurrection from the dead, finally, was culturally idiosyncratic to the point of being incomprehensible to all but religious Jews.[36]

34. Cf. Mussner 1984: 130: "It is the prayer of the *Jew* Jesus with which every Jew without inner reservation can pray. . . . The Our Father is the great 'bridge prayer' between the Jewish and the Christian communities." Cf. further Finkel 1981 and Heinemann 1978.

35. For recent surveys of this point see Davies and Sanders 1999: 649–58, 663–64; Tomson 2001b; and Bockmuehl 2000a and the literature cited there. Kister 2001 points out the extent to which even such supposedly antinomian views as those expressed in Mark 7:15 or the argument about the "straining of gnats" (Matt. 23:24), although clearly controversial in Jesus's pre–AD 70 debate with "Pharisees," became in fact part of the rabbinic mainstream. I am wholly unpersuaded by the argument of Meier 2003: 67–79 that the Qumran and rabbinic texts on divorce are irrelevant ("not *ad rem*"; 77) to Jesus's teaching.

36. For the *Sitz im Leben* of the New Testament's resurrection language, see my comments in Bockmuehl 2001b as well as the comprehensive documentation in Wright 2003.

The preceding three paragraphs give a deliberately synthetic, cumulative reading. The constituent features need not in every case be unambiguously authentic or straightforwardly retrievable in order to secure the overall picture of a Jesus whose Jewishness of faith and praxis inalienably defines his identity as the "what" of the "who." Some cited assertions are peculiar to Matthew, while others are wholly absent from John. The argument capitalizes on a Jewish cultural and religious way of life that Jesus shared with the apostolic Palestinian communities that first passed on his tradition (settings that historical criticism often cannot reliably distinguish in practice). A vigorous historical case can indeed be made for virtually all of the cited traditions—including the interesting correlation, observed also at Qumran and among the Pharisees, of an integrated concern for both eschatological hope and Jewish praxis (or halakah). It is particularly significant that the preservation of such obsolete elements in the Gospels arguably runs against the grain of redaction: they have become politically incorrect for evangelists committed in every case to the gospel's post-Easter outreach to *Gentiles*.

This strikingly Jewish profile of Jesus is one of the more important illustrations of the fact that, contrary to much scholarly posturing, the evangelists do *not* primarily envisage their works as convenient instruments of cultural and religious *aggiornamento*. Mark may tinker somewhat unsystematically with food laws (Mark 7:1–19) and Matthew may elaborate the tradition's hostility to Pharisees (Matt. 23:1–36). The past of Jesus is indeed applied to the writers' present: but just as vital, both historically and theologically, is that his past and their present are not the same (see Lemcio 1991, which remains a useful primer on this point). Even the Fourth Gospel's controversially attenuated depiction of Jesus's Jewish particularity acknowledges the opposition of most of "the Jews" (or "Judeans"?) while still affirming Jesus as "the king *of Israel*" (John 1:49; 12:13).[37] What is striking in the Gospels is not so much their adaptation to the needs of post-70

37. On the much-debated topic of "Jews" and "Israel" in John note, among others, Harvey 1996: 245–50 and Devillers 1998.

Gentile communities but precisely the remarkable *lack* of such accommodation, whether linguistically, religiously, geographically, historically, legally, or theologically. At least as documents for the constitution of a Gentile church and of a faith in a risen and present Christ, the Gospels remain extraordinarily anachronistic in their presentation of a Jesus who manifests a great deal more Jewish particularity than was often found congenial by Gentile Christians.[38] Needless to say, the number of controversial topics clamoring for discussion here is enormous, most of them impossibly complex for a short study.

To conclude this section, and as something of a control on the bird's-eye-view reconstruction just offered, I wish briefly to single out two concerns of Jesus's ministry likely to be of particular importance for his distinctive identity, namely, his views of Israel and of himself. It seems appropriate to view the key issues here through the lens of two pivotal texts as cases in point, one pertaining to his view of the mission of the Twelve.[39]

The Destiny of the Twelve

All four Gospels affirm that Jesus singled out twelve men as an inner core of the larger group of disciples, although relatively less is made of this in John. Their appointment is generally regarded as authentic by all except those who fail to find it in Q or the *Gospel of Thomas* and therefore ascribe it to the evangelists (thus Crossan 1998: 337).[40] The symbolism of the

38. Unless this is a deliberately archaizing move, which in its persistence across the Synoptic tradition seems unlikely both intrinsically and in its presupposition that later evangelists remained *au fait* with the intricacies of Palestinian Jewish halakic debate.

39. My choice of texts in what follows is on one level arbitrary: many others could be said to be at least equally apropos (including several intriguing Matthean texts on Israel and Johannine ones on Jesus's self-understanding). At the same time, one could say in defense of my choice that it attempts to represent a balance of the Synoptic tradition's sources (double and triple attestation), forms (an individual logion from Q and an extended parable from Mark), and narrative thrust (in that it brings this question to a point during Jesus's last week in Jerusalem).

40. See Meier 2001 for a nuanced, robust defense of the Twelve as an important part of the public ministry of Jesus in discussion with recent criticism. He rightly re-

Twelve, too, is not in serious doubt. When seen on the canvas of
its scriptural and Jewish setting, this eschatological institution
of the Twelve conveys a theocentric and specifically *messianic*
reconstitution of the entire biblical Israel under the leadership
of tribal judges and their king.[41] The theme of twelve phylarchs
or tribal princes under their king continued to be an important
part of Jewish interpretation in the early Roman period and
specifically features as part of both eschatological hope and
halakic prescription at Qumran.[42] Similarly, the *Testaments of
the Twelve Patriarchs* expects the sons of Jacob at the resurrection to rule over their respective tribes—and such judging
as the exercise of authority and government seems to be what
our logion intends too.[43] Here the judges rule over their tribes
within the kingdom of the Son of Man, just as the synagogue's
ancient *Amidah* prayer anticipates the restoration of the tribal
judges and the Davidic king (*Prayer of Eighteen Benedictions*,
nos. 11, 14). The Jesus tradition's stress not on "princes" but
on "apostles" who are "sent" is distinctive but still makes sense
against this background—indeed it is precisely the *sending* of
these twelve that chiefly authorizes and constitutes them as
"apostles":[44]

gards Luke's omission of the Twelve (383–84) as explicable on grounds of style and
perhaps embarrassment at Judas's presence at the Last Supper.

41. Cf. Horbury 2003a: 157–88; Davies and Sanders 1999: 635–36; and Davies
and Allison 1988–97: 3.58n134, who note Shabbetai Zvi's choice of twelve disciples
representing the twelve tribes.

42. 1QM 2.1–3; 3.3; 5.1–2; 4Q164 (4QpIsa[d]) 1.7 on Isa. 54:12. For Qumran
halakah see 11QTemple 57.11–15; 1QS 8.1; and 4Q159 (4QOrdinances[a]) frags.
2–4, lines 3–4.

43. *Testament of Judah* 25.1–2; cf. *Testament of Benjamin* 10.7; *Testament of
Zebulun* 10.2; also *Testament of Abraham* A 13.6. See further Horbury 2003a: 167–68
and Davies and Allison 1988–97: 3.55–56, 55n119. An eternal heavenly role for the
twelve patriarchs is also envisaged in Philo, *Questions and Answers on Exodus* 2.114.
Under this heading of the phylarchs' judging, it is also worth considering Jesus's as-
signments of the keys of the kingdom (Matt. 16:19), "binding and loosing" (18:18),
and also perhaps the role of James and the apostolic "court" of Acts 15.

44. So, rightly, Horbury 2003a: 181, with additional reference to Gal. 2:8 and the
apparently "apostolic" elders of Luke 10:1. The sending of empowered emissaries
(*shelukhim*) has, incidentally, been an important feature of Habad, the Jewish messianic
movement around the Lubavitcher Rebbe, Menahem Schneerson (1902–94).

Then Peter said in reply, "Look, we have left everything and followed you. What then will we have?" Jesus said to them, "Truly I tell you, at the renewal of all things, when the Son of Man is seated on the throne of his glory, you who have followed me will also sit on twelve thrones, judging the twelve tribes of Israel [καθήσεσθε καὶ ὑμεῖς ἐπὶ δώδεκα θρόνους κρίνοντες τὰς δώδεκα φυλὰς τοῦ Ἰσραήλ]." (Matt. 19:27-28 NRSV)

You are those who have stood by me in my trials; and I confer on you, just as my Father has conferred on me, a kingdom, so that you may eat and drink at my table in my kingdom, and you will sit on thrones judging the twelve tribes of Israel [καὶ καθήσεσθε ἐπὶ θρόνων τὰς δώδεκα φυλὰς κρίνοντες τοῦ Ἰσραήλ]. (Luke 22:28–30 NRSV)

Our saying occurs in two very different settings during Jesus's last week in Jerusalem. Matthew includes it in a discussion of the costs and rewards of discipleship following Jesus's encounter with the rich young man (cf. Mark 10:17–31 ‖ Luke 18:18–30), while Luke makes it part of his unique discourse after the Last Supper on the subject of greatness in the kingdom (cf. Mark 10:42–45 ‖ Matt. 20:25–28). Since it belongs to the remainder of a subtraction of Mark from Matthew's agreement with Luke, it fits the definition of Q and is therefore typically included at the very end of that supposed sayings document.[45] In fact, however, neither the classic Two-Source Hypothesis nor any of its major rivals (literary dependence of Luke on Matthew or of Matthew on Luke) offers a satisfactory genetic explanation of what is more likely a case of independent, quite possibly oral, transmission of the same saying in different settings.[46] At the same time, the present context of the Lukan version seems more generalized and could be secondary to that in Matthew.

Significantly, circumstances appear to have conspired to ensure that this leading constitutional role of the Twelve for practical purposes disappeared soon after the resurrection: inasmuch as it continued at all (they are last mentioned in Acts 6:2; cf. 1 Cor.

45. Although sometimes contested and often neglected, the inclusion of this saying appears to be a majority view. See Bammel 1970 and more recently Tuckett 2000, as well as most fully Hoffmann and Heil 1998.

46. A major case for the orality of much of the early Gospel tradition is advanced by Dunn 2003 and 2005.

15:5), it rapidly gave way to a temporary troika of "pillars" involving an outsider, James the Just, along with Simon Peter and John the son of Zebedee from the original group. Only Revelation 21:14 envisages a future "architectural" role for the (now idealized) Twelve as foundations of the new Jerusalem's wall—a role that resembles that of Peter in Matthew 16:18, of the "pillars" in Galatians 2:9, and of James the Just in Hegesippus (Eusebius, *Ecclesiastical History* 2.23.7–8).[47] This virtual disappearance of the Twelve renders the persistence of Jesus's promise to them all the more remarkable (and the promise itself more probably authentic, whatever its original setting).[48]

More interestingly for our purposes, this prediction graphically demonstrates the vital importance of the restoration of biblical Israel's twelve tribes for Jesus's message and expectation—a message deeply rooted in the Old Testament and of some continuing interest in the early church, even after the demise of the Twelve.[49] This was the hoped-for outcome of Jesus's mission on his heavenly Father's behalf, which would culminate in the Son of Man's messianic rule as Israel's king.[50] It is significant that the plural "thrones" of the "tribes" *in Jerusalem* are anticipated in Psalm 122:2–5, a psalm of ascent sung by festival pilgrims (similarly Tomson 2001a: 372 and Horbury 2003a: 138) and thus highly suitable

47. Note, however, the possibility that some sources may implicitly associate James the Just himself with a council of twelve; see Horbury 2003a: 178–79 (citing van den Broek 1988: 63–65 and Bauckham 1990: 74–75), who also notes the repeated appointments of bishops with twelve elders in Jewish Christian texts like *Pseudo-Clementine Recognitions* 3.68; 6.15; *Homilies* 11.36. See further Zwiep 2004 on the continued significance of the Twelve in Palestinian Christianity.

48. So Sanders 1985: 98–106; Davies and Allison 1988–97: 3.58; Meier 2001: 386; and many others.

49. For the Twelve in the ministry of Jesus, see the extensive and programmatic statements of Meier 1991–2001: 3.125–97 and 2001. Continuing interest in the twelve tribes is attested by Paul in Acts 26:7 and by others in James 1:1; Rev. 7:5–8; 14:1–3; 21:12; cf. *Shepherd of Hermas, Similitude* 9.17; *Barnabas* 8.3; *Protevangelium of James* 1.1; Irenaeus, *Against Heresies* 4.21.3; *Diatessaron* 48.39 ("twelve tribes of angels"); and Hippolytus, *Refutation of All Heresies* 5.3 on the Naassenes.

50. That the eschatological Son of Man here can be only Jesus is strongly argued by Tuckett 2000: 111, 114. Cf. also his argument against Crossan's view that Dan. 7 cannot be invoked in support of Jesus as apocalyptic Son of Man (Tuckett 1999: 272–73).

for the Passover setting of both the Lukan and Matthean narrative contexts. These thrones for the phylarchs, surrounding the Son of Man's "throne of glory," also evoke the heavenly thrones of the saints around that of the Ancient of Days in Daniel 7:9.[51]

At the same time, this hope for national restoration does not for Jesus assume militant political fervor of the kind reflected in texts like the *Psalms of Solomon* or Qumran's *War Scroll* and that is at least compatible with the *Amidah's* petitions for the eschatological restoration of the judges and of the Davidic throne in Jerusalem (*Prayer of Eighteen Benedictions*, nos. 11, 14).[52] The potential for militancy was tempered in Jesus's case by his vision of the kingdom of God that, although no less tangible or political, is nevertheless characterized by an eschatological mission to gather in the leaderless "lost sheep" of the house of Israel (Mark 6:34; Matt. 9:36; 10:6; 15:24). This is a mission conceived in terms of good news to the poor, the blind, the deaf, the lame, and the lepers. That kingdom of the lost sheep of Israel is the one Jesus would rule and whose tribes the Twelve would judge.

The Mission of the Son

If the previous passage seemed complicated, the interpretative jungle is a great deal more impenetrable here: critical problems abound, and the academic bibliography on Mark 12:1–9 is vastly overpopulated even by the standards of the anthill known as New Testament studies.

The narrative context is familiar and straightforward. Jesus has been challenged by the religious authorities about his authorization to act as he did in the temple. His reply launches into an evidently programmatic parable, which characterizes his understanding of himself, his mission, and his identity in terms of an Old Testament symbol for Israel and its leadership that was well known

51. So a number of commentators; cf. Horbury 2003a: 137–38 and 1998b: 99, who points out that the targum interprets Ps. 122:3 of the heavenly Jerusalem (*yerushalayim de-mitbanya birqi'a*).

52. Note the Messiah's "gathering" and "judging" of the tribes of Israel in *Psalms of Solomon* 17.26 (and then of the nations in 17.29).

and understood by Jesus's contemporaries (Isa. 5; cf. 4Q500). The story here is given in the version of Mark 12:1–9, which most commentators regard as having shaped the two Synoptic parallels (Matt. 21:33–41 and Luke 20:9–16; cf. *Gospel of Thomas* 65):

> A man planted a vineyard, put a fence around it, dug a pit for the wine press, and built a watchtower; then he leased it to tenants and went to another country. When the season came, he sent a slave to the tenants to collect from them his share of the produce of the vineyard. But they seized him, and beat him, and sent him away empty-handed. And again he sent another slave to them; this one they beat over the head and insulted. Then he sent another, and that one they killed. And so it was with many others; some they beat, and others they killed. He had still one other, a beloved son [υἱὸν ἀγαπητόν]. Finally he sent him to them, saying, "They will respect my son." But those tenants said to one another, "This is the heir [οὗτός ἐστιν ὁ κληρονόμος]; come, let us kill him, and the inheritance will be ours." So they seized him, killed him, and threw him out of the vineyard. What then will the owner of the vineyard do? He will come and destroy the tenants and give the vineyard to others. (NRSV)

For present purposes we may simply concentrate on three essential features of this parable, which are common to all three Synoptic versions.

First, as is typical in Jesus's parables, the underlying frame of reference is uncompromisingly *centered on God, God's people, and God's word.* The main protagonist is the God of Israel, and human action is in response or disobedience to the divine command. In keeping with its formative scriptural antecedents (Isa. 5:2, 7, a "love song" to God) and interpretative tradition,[53] the

---

53. Cf. similarly Isa. 27:2–5; Jer. 2:21; 12:10; Ezek. 15:6; 19:10, 12–14; Hos. 10:1; Ps. 80:8–16; although some of these speak of a vine rather than a vineyard. The vineyard theme is continued in subsequent Jewish texts, including *Targum Jonathan* on Isa. 5 and on the other passages cited; 4Q500 (on which see Baumgarten 1989; Brooke 1995; and C. A. Evans 2000); Tosefta, tractates *Sukkah* 3.15 and *Me'ilah* 1.16; and a number of later midrashic parables (*Pesiqta of Rab Kahana* 3.9; 16.9). Matthew employs the same theme in 20:1–16 and 21:28–32. See also C. A. Evans 2003 in response to the argument of Kloppenborg Verbin 2002 that the vineyard reference in Mark 12 is merely Septuagintal (and by implication secondary).

vineyard is clearly Israel—or rather, as George Brooke phrases it: Jerusalem, centered on the temple, as "Israel in miniature."[54] The tenants represent the religious and political leadership.[55] This much is widely agreed among commentators, as is the Palestinian social context of wealthy absentee landlords (though that is hardly essential to an understanding of the parable; Hengel 1968; Horsley 1995: 132–37; 2003: 94). God owns and plants Jerusalem-Israel as his vineyard. Given the immediately preceding narrative context of Jesus's demonstration in the temple, the details of the parable are by no means merely cosmetic: it is significant that God supplies the vineyard with a winepress and protects it with a watchtower (here also with a fence), items that in contemporary Jewish interpretation stand for the altar and the temple, respectively.[56] God sends a series of servants (more in Mark and Matthew than the three in Luke and two in *Gospel of Thomas* 65), patiently but insistently requiring the harvest that is the owner's rightful due.[57] Then finally God sends his only Son, who also goes willingly into the vineyard. Here the family resemblance is obvious, for the Son alone is explicitly identified in terms of the one he represents: "This is the heir." The tenants can see the Father in the Son, rather as one might find it expressed in "higher" Johannine Christology (see John 8:19; 10:30; 12:45; 14:7, 9; 15:23—or for that matter Matt. 11:27 ‖ Luke 10:22).

54. Brooke 1995: 283–85 shows the prevalence of the link between vineyard, community, and temple in 4Q500, arguing that the same correlation is implied in Mark 12:1–9.

55. This is less immediately obvious from the Old Testament antecedents (cf. Isa. 3:14 and Song 8:11–12), but has a certain intrinsic plausibility and is clearly so understood in the narrative frame of all three Synoptic versions (Mark 12:12 ‖ Matt. 21:46 ‖ Luke 20:19).

56. So explicitly Tosefta, tractates *Sukkah* 3.15 (attributed to R. Yose ben Halafta, second century) and *Me'ilah* 1.16 (Isa 5:1–2); similarly *Targum Jonathan* on Isa. 5:2 (on the importance of which see already Juel 1977: 136–37). The same is apparently already presupposed in 4Q500, evidently a liturgical text; see Weren 1998: 16; C. A. Evans 2000; 2003: 107–9. Whether the fence in the parable represents Torah interpretation, as it does in Mishnah, tractate *Abot* 1.1, is perhaps less obvious.

57. Horsley 2003: 94–95 is right to note that by turning the rulers into the *tenants* of the vineyard, the parable adopts a position that would strike many of the original hearers as provocatively inverting their socioeconomic reality.

Second, and despite the tenants' reckless obstinacy, God's desire for the vineyard is fully vindicated. When the Son is killed and thrown out of the vineyard (i.e., Jerusalem; cf. also Heb. 13:12–13), God brings his purpose for it to fruition in removing the tenants who failed to honor the Father in the Son. The Son's self-giving death stirs the Father to action that is both redemptive (of the vineyard) and destructive (of those entrusted with its care). In all three Synoptic versions, the parable is thus in different ways at once *antisupersessionist and supersessionist* in intent.[58] The whole object of the action, whether of God, of the servants, or of God's Son, is the protection and prospering of the vineyard of Israel in the purpose for which it was made.

Christian interpreters even in recent years often read this parable as if it ends with the owner's destruction of the *vineyard* and the transfer of his favor to a new and different one. It does not. Indeed the parable is *deeply antisupersessionist in relation to Israel.* In all three Gospels the vineyard is saved—a point that echoes ancient Jewish interpretation but is nonetheless remarkable because in several Old Testament antecedents the opposite appears to be the case. Indeed, in this respect the conclusion of the parable differs strikingly from that of Isaiah 5:5–6. There is indeed a radical supersession and even replacement, apparently without remnant—but it applies to the *tenants* in charge, Israel's religious and political guardians, the "shepherds" who destroy and trample down the vineyard, to cite another prophet's striking image (Jer. 12:10). The vineyard itself is entrusted to "others" (Mark 12:9) who will care for it properly.

Matthew famously adds that it is given "to a people" (ἔθνει; 21:43). Contrary to a widespread misreading, however, even for Matthew those from whom the vineyard is taken are not "Israel" but its failed leaders (21:45), and the people to whom it is given is emphatically *not* another or a different *ethnos* but rather the restored nation, the twelve tribes whom the disciples will "judge" (i.e., govern) in the eschaton (19:28). This is the "people" who will

58. For a useful survey of the definitional problems surrounding supersession, see B. Marshall 2001: 232.

indeed render to God the vineyard's harvest in due season (οἵτινες ἀποδώσουσιν αὐτῷ τοὺς καρποὺς ἐν τοῖς καιροῖς αὐτῶν; 21:41).[59] In the face of persistent assertions to the contrary, it is worth pointing out that even Matthew 21:43 does *not* in fact evacuate the vineyard of Jews and give it to Gentiles.[60] Matthew consistently designates Gentiles with the plural *ethnē*, while the use of singular *ethnos* for Israel has parallels in other Gospels (Luke 7:5; 23:2; John 11:48–52). Instead, the vineyard is preserved and made fruitful by being taken from the charge of the chief priests and Pharisees (so throughout Matt. 21:23–45) and given to the "people" who will bear its fruit. As the reaction of the Pharisees in 21:45 shows, it is clear to the evangelist that for all its robust subversiveness this parable intends a definitive break *within* Israel rather than over against it: the enemy within is the current Pharisaic and priestly leadership.

Third and most poignantly for the identity of Jesus, *the mission of the Son of God is to give his life in the service of Israel's rescue from oppression*, for the restoration of its relationship with God. He stands in this respect in solidarity with other servants who have gone before. They suffer too, and some of them die (in Mark and Matthew). The last messenger differs in that he is uniquely the heir and "beloved Son," who ushers in both judgment on God's enemies and redemption for his vineyard. His is the ultimate sacrifice, the one that prompts God's rescue of the vineyard. He also markedly differs from the others in that the tenants recognize his true identity ("this is the heir") and murder him and cast him out precisely for this: the aim is nothing short of disinheriting God.

Not all these points need specific allegorical correlation, and commentators are right when they point out the increasing christological detail that seems to have entered successive Synoptic versions of the parable. Nevertheless, it is the identity of the Son that

59. Post–AD 70 Jewish interpretation draws specific attention to the destruction, not of the vineyard, but of the vineyard's *watchtower* (i.e., the temple); cf. Juel 1977: 136–37 on the targum.

60. Kvalbein 2000 critiques Luz as paradigmatic of Matthean interpreters in this respect (47n9 lists others); cf. Frankemölle 1998a: 329–63 and S. McKnight 1993.

stands out. His is the defining mission; as the heir he represents all that the Father means to the vineyard. Recalling Abraham's gift of that other "beloved son," Isaac, as understood in contemporary Jewish interpretation, so here by not withholding even his only Son the Father gives everything he has to plead for reconciliation with his own vineyard.[61] Through the Son's self-giving sacrificial suffering, death, and expulsion, God takes action to save the vineyard from its unlawful oppressors.

Israel's Christ in History and Christian Memory

Our journey in this chapter has led from methodological qualms about the notion of a Jewish identity of Jesus to an assessment of its rediscovery in twentieth-century historical-Jesus scholarship. From there, we progressed to a reconstruction of the practical profile of Jesus's Israel-centered mission and message, with an assessment of two sample implementations of this concern in his eschatology and self-understanding.

The vastness of our topic dictates that many problems and texts remain unaddressed.[62] And in all this one needs to bear in mind

61. The Jewish history of interpretation of Gen. 22 is notoriously complex. See already the pleonastic rendition of Gen. 22:2 Septuagint (τὸν υἱόν σου τὸν ἀγαπητόν, ὃν ἠγάπησας, τὸν Ἰσαάκ); Josephus, *Antiquities* 1.232; 4 Macc. 13:12; 16:20 (cf. 7:14); Pseudo-Philo, *Biblical Antiquities* 32.2–4. See also 4Q225 in a welter of recent discussion (Vermes 1996 with the critique of Fitzmyer 2002; also VanderKam 1997; García Martínez 2002; and Kugler 2003). Rom. 8:32 makes a similar point about Christ; cf. Dahl 1969.

62. One of these might be whether membership in "the house of Israel" was for Jesus a concept of what is nowadays called "ethnicity" or whether it (also) designated a matter of practical and spiritual allegiance, habitus, and religious separation, as it came to be at Qumran and in the early church. Other controversies include the place of Gentiles, the approach to purity and Sabbath halakah, the nature of Jesus's own envisaged kingship over Israel, and the extent to which his ministry presupposes a deliberate theology of the land. An important additional "text" to consider would be that of the temple demonstration itself, which has over the last twenty years become a kind of pièce de résistance for historical-Jesus scholarship—and for the ongoing debate between supersessionist and antisupersessionist readings. Its omission here, aside from the perfunctory excuse of the author's lack of time, space, and talent, may possibly be justified on the grounds that (unlike the two earlier texts) this episode appears intrinsically ambivalent even in the New Testament, being understood

the difficulty of speaking about "Judaism" at this time, before
the events of AD 70 and 135 led in due course to the ascendancy
of a normative rabbinic movement and a gradual but ineluctable
diminution of the spectrum of available options for faithful Jewish life and worship.

While these and other issues continue in inevitable suspense,
it seems clear that the identity of Jesus remains incomprehensible
apart from the evangelists' apostolic memory and testimony to the
migrant prophet and Messiah from Nazareth "on a mission from
God": he walked the biblical holy land in search of the lost sheep
of the house of Israel, wept over Jerusalem and protested against
its temple's corruption, and finally bound his own fate to that city
and to the redemption of the twelve tribes of Israel. To recover a
shared vision of the object of New Testament study will require us
to take seriously the text's implied reading on this point, sometimes
reading against the grain of much historic Christian protestation
to the contrary. What I have called theological "gene therapy" is
emphatically not a matter just of letting historical criticism trump
the voice of Scripture or the creeds. Nor is it a case of creating a
new doctrinal mutant, a kind of "designer Christianity" in our own
postmodern image, resplendent in the assurance of the superior
insights and innovations of our own age. On the contrary, it is
quite simply to return to the text and its implied reading: holding
the church accountable to its own most basic confession about a
two-testament Scripture that bears witness to the Messiah of God's
elect people. The New Testament documents, both early and late,
recall that the Word became *Jewish* flesh and lived, died, and rose

---

in strikingly different terms by John (replacement; 2:21) and Mark (sanctification;
11:15–17). This ambivalence is contested by some authors (Telford 1980) on the basis
of Mark's characteristic and unparalleled "sandwiching" of the temple episode with
the cursing of the fig tree (11:12–14, 20–25). For Mark the latter is indeed uniquely
symbolic (note 11:13b), but it is important not to overinterpret it. The primary point
is not the supersession of Judaism or even of the temple (by Jesus), but the power of
true faith, prayer, and forgiveness (note 11:22–25 and v. 26 [variant reading]). That
this stands in evident contrast to the scene in the temple is not in doubt; the point is
simply that Mark preserves, whether deliberately or out of loyalty to his tradition,
an account of the temple action that stresses the restoration and resanctification of
the court of the Gentiles, *pars pro toto*, as the house of prayer that the entire temple
was meant to be.

among us. Amid a good deal of attention deficit and hyperactive disorder among biblical scholars, this may indeed prove to be the abiding contribution of the recent wave of Jesus scholarship.

In the parable of the wicked tenants, Jesus understands his identity as unique Son of the Father to be inextricably linked to his mission for the deliverance and renewal of Israel. His ministry signally touched a handful of individual Gentiles, and his message included the promise that a (perhaps deliberately ambiguous) mass of otherwise unspecified exiles would arrive from the east and the west to join with Abraham, Isaac, and Jacob in the messianic banquet (Matt. 8:11 ‖ Luke 13:29). No theologically conscionable construal of Jesus's identity, however, can finally bypass this vital and personified commitment to the salvation of Israel, centered on the city over which Jesus lamented and where he died.[63] Jesus's Apostle to the Gentiles saw his own mission as directly instrumental to that same end (Rom. 9:5; 11:1–2, 26),[64] a point obscured for centuries under the forgetful Gentile superiority complex that Paul himself explicitly condemned (11:18–24).

In our own time, it has taken the twentieth century's near destruction of the vineyard to awaken the church to the New Testament's implication that, as Pope John Paul II put it in his historic visit to Rome's great synagogue in 1986, the covenant remains unbroken. Judaism, he said on that occasion, is profoundly "intrinsic" to Christianity, just as Jews are uniquely the favored and elder brothers of Christians. "This people continues in spite of everything to be the people of the covenant and, despite human infidelity, the Lord is faithful to his covenant."[65] That is

63. For the author to the Hebrews it is indeed significant that Jesus died *outside* the city, a fact that encourages the quest for the heavenly Jerusalem (Heb. 13:12–14). But while that undoubtedly relativizes the importance of the temporal reality, it is far from obvious that the author envisages the supersession to be strictly discontinuous in the sense sometimes envisaged.

64. This point is harder to establish for Paul's view of Jerusalem, despite the efforts of Munck 1959 and others. See, however, the substantial argument of Horbury 2003a: 189–226; cf. also Bockmuehl 2001a: 31. Paul also notes the relevance for Christology of Jesus's Davidic descent (Rom. 1:3; cf. 2 Tim. 2:8) and Jewish flesh (Rom. 9:5; cf. Gal. 4:4–5).

65. Cited in Pontifical Biblical Commission 2002: 196–97 §86. Cf. similarly Barth's famous comment on Rom. 11:17 in *Church Dogmatics* 2/2.286–87 (also quoted in

to say, Gentile amnesia on this point is in fact a denial of Jesus and of Christianity as much as it is a denial of Judaism. It rides roughshod over the "textual intention," the implied reading we discussed in chapters 1–3. The history of Christian thought and praxis, as we saw at the beginning of this chapter, suggests a quasigenetic predisposition against a Jewish Jesus—and for that reason variously against an incarnate Jesus, born of a Palestinian Jewish mother named Miriam, one who sought the lost sheep of the house of Israel, one who held that God's word in Scripture cannot be broken, one who physically suffered and died under Pontius Pilate, one who was raised on the third day.

That disposition, then, may indeed necessitate a measure of theological gene therapy if the church is to reappropriate the meaning and significance of the Word made—and raised—Jewish flesh.[66] The Fourth Evangelist grasps the meaning of that Word most provocatively when he finds in the historic soil of Palestine the Bethel of Jesus—and Jacob's ladder made tangible in the thirsting, weeping, bleeding Son of Man upon whom the angels descend and ascend as they gaze on the "place of God" on earth as it is in heaven (John 1:51; cf. Gen. 28:12).

By no means all the church fathers would have concurred. Cyril of Alexandria arguably fueled anti-Judaism in his city through his view of a Jesus who is less than Jewish by virtue of being less than fully human.[67] Writing in the same city a century earlier, Origen saw fit to patronize no less a figure than the apostle Peter because he continued at least for a while to live as a Jew, having "not yet learned from Jesus to ascend from the law that is regulated according to the letter, to that which is interpreted according to the Spirit" (ὡς μηδέπω ἀπὸ τοῦ Ἰησοῦ μαθὼν ἀναβαίνειν ἀπὸ τοῦ κατὰ

Mussner 1984: 132) and more fully the Christology of Marquardt 1990. Specifically on the idea of the unbroken covenant, see also Frankemölle 1998a and 1998b.

66. This point is also stressed in an important essay by Jenson 2003b: 12. It stands in apparent tension with a view like that of Coakley 2002: 162–65, who appeals to Gregory of Nyssa (against Augustine and Origen) in support of an unstable but departicularized (viz., sexless) eschatological body, including by implication that of Jesus.

67. This point is extensively demonstrated in Wilken 1971: 62–68, 114–18, 218–21, 226–28. I owe this reference to Mark W. Elliott.

τὸ γράμμα νόμου ἐπὶ τὸν κατὰ τὸ πνεῦμα). Adopting John 16:12 as his motto, Origen went on to conclude that because as Jews the apostles had been brought up "according to the letter" of the law of Moses, Jesus was unable to tell them the *true* law: knowing the difficulty of rooting out opinions that people hold almost from birth, he decided instead to postpone for the postresurrection period the (supposedly Pauline) insight that these opinions were in fact mere "loss and dung." As for Peter, he was still mired in his superstitious Jewish observance (ἔτι δεισιδαιμονοῦντα) until the vision of Acts 10 at last enlightened him (*Against Celsus* 2.1–2).[68] This sort of disquisition, however tempered in Origen's case by personal acquaintance with Jews and assiduous study of Hebrew and Jewish sources, stands in continuity with the depressingly familiar litany of patristic anti-Judaism, amply documented in the scholarly literature and to some extent an integral part of Gentile Christian self-definition and apologetics (internally as well as externally vis-à-vis both Judaism and paganism).[69] The apostolic church had embodied the Abrahamic mission and the command of Jesus by pioneering at great personal cost a Jewish welcome of Noahide Gentiles as Gentiles. Subsequent Gentile Christianity generally failed to return the compliment. It did so for reasons that were sometimes understandable and may have a good deal to do with the painful aftermath of the First Jewish War and especially the Second Jewish War against Rome (so Tomson 2003)—an aftermath that in turn served to highlight and magnify signs of conflict between church and synagogue in the New Testament itself.

But things are perhaps not so different today. Much as it likes to believe that it has absolved itself of this unpleasant history by demonstrative breast-beating over tacit complicity in the past, a good deal especially of Protestant scholarship in the West arguably aggravates such tendencies in its attitudes to the Bible in general and the Old Testament in particular, attitudes whose self-assured neglect of Scripture's implied readers, implied readings, and ef-

68. For Origen's view of Judaism cf. De Lange 1976: 39–47.
69. Useful digests of twentieth-century scholarship on this subject appear in Carleton Paget 1997 and Stroumsa 1996.

fective history the early church would have strongly repudiated. Notable recent writers on Christian biblical theology rightly draw attention to the importance of the Old Testament's *intrinsic* canonical voice. What, in other words, are the fundamental themes of the Old Testament per se and *as a whole*, as Christian Scripture and yet also as intrinsically Israelite, compatible with yet distinguishable from its Christianly significant reception in the New Testament? Even for a purely Christian biblical theology, it matters to ask if the Old Testament has an abiding voice of its own within the Christian Bible.[70]

Two examples bear this out. First, the familiar uncomprehending mockery of Leviticus in the prominent hermeneutical feuds of certain mainline Protestant churches is but one instance of a thinly veiled form of popular Marcionism, which seeks to distance the self-evidently hidebound "oldness" of the Old Testament from the radical and therefore superior newness of the New.[71]

A second case in point may be the studied refusal, at a time of politically correct Christian admiration for Judaism (from a distance), to come to theologically articulate terms with the existence of a Jewish Jesus's small but growing number of Jewish followers today. That such reflection is a biblical and theological desideratum is both patently obvious from the New Testament and at the same time crucial for any further substantive progress in contemporary Christian-Jewish understanding. Given the history of relations between Christianity and Judaism, even to recognize the existence of Jewish believers in Jesus is a task no less complex

70. For a history of this "struggle to read the Old Testament as Christian Scripture," see most recently Childs 2004; other leading recent contributors to this lively debate include Hübner 1988; Stuhlmacher 1997; Hengel 2002; and Seitz 1998 and 2001. Curiously, Goldingay 2003: 24–28 rejects the possibility of New Testament theology altogether, but nevertheless defends the exercise of an Old Testament theology (still designated by this Christian nomenclature!) to which the New Testament adds nothing but a series of Christian "ecclesial footnotes."

71. There may be wisdom in the early Christian nomenclature of reading not Old and New Testaments but "the Law and the Prophets together with the Gospels and apostolic Letters" (Tertullian, *Prescription against Heretics* 36.5; in the East cf. similarly *Apostolic Constitutions* 8.5, although elsewhere "Law and Prophets" were not always read in the liturgy). On the volatile ancient concept of Christian "newness," see esp. Kinzig 1994a and 1994b.

and daunting than that of a mutual political recognition between today's warring nations and factions in the holy land.

Contrary to the arbiters of political correctness, however, what is difficult or "controversial" need not therefore be wrong or even detrimental to friendship and open dialogue. Indeed, as one leading Jewish observer notes about the reciprocal problem of conversions, "These inevitable facts will, of course, make for tensions, but the authenticity of any new Jewish-Christian relationship is energized by this tension as much as it is energized by the rediscovery of much commonality" (Novak 1998: 60, on Soulen 1996).[72] Jewish believers in Jesus who remain faithful to their Jewish identity are in a unique position to attest, cement, and protect both what is shared and what is distinctive in this unique relationship.[73] Indeed, a theologically articulate recognition of their existence would furnish powerful proof of the Great Commission's reminder that Jesus's messiahship genuinely confirms, and does not subvert, Israel's place as the elect "people of the covenant" to whom "the Lord is faithful."[74]

Christians and Jews believe in the same God of Israel and read common Holy Scriptures. They have done so since antiquity, often mutually influencing each other's reading.[75] Although in painfully different ways, Christians and Jews both relate to Jesus as "one of ours." And a key factor that uniquely relates them to each other as human communities is that some believing Jews are believers in Jesus and some believing Christians are believing Jews. It is of ecclesiological, covenantal, and arguably eschatological significance that neither faith can have this relationship with any other religious group.

72. Recent Jewish attempts to engage Jewish Christianity in a courageously constructive manner include Wyschogrod 1995 and Cohn-Sherbok 2000.

73. See Rudolph 2005 for a theologically articulate reflection on this question from the perspective of messianic Judaism.

74. Thus the recent Pontifical Biblical Commission 2002: 197 §86; cf. similarly Michael Wyschogrod, cited in Soulen 1996: 11. Note also von der Osten-Sacken 1982: 144–67 (ET 1986: 101–17) on the theological importance of Jewish Christianity; see further Rudolph 2005.

75. Note the Jewish and Christian readings of the Binding of Isaac discussed in Kessler 2004.

Scripture itself, as shared Word of Life for Jews and Gentiles, precludes the very possibility of asking the outsider's *Judenfrage* ("Jewish question"). Instead, it compels those who convert to faith in the Messiah to stop wondering "what to make of the Jews," but rather to remember and recognize *themselves* as having their identity in relation to the chosen people.[76]

I wish to close, however, on another note that has been largely implicit thus far. The abiding significance of this remembered Israelite identity of Jesus is vitally underscored by his *resurrection*. Far from being the brainchild of a Pauline rush into a Hellenistic savior cult, this is itself a deeply and irreversibly Jewish affirmation, in both the pre- and post-Easter contexts of the New Testament. Indeed, no Roman soldier said to be guarding the tomb that first Easter Sunday morning could have described the events in terms of "resurrection": that language was simply unavailable.[77] Only a Jew, indeed only a religious, possibly Pharisaic Jew, could predict—or for that matter remember—someone being "resurrected."

It is clearly true that the reality of a resurrection after three days inevitably strained and transformed all the available *Jewish* linguistic registers, too, as Rowan Williams rightly suggests (1996: 91; cf. Bockmuehl 2001b: 113). But it remains significant that scholars who otherwise accept the Jewish identity of Jesus are often content to sideline or ignore his resurrection as irrelevant.[78] Even those who do take it seriously do not always make enough of one crucial fact: the one who is raised is none other than the crucified Messiah of Israel and "King of the Jews." For the early Christians it was the resurrection that confirmed this identity; indeed it is theologically vital for the New Testament witnesses that Jesus's identity did not change on Easter Sunday (Acts 2:36; 17:3; 26:3;

76. Cf. the shrewd observations of Hütter 2004: 210–11, who also (217, 217nn23–24) rightly draws analogies to the work of John H. Yoder and especially to George Lindbeck's call for a more Israel-focused ecclesiology (citing Lindbeck 2003; cf. also B. Marshall 2001).

77. Cf. further Bockmuehl 2001b: 111–14; also Wright 2003 (on which see Bockmuehl 2004a).

78. Meier 1991–2001, ironically, says less about it than do Borg (in Borg and Wright 1999: 129–42) and other members of the Jesus Seminar, who believe its historicity to be both nonexistent and irrelevant.

cf. Luke 24:26; Rom. 1:3–4; Phil. 2:9–11; John 20:28–31).[79] In the
resurrection God makes Jesus visibly "both Lord and Messiah"
of Israel (Acts 2:36), the Son of David who is "Son of God with
power" (Rom. 1:3–4)—and, in one of the most radically Jewish
and radically Nicene of all early christological affirmations, God
bestowed on him "the name that is above every name"—the very
name of YHWH (Phil. 2:9; cf. Eph. 1:20–21; Heb. 1:3b–4; John
17:11–12; Rev. 1:4, 8).[80] For the early Christians, in other words,
it is "seeing the Word" in the resurrection that crucially confirms
Jesus the Jew as Messiah and Lord God of Israel.[81] In the early
church's memory of the apostolic witness—including that of the
Apostle to the Gentiles—the New Testament's implied readers had
a firm grasp of this truth: "Remember Jesus Christ, raised from
the dead, descendant of David" (2 Tim. 2:8).

79. Wright 2003: 553–83 does begin to grapple with the specific significance of
the resurrection for the messiahship and lordship of Jesus.
80. For fuller development of this interpretation, see my commentary (Bockmuehl
1997: 141–48); cf. further Bauckham 1998c (with 1998a: 51–53); McDonough 1999:
201–17 with reference to Rev. 1:4 (cf. esp. 200–201 on *Targum Pseudo-Jonathan* on
Deut. 32:39); and more broadly the seminal new study by Gieschen 2003. Note further
Hurtado 2003: 112–14, as well as the evidence for a "high" pre-Christian messianism
developed in Horbury 1998b: 86–108.
81. Cf. also the important argument of B. Marshall 2001: 245–47 illustrating the
extent to which New Testament (esp. Johannine) and patristic texts identify the God
of Israel with the Logos and the Son, i.e., the Second Person of the Trinity.

EPILOGUE

Seeing the Word of Life

> We proclaim to you the one who was from the beginning. This is he whom we heard, and we saw him with our eyes: we saw and we felt with our hands. He is the Word of Life. (1 John 1:1 Peshitta)[1]

After all is said and done, what then might encourage a fresh focus on subject-appropriate New Testament study in this new century? This book has managed to sketch only a few signposts on the way to such renewed ways of seeing, beginning with Simon Marmion's bold fifteenth-century observation of the evangelist painting the Word of Life. But perhaps preliminary results are quite in order. This volume stands only at the beginning of a new series on theological interpretation, not at the end. It seems appropriate, then, to offer a summary epilogue rather than a full conclusion.

Our journey began by suggesting a diagnosis of a discipline that is now widely felt to lack agreed criteria not just for appropriate

---

1. The Syriac syntax sustains a powerfully Johannine ambiguity in using the masculine pronoun throughout, and especially in the last phrase: *haw di-itawohi melta de-hayye*. Although closer to the original, the New American Bible likewise supplies a predicate complement for the verbless Greek περί: "What was from the beginning . . . we speak of the Word of Life."

methods and results, but in many cases about even the very subject to be studied. What future can there be for scholarly New Testament studies amid the ruins of so many "assured results" of the past? Two initiatives in particular, I suggested, may hold promise for a reenergized, common conversation about the New Testament: first, to investigate the implied readership and the implied readings that arise from its engagement with the text; and, second, to harness the New Testament's plural and diverse effects as a resource for renewed reflection on its interpretation. I have argued, in other words, that the question of the implied readers is linked, both *exegetically* and *historically*, to that of implied readings. More specifically, both of these questions are illuminated by the study of how the apostolic voices were in fact remembered, heard, and heeded in the early postapostolic period—and vice versa.

We explored this in several hermeneutical and historical chapters. If there is an implied reader, does the New Testament help us discover the interpretative stance of that implied exegete vis-à-vis a text presented as divine revelation? Chapter 2 argued that the scriptural text itself favors a certain kind of exegetical posture that fosters attentive textual observation leading to a close cohesion of exegesis and theology in a personally and corporately engaged interpretation.

Chapter 3 moved from implied readers to "textual intention" and implied readings. The undeniable diversity of biblical voices was seen to tolerate, indeed to invite, a reading that is in some sense already canonical—but in a way that enriches, rather than closes down, genuinely open understanding. Far from a moribund attempt at repressing polyphony, such interpretation follows the "effective" contours of both the discrete strings and the harmonic chords in the canon's implied readings.

For the implied reader, hearing and reception involves an appropriation of tensions and convergence within the polyphonous Scripture—a task that in turn calls for more attentive observation, both of such readers and of their texts, than New Testament scholarship may have been used to. This problem was examined in relation to two case studies, one of a general trend and the other of an individual scholar. In reflecting on the nineteenth-century

Tübingen School's influence on New Testament interpretation, chapter 4 asked whether and how we should negotiate between the tensions straining the Petrine and Pauline missions on the one hand and, on the other, the tradition's unequivocal reception of their partnership in the gospel. Might the latter provide a guide for reading the former, as well as vice versa, but without submerging either one beneath the other? In chapter 5 our second, rather different case study of the relationship between implied readings and implied readers concerned the work of a now-little-known British twentieth-century New Testament scholar, Sir Edwyn Hoskyns. His insistence on the text as linking Christian origins with Christian faith provides an alternative approach to my point about the possible correspondences between the beliefs and events that gave rise to the text and the implied effects it generates.

Finally, we looked in two further chapters at the place of *apostolic memory* as offering one means of access to this early effective history. In chapter 6, I suggested that memory of the apostolic generation tended to order the diversity of actual and implied readers and readings toward the identity of Jesus Christ, whom the New Testament authors remember and of whom they all speak. After a methodological account of this concern in the early church, the final chapter showed how such apostolic memory of Jesus serves both to confirm and to correct subsequent interpretations, especially of the Jewish identity of the historical Jesus of Nazareth, who for the early Christians was the same person as the risen and exalted Christ of Israel.

Throughout these chapters, my aim has been to encourage this way of watching the biblical authors, as Simon Marmion does in the miniature with which we began. To do this will require two things at once: to recover and sharpen our focus on that incarnate Jewish God-child at the heart of all the New Testament portraits, and to broaden our field of vision for the diversity and distinctiveness in which they are presented. Marmion exquisitely illustrates how, in the often humdrum ordinariness of their words and characters, they invite us to see and touch the Word of Life.

In doing this, I have argued, students of Christian faith, of other faiths, or of no faith can find their own understanding of the New

Testament honed and interrogated by a plural but common conversation about the object of these writings. While emphatically
plural, the commonality of such discourse is bound to be more
fruitful where we do *not* bracket or hold back from discussing what
the texts themselves intend. Non-Christian outsiders' questions of
criticism and even of subversion may well energize this discussion,
perhaps all the more so where these outside participants are themselves insiders of other world faiths. But so will the voice of those
who represent the continuity of implied readers, for whom this
Scripture has spoken, and continues to speak, that Word of Life.

In reflecting on the possibility of finding a meeting place between
the diversity both of biblical authors and of their interpreters, New
Testament study in the twenty-first century will require a quantum
leap beyond the tired clichés of the "unity and diversity" problem
as it was handled in the past. Advocates of easy harmonies of tension and contradiction, like those of relentlessly conflict-driven
polarizations, routinely underrate their epistemologically sinister
potential. Similarly, we are unlikely to advance our conversation
with ideologically prescriptive developmentalism or, on the other
hand, historically oblivious models of doctrinal and ecclesial assertion. Unity is impossible where truth is suppressed—but so is
truth in the absence of difference.

We will do well to rediscover that the tensions and differences,
both between the authors of Scripture and between its implied
readers, may be better understood not as reductive or subversive
assertions of power, but as quests for hermeneutical faithfulness
to the object of the text, the *intentio operis*. The biblical writers
unapologetically presume a readership converted, or converting,
to the conviction that their subject makes all the difference in the
world—and that their claims for it are true. Just as unapologetically, however, some of these same writers remain markedly hospitable to a recognition and engagement with outsiders concerned
to know the truth. While it is perhaps most characteristic of Luke,
this epistemic hospitality ranges in fact from the magi of the New
Testament's first page all the way to its last page: there the nations
are healed and bring their glory into the city of God—and they
see the life-giving Word, face to face.

WORKS CITED

Abramowski, Luise. 1990. "The 'Memoirs of the Apostles' in Justin." Pages 323–35 in *The Gospel and the Gospels*. Edited by P. Stuhlmacher. Grand Rapids: Eerdmans.

Achtemeier, Paul J. 1990. "*Omne verbum sonat*: The New Testament and the Oral Environment of Late Western Antiquity." *Journal of Biblical Literature* 109:3–27.

Aichele, George, ed. 1995. *The Postmodern Bible*. New Haven: Yale University Press.

———. 2001. *The Control of Biblical Meaning: Canon as Semiotic Mechanism*. Harrisburg, PA: Trinity.

Alexander, Loveday. 1990. "The Living Voice: Scepticism towards the Written Word in Early Christian and in Graeco-Roman Texts." Pages 221–47 in *The Bible in Three Dimensions: Essays in Celebration of Forty Years of Biblical Studies in the University of Sheffield*. Edited by D. J. A. Clines et al. Journal for the Study of the Old Testament: Supplement Series 87. Sheffield: JSOT Press.

Alexander, T. Desmond, and Brian S. Rosner. 2000. *New Dictionary of Biblical Theology*. Downers Grove, IL: InterVarsity.

Allison, Dale C., Jr. 1998. *Jesus of Nazareth: Millenarian Prophet*. Minneapolis: Fortress.

———. 2000. "The Secularizing of the Historical Jesus." *Perspectives in Religious Studies* 27:135–52.

Amitzur, Hagi. 1996. "Justinian's Solomon's Temple in Jerusalem." Pages 160–75 in *The Centrality of Jerusalem*. Edited by M. Poorthuis and C. Safrai. Kampen: Kok Pharos.

Anonymous. 1940. *Die Botschaft Gottes*. Institut zur Erforschung des jüdischen Einflusses auf das Deutsche Kirchliche Leben. Weimar: Verlag deutsche Christen.

233

Aragione, Gabriella. 2004. "Justin, 'philosophe' chrétien, et les '*Mémoires des apôtres* qui sont appelés Évangiles.'" *Apocrypha* 15:41–56.

Arnal, William. 2005. "The Cipher 'Judaism' in Contemporary Historical Jesus Scholarship." Pages 24–54 in *Apocalypticism, Anti-Semitism, and the Historical Jesus: Subtexts in Criticism.* Edited by J. S. Kloppenborg and J. W. Marshall. Journal for the Study of the Historical Jesus Supplement 1. London: T&T Clark.

Assmann, Jan. 1982. *Das kulturelle Gedächtnis: Schrift, Erinnerung und politische Identität in frühen Hochkulturen.* Munich: Beck.

————. 2000. *Religion und kulturelles Gedächtnis: Zehn Studien.* Munich: Beck.

Auzépy, Marie-France. 1997. *La vie d'Etienne le Jeune.* Birmingham Byzantine and Ottoman Monographs 3. Aldershot: Variorum.

Ayres, Lewis, and Stephen E. Fowl. 1999. "(Mis)Reading the Face of God: *The Interpretation of the Bible in the Church.*" *Theological Studies* 60:513–28.

Bacci, Michele. 2000. "With the Paintbrush of the Evangelist Luke." Pages 79–90 in *Mother of God: Representations of the Virgin in Byzantine Art.* Edited by M. Vassilaki. Milan: Skira.

Bachmann, Michael. 1999. *Antijudaismus im Galaterbrief? Exegetische Studien zu einem polemischen Schreiben und zur Theologie des Apostels Paulus.* Novum Testamentum et Orbis Antiquus 40. Freiburg: Universitätsverlag; Göttingen: Vandenhoeck & Ruprecht.

Bailey, Kenneth E. 1995a. "Informal Controlled Oral Tradition and the Synoptic Gospels." *Themelios* 20:4–11.

————. 1995b. "Middle Eastern Oral Tradition and the Synoptic Gospels." *Expository Times* 106:363–67.

Baird, William. 1992–2003. *History of New Testament Research.* 2 vols. Minneapolis: Fortress.

Baldwin, Matthew C. 2005. *Whose Acts of Peter? Text and Historical Context of the Actus Vercellenses.* Wissenschaftliche Untersuchungen zum Neuen Testament 2/196. Tübingen: Mohr.

Balla, Peter. 1998. *Challenges to New Testament Theology: An Attempt to Justify the Enterprise.* Peabody, MA: Hendrickson.

Bammel, Ernst. 1970. "Das Ende von Q." Pages 39–50 in *Verborum veritas: Festschrift für Gustav Stählin.* Edited by O. Böcher and K. Haacker. Wuppertal: Brockhaus.

Barash, J. A. 1997. "The Sources of Memory." *Journal of the History of Ideas* 58:707–18.

Barnard, Leslie W. 1967. *Justin Martyr: His Life and Thought.* Cambridge: Cambridge University Press.

Baroin, Catherine. 1998. "Erinnerung, Gedächtnis." Translated by T. Heinze. Pages 70–71 in vol. 4 of *Der neue Pauly.* Edited by H. Cancik and H. Schneider. Leiden: Brill.

Barr, James. 1961. *The Semantics of Biblical Language.* Oxford: Oxford University Press.

———. 1983. *Holy Scripture: Canon, Authority, Criticism.* Oxford: Clarendon.

———. 1999. *The Concept of Biblical Theology: An Old Testament Perspective.* London: SCM.

Barrett, C. K. 1963. "Cephas and Corinth." Pages 1–12 in *Abraham unser Vater: Juden und Christen im Gespräch über die Bibel: Festschrift für Otto Michel zum 60. Geburtstag.* Edited by O. Betz, M. Hengel, and P. Schmidt. Arbeiten zur Geschichte des Spätjudentums und Urchristentums 5. Leiden: Brill.

———. 1975. "Albert Schweitzer and the New Testament." *Expository Times* 87:4–10. Reprinted on pages 63–75 in Barrett's *Jesus and the Word: And Other Essays.* Edinburgh: T&T Clark, 1995.

———. 1995. "Hoskyns and Davey." Pages 55–62 in Barrett's *Jesus and the Word: And Other Essays.* Edinburgh: T&T Clark.

———. 1997. "Christocentricity at Antioch." Pages 323–39 in *Jesus Christus als die Mitte der Schrift: Studien zur Hermeneutik des Evangeliums.* Edited by C. Landmesser et al. Beihefte zur Zeitschrift für die neutestamentliche Wissenschaft 86. Berlin: de Gruyter.

Barth, Karl. 1933. *The Epistle to the Romans.* Translated by E. C. Hoskyns. London: Oxford University Press.

Barthes, Roland, ed. 1974. *Structural Analysis and Biblical Exegesis: Interpretational Essays.* Pittsburgh Theological Monograph Series 3. Pittsburgh: Pickwick.

Bartholomew, Craig G., et al., eds. 2002. *A Royal Priesthood? The Use of the Bible Ethically and Politically: A Dialogue with Oliver O'Donovan.* Scripture and Hermeneutics Series 3. Carlisle: Paternoster; Grand Rapids: Zondervan.

———, eds. 2004. *Out of Egypt: Biblical Theology and Biblical Interpretation.* Scripture and Hermeneutics Series 5. Bletchley, Milton Keynes, UK: Paternoster; Grand Rapids: Zondervan.

Barton, John. 2003. "Unity and Diversity in the Biblical Canon." Pages 11–26 in *Die Einheit der Schrift und die Vielfalt des Kanons/The Unity of Scripture and the Diversity of the Canon.* Edited by J. Barton and M. Wolter. Berlin: de Gruyter.

Barton, Stephen C. 1999. "New Testament Interpretation as Performance." *Scottish Journal of Theology* 52:179–208.

Bartov, Omer. 1993. "Intellectuals on Auschwitz: Memory, History, and Truth." *History and Memory* 5:87–117.

Basset, Jean-Claude. 1988. "L'anamnèse: Aux sources de la tradition chrétienne." Pages 91–104 in vol. 2 of *La mémoire des religions.* Edited by P. Borgeaud. Religions en Perspective. Geneva: Labor & Fides.

Bassler, Jouette M., David M. Hay, and E. Elizabeth Johnson, eds. 1991–97. *Pauline Theology.* 4 vols. Minneapolis: Fortress.

Bate, Jonathan. 1998. *The Genius of Shakespeare.* New York: Oxford University Press.

Bauckham, Richard. 1983. *Jude, 2 Peter*. Word Biblical Commentary 50. Waco: Word.

———. 1990. *Jude and the Relatives of Jesus in the Early Church*. Edinburgh: T&T Clark.

———. 1998a. *God Crucified: Monotheism and Christology in the New Testament*. Didsbury Lectures 1996. Carlisle: Paternoster.

———. 1998b. "John for Readers of Mark." Pages 147–71 in *The Gospels for All Christians*. Edited by R. Bauckham. Grand Rapids: Eerdmans.

———.1998c. "The Worship of Jesus in Philippians 2:9–11." Pages 128–39 in *Where Christianity Began: Essays on Philippians 2*. Edited by R. P. Martin and B. J. Dodd. Louisville: Westminster John Knox.

———. 2003. "The Eyewitnesses and the Gospel Tradition." *Journal for the Study of the Historical Jesus* 1:28–60.

———. 2006. *Jesus and the Eyewitnesses: The Gospels as Eyewitness Testimony*. Grand Rapids: Eerdmans.

Baudrillard, Jean. 1987. *Forget Foucault*. Translated by S. Lotringer. New York: Semiotext(e).

Bauer, Walter. 1972. *Orthodoxy and Heresy in Earliest Christianity*. Translated by the Philadelphia Seminar on Christian Origins. Edited by R. A. Kraft and G. Krodel. Philadelphia: Fortress.

Bauerschmidt, Frederick Christian. 1999. "The Word Made Speculative? John Milbank's Christological Poetics." *Modern Theology* 15:417–32.

Baum, Armin Daniel. 1998. "Papias, der Vorzug der Viva Vox und die Evangelienschriften." *New Testament Studies* 44:144–51.

Baumgarten, Joseph M. 1989. "4Q500 and the Ancient Conception of the Lord's Vineyard." *Journal of Jewish Studies* 40:1–6.

Baur, Ferdinand Christian. 1831. "Die Christuspartei in der korinthischen Gemeinde, der Gegensatz des petrinischen und paulinischen Christenthums in der alten Kirche, der Apostel Paulus in Rom." *Tübinger Zeitschrift für Theologie* 4:61–206.

———. 1845. *Paulus, der Apostel Jesu Christi: Sein Leben und Wirken, seine Briefe und seine Lehre*. Stuttgart: Becher & Müller.

———. 1878. *The Church History of the First Three Centuries*. 2 vols. 3rd edition. Translated by A. Menzies. London: Williams & Norgate.

———. 2003. *Paul the Apostle of Jesus Christ: His Life and Works, His Epistles and Teachings*. Translated by E. Zeller and A. Menzies. Peabody, MA: Hendrickson.

Begg, Christopher. 2005. *Flavius Josephus: Judean Antiquities Books 5–7*. Flavius Josephus: Translation and Commentary 4. Leiden: Brill.

Begg, Christopher, and Paul Spilsbury. 2005. *Flavius Josephus: Judean Antiquities Books 8–10*. Flavius Josephus: Translation and Commentary 5. Leiden: Brill.

Benoît, André. 1960. "Écriture et tradition chez Saint Irénée." *Revue d'histoire et de philosophie religieuses* 40:32–43.

Berger, Klaus. 1988. *Hermeneutik des Neuen Testaments*. Gütersloh: Mohn.

———. 1995a. "Loyalität." *Zeitschrift für Theologie und Kirche Beiheft* 9:120–32.

———. 1995b. *Theologiegeschichte des Urchristentums: Theologie des Neuen Testaments*. 2nd edition. Tübingen: Francke.

Berlin, Isaiah. 1999. *Concepts and Categories: Philosophical Essays*. Edited by H. Hardy. London: Pimlico.

Berlinerblau, Jacques. 2005. *The Secular Bible: Why Nonbelievers Must Take Religion Seriously*. Cambridge: Cambridge University Press.

Bethge, Eberhard. 1983. *Dietrich Bonhoeffer: Theologe, Christ, Zeitgenosse*. 5th edition. Munich: Kaiser.

Betz, Hans Dieter. 2003. "Mein Weg in die neutestamentliche Wissenschaft." Pages 41–48 in *Neutestamentliche Wissenschaft: Autobiographische Essays aus der evangelischen Theologie*. Edited by E.-M. Becker. Tübingen: Francke.

Bisconti, Fabrizio. 2001. "L'origine dell'iconografia di Pietro e Paolo." Pages 393–401 in *Pietro e Paolo: Il loro rapporto con Roma nelle testimonianze antiche*. Edited by P. Grech. Studia Ephemeridis Augustinianum 74. Rome: Institutum Patristicum Augustinianum.

Bleich, David. 1988. *The Double Perspective: Language, Literacy, and Social Relations*. New York: Oxford University Press.

Bockmuehl, Markus. 1990. *Revelation and Mystery in Ancient Judaism and Pauline Christianity*. Wissenschaftliche Untersuchungen zum Neuen Testament 2/36. Tübingen: Mohr.

———. 1995. "A Commentator's Approach to the 'Effective History' of Philippians." *Journal for the Study of the New Testament* 60:57–88.

———. 1997. *A Commentary on the Epistle to the Philippians*. Black's New Testament Commentaries. London: Black.

———. 1998a. "Humpty Dumpty and New Testament Theology." *Theology* 101:330–38.

———. 1998b. "'To Be or Not to Be': The Possible Futures of New Testament Scholarship." *Scottish Journal of Theology* 51:271–306.

———. 2000a. "Halakhah and Ethics in the Jesus Tradition." Pages 3–15 in Bockmuehl's *Jewish Law in Gentile Churches: Halakhah and the Beginning of Christian Public Ethics*. Edinburgh: T&T Clark.

———. 2000b. *Jewish Law in Gentile Churches: Halakhah and the Beginning of Christian Public Ethics*. Edinburgh: T&T Clark.

———. 2000c. "Peter, Paul, and Fred: The Icon of the Apostles in the Discipline that F. C. Baur Built." *Princeton Theological Review* 7.4:4–9.

———. 2001a. "1 Thessalonians 2:14–16 and the Church in Jerusalem." *Tyndale Bulletin* 52:1–31.

———. 2001b. "Resurrection." Pages 102–18 in *The Cambridge Companion to Jesus*. Edited by M. Bockmuehl. Cambridge: Cambridge University Press.

———. 2002. Review of Bruce J. Malina, *The New Testament World: Insights from Cultural Anthropology*. *Bryn Mawr Classical Review*, no. 2002.04.19:

http://ccat.sas.upenn.edu/bmcr/2002/2002-04-19.html (accessed April 17, 2006).

———. 2003a. "The Jewish People and Their Sacred Scriptures in the Christian Bible: Response." *Scripture Bulletin* 33:15–28.

———. 2003b. "Reason, Wisdom and the Implied Disciple of Scripture." Pages 53–68 in *Reading Texts, Seeking Wisdom: Scripture and Theology.* Edited by D. F. Ford and G. N. Stanton. London: SCM.

———. 2003c. "Syrian Memories of Simon Peter: Ignatius, Justin and Serapion." Pages 126–46 in *The Image of the Judaeo-Christians in Ancient Jewish and Christian Literature: Papers Delivered at the Colloquium of the Institutum Iudaicum, Brussels, 18–19 November, 2001.* Edited by P. J. Tomson and D. Lambers-Petry. Tübingen: Mohr.

———. 2004a. "Compleat History of the Resurrection: A Dialogue with N. T. Wright." *Journal for the Study of the New Testament* 26:489–504.

———. 2004b. "What's under the Microscope? Revisiting E. C. Hoskyns on the Object of New Testament Study." *Theology* 107:3–13.

———. 2005a. "The Making of Gospel Commentaries." Pages 274–95 in *The Written Gospel.* Edited by M. Bockmuehl and D. A. Hagner. Cambridge: Cambridge University Press.

———. 2005b. Review of James D. G. Dunn, *Jesus Remembered. Journal of Theological Studies,* n.s., 56:140–49.

———. 2005c. "Why Not Let Acts Be Acts? In Conversation with C. Kavin Rowe." *Journal for the Study of the New Testament* 28:163–66.

———. forthcoming. "The Dead Sea Scrolls and Ancient Commentary." In *Text, Thought, and Practice in Qumran and Early Christianity: Proceedings of the Ninth International Symposium of the Orion Center for the Study of the Dead Sea Scrolls and Associated Literature.* Edited by D. R. Schwartz and R. Clements. Studies on the Texts of the Desert of Judah. Leiden: Brill.

Boghossian, Paul. 1996. "The Sokal Hoax." *Times Literary Supplement,* Dec. 13:14.

Boismard, M. E., Justin Taylor, and A. Lamouille. 1990–. *Les actes des deux apôtres.* 6 vols. to date. Études bibliques 12–14, 23, 26, 41. Paris: Gabalda.

Boobbyer, Philip. 2002. "Moral Judgements and Moral Realism in History." *Totalitarian Movements and Political Religions* 3:83–112.

Borg, Marcus J. 1987. *Jesus: A New Vision: Spirit, Culture, and the Life of Discipleship.* New York: Harper & Row.

Borg, Marcus J., and N. T. Wright. 1999. *The Meaning of Jesus: Two Visions.* London: SPCK.

Borges, Jorge Luis. 1944. *Ficciones (1935–1944).* Buenos Aires: Sur.

Boring, M. Eugene. 1996. "Gospel and Church in 2 Peter." *Mid-Stream* 35:399–414.

Böttrich, Christfried. 2001. *Petrus: Fischer, Fels und Funktionär.* Biblische Gestalten 2. Leipzig: Evangelische Verlagsanstalt.

―――. 2002. "Petrus und Paulus in Antiochien (Gal 2,11–21)." *Berliner theologische Zeitschrift* 19:224–39.

―――. 2004. "Petrus-Bischofsamt-Kirche." *Zeitschrift für Neues Testament* 7.13:44–51.

Boyarin, Daniel. 2004. *Border Lines: The Partition of Judaeo-Christianity*. Divinations. Philadelphia: University of Pennsylvania Press.

Bradshaw, Paul F., Maxwell E. Johnson, and L. Edward Phillips. 2002. *The Apostolic Tradition: A Commentary*. Hermeneia. Minneapolis: Fortress.

Brändén, Irina. 2002. *Mariakult och Mariabilder i Konstantinopel*. Forskarkurs i bysantinologi 9–21 juni 2002. Swedish Research Institute of Istanbul. http://www.srii.org/IrinaBr%3Dnd%3Dn.pdf (accessed April 17, 2006).

Brändle, Rudolf. 1992. "Petrus und Paulus als nova sidera." *Theologische Zeitschrift* 48:207–17.

Brandt, Hartwin. 2002. *Wird auch silbern mein Haar: Eine Geschichte des Alters in der Antike*. Beck's archäologische Bibliothek. Munich: Beck.

Brett, Mark G. 1991. *Biblical Criticism in Crisis?* Cambridge: Cambridge University Press.

Brierley, Peter W. 2000. *The Tide Is Running Out: What the English Church Attendance Survey Reveals*. London: Christian Research.

Broek, R. van den. 1988. "Der Brief des Jakobus an Quadratus und das Problem der judenchristlichen Bischöfe von Jerusalem (Eusebius, H.E. IV,5,1–3)." Pages 56–65 in *Text and Testimony: Essays on New Testament and Apocryphal Literature in Honour of A. F. J. Klijn*. Edited by T. Baarda et al. Kampen: Kok.

Brooke, George J. 1995. "4Q500 1 and the Use of Scripture in the Parable of the Vineyard." *Dead Sea Discoveries* 2:268–94.

Brown, David. 1999. *Tradition and Imagination: Revelation and Change*. Oxford: Clarendon.

―――. 2000. *Discipleship and Imagination: Christian Tradition and Truth*. Oxford: Oxford University Press.

Brown, Peter. 1981. *The Cult of the Saints: Its Rise and Function in Latin Christianity*. Haskell Lectures on History of Religions, n.s., 2. Chicago: University of Chicago Press; London: SCM.

Brueggemann, Walter. 1993. *The Bible and Postmodern Imagination: Texts under Negotiation*. London: SCM.

―――. 2001. "Canon Fire: The Bible as Scripture." *Christian Century* 118:22–26.

―――. 2002. "Biblical Authority: A Personal Reflection." Pages 5–31 in *Struggling with Scripture*. Edited by W. Brueggemann et al. Louisville: Westminster John Knox.

Bultmann, Rudolf. 1951. *Theology of the New Testament*. Translated by K. Grobel. New York: Scribner.

Burge, Gary M. 2003. *Whose Land? Whose Promise? What Christians Are Not Being Told about Israel and Palestinians*. Carlisle: Paternoster.

Butterfield, Herbert. 1931. *The Whig Interpretation of History*. London: Bell.

Byrskog, Samuel. 2000. *Story as History—History as Story: The Gospel Tradition in the Context of Ancient Oral History.* Wissenschaftliche Untersuchungen zum Neuen Testament 123. Tübingen: Mohr.

———. 2004. "A New Perspective on the Jesus Tradition: Reflections on James D. G. Dunn's *Jesus Remembered.*" *Journal for the Study of the New Testament* 26:459–71.

Caird, G. B. 1994. *New Testament Theology.* Edited by L. D. Hurst. Oxford: Clarendon.

Cameron, Ron. 1992. "Thomas, Gospel of." Pages 535–40 in vol. 6 of *The Anchor Bible Dictionary.* Edited by D. N. Freedman et al. New York: Doubleday.

Campbell, Douglas A. 2002. "Apostolic Competition at Corinth?" *Journal of Beliefs and Values* 23:229–31.

———. 2005. *The Quest for Paul's Gospel: A Suggested Strategy.* Journal for the Study of the New Testament: Supplement Series 274. London and New York: T&T Clark.

Cannadine, David. 1992. *G. M. Trevelyan: A Life in History.* London: HarperCollins.

Cantalamessa, Raniero. 2002. *Life in Christ: The Spiritual Message of the Letter to the Romans.* Translated by F. L. Villa. Collegeville, MN: Liturgical Press.

Carleton Paget, James. 1997. "Anti-Judaism and Early Christian Identity." *Zeitschrift für Antikes Christentum* 1:195–225.

———. 2001. "Quests for the Historical Jesus." Pages 138–55 in *The Cambridge Companion to Jesus.* Edited by M. Bockmuehl. Cambridge: Cambridge University Press.

Carroll, Robert P. 1998. "Poststructuralist Approaches: New Historicism and Postmodernism." Pages 50–66 in *The Cambridge Companion to Biblical Interpretation.* Edited by J. Barton. Cambridge: Cambridge University Press.

Carruthers, Mary. 1990. *The Book of Memory: A Study of Memory in Medieval Culture.* Cambridge Studies in Medieval Literature 10. Cambridge: Cambridge University Press.

Carson, D. A., Peter Thomas O'Brien, and Mark A. Seifrid, eds. 2001–4. *Justification and Variegated Nomism: A Fresh Appraisal of Paul and Second Temple Judaism.* 2 vols. Wissenschaftliche Untersuchungen zum Neuen Testament 2/140, 181. Tübingen: Mohr; Grand Rapids: Baker.

Chadwick, Henry. 1959. *The Circle and the Ellipse: Rival Concepts of Authority in the Early Church.* Oxford: Clarendon.

———. 1962. "Pope Damasus and the Peculiar Claim of Rome to St Peter and St Paul." Pages 313–18 in *Neotestamentica et patristica: Eine Freundesgabe, Herrn Professor Dr. Oscar Cullmann zu seinem 60. Geburtstag überreicht.* Edited by A. N. Wilder. Novum Testamentum Supplement 6. Leiden: Brill.

Chancey, Mark A. 2002. *The Myth of a Gentile Galilee: The Population of Galilee and New Testament Studies.* Society for New Testament Studies Monograph 118. Cambridge: Cambridge University Press.

————. 2005. *Greco-Roman Culture and the Galilee of Jesus.* Society for New Testament Studies Monograph Series 134. Cambridge: Cambridge University Press.

Chapman, Stephen B. 2002. Review of George Aichele, *The Control of Biblical Meaning: Canon as Semiotic Mechanism. Theology Today* 59:113–15.

Chesterton, G. K. 1955. *The Everlasting Man.* Garden City: Image.

Childs, Brevard S. 1962. *Memory and Tradition in Israel.* London: SCM.

————. 1970. *Biblical Theology in Crisis.* Philadelphia: Westminster.

————. 1984. *The New Testament as Canon: An Introduction.* London: SCM.

————. 1992. *Biblical Theology of the Old and New Testaments: Theological Reflection on the Christian Bible.* London: SCM.

————. 1995. "On Reclaiming the Bible for Christian Theology." Pages 1–17 in *Reclaiming the Bible for the Church.* Edited by C. E. Braaten and R. W. Jenson. Grand Rapids: Eerdmans.

————. 1997. "Toward Recovering Theological Exegesis." *Pro ecclesia* 6:16–26.

————. 2002. *Biblical Theology: A Proposal.* Facets. Minneapolis: Fortress.

————. 2004. *The Struggle to Understand Isaiah as Christian Scripture.* Grand Rapids: Eerdmans.

Churchill, Winston. 1991. "The Dream." Pages 362–71 in *The Oxford Book of Essays.* Edited by J. Gross. Oxford: Oxford University Press.

Clark, Andrew C. 2001. *Parallel Lives: The Relation of Paul to the Apostles in the Lucan Perspective.* Paternoster Biblical and Theological Monographs. Carlisle: Paternoster.

Clines, David J. A. 1993. "Possibilities and Priorities of Biblical Interpretation in an International Perspective." *Biblical Interpretation* 1:67–87.

Coakley, Sarah. 2002. *Powers and Submissions: Spirituality, Philosophy and Gender.* Challenges in Contemporary Theology. Oxford: Blackwell.

Cobham, J. O. 1958a. "E. C. Hoskyns: The Sunderland Curate." *Church Quarterly Review* 158:280–95.

————. 1958b. "Sir Edwyn Hoskyns on Justification by Faith: His Sermons on the 39 Articles." *Church Quarterly Review* 159:325–40.

Coggins, Richard. 1993. "A Future for the Commentary?" Pages 163–75 in *The Open Text: New Directions for Biblical Studies?* Edited by F. Watson. London: SCM.

Cohn-Sherbok, Dan. 2000. *Messianic Judaism.* London: Cassell.

Coleman, Janet. 1992. *Ancient and Medieval Memories: Studies in the Reconstruction of the Past.* Cambridge: Cambridge University Press.

Collins, John J. 2005. *The Bible after Babel: Historical Criticism in a Postmodern Age.* Grand Rapids: Eerdmans.

Corley, Kathleen E. 2002. *Women and the Historical Jesus: Feminist Myths of Christian Origins.* Santa Rosa, CA: Polebridge.

Countryman, Louis William. 2003. *Interpreting the Truth: Changing the Paradigm of Biblical Studies.* Harrisburg, PA: Trinity.

Courtonne, Yves, ed. 1957–66. *Saint Basile: Lettres*. 3 vols. Paris: Belles Lettres.

Crossan, John Dominic. 1985. *Four Other Gospels: Shadows on the Contour of Canon*. Minneapolis: Winston.

———. 1991. *The Historical Jesus: The Life of a Mediterranean Jewish Peasant*. San Francisco: Harper.

———. 1998. *The Birth of Christianity: Discovering What Happened in the Years Immediately after the Execution of Jesus*. San Francisco: Harper.

Crossan, John Dominic, and Jonathan L. Reed. 2001. *Excavating Jesus: Beneath the Stones, behind the Texts*. San Francisco: Harper.

Cummins, Stephen A. 2004. "The Theological Interpretation of Scripture: Recent Contributions by Stephen E. Fowl, Christopher R. Seitz, and Francis Watson." *Currents in Biblical Research* 2:179–96.

Cunningham, Valentine. 2002. *Reading after Theory*. Blackwell Manifestos. Oxford: Blackwell.

Dahan, Gilbert. 2000. "Le commentaire médieval de la Bible: Le passage au sens spirituel." Pages 213–30 in *Le commentaire entre tradition et innovation: Actes du colloque international de l'Institut des traditions textuelles, Paris et Villejuif, 22–25 septembre 1999*. Edited by M.-O. Goulet-Cazé and T. Dorandi. Bibliothèque d'histoire de la philosophie, n.s. Paris: Vrin.

Dahl, Nils Alstrup. 1948. "Anamnesis." *Studia theologica* 2:69–95.

———. 1969. "The Atonement: An Adequate Reward for the Akedah? (Ro 8:32)." Pages 15–29 in *Neotestamentica et Semitica: Studies in Honour of Matthew Black*. Edited by E. E. Ellis et al. Edinburgh: T&T Clark.

Daley, Brian E. 2003. "Is Patristic Exegesis Still Usable? Some Reflections on Early Christian Interpretation of the Psalms." Pages 69–88 in *The Art of Reading Scripture*. Edited by E. F. Davis and R. B. Hays. Grand Rapids: Eerdmans.

Damrosch, David. 1995. *We Scholars: Changing the Culture of the University*. Cambridge: Harvard University Press.

Danker, Frederick W., and Walter Bauer. 2000. *A Greek-English Lexicon of the New Testament and Other Early Christian Literature*. 3rd edition. Chicago: University of Chicago Press.

Daube, David. 1990. "*Zukunftsmusik*: Some Desirable Lines of Exploration in the New Testament Field." Pages 360–80 in *The Interrelations of the Gospels: A Symposium Led by M.-É. Boismard, W. R. Farmer, F. Neirynck, Jerusalem 1984*. Edited by M.-É. Boismard et al. Bibliotheca Ephemeridum Theologicarum Lovaniensium 95. Louvain: Louvain University Press.

Davies, Philip R. 1995. *Whose Bible Is It Anyway?* Sheffield: Sheffield Academic Press.

———. 2004. *Whose Bible Is It Anyway?* 2nd edition. London and New York: T&T Clark.

Davies, W. D., and Dale C. Allison Jr. 1988–97. *A Critical and Exegetical Commentary on the Gospel according to Saint Matthew*. 3 vols. International Critical Commentary. Edinburgh: T&T Clark.

Davies, W. D., and E. P. Sanders. 1999. "Jesus: From the Jewish Point of View." Pages 618–77 in *The Cambridge History of Judaism*, vol. 3: *The Early Roman Period*. Edited by W. Horbury et al. Cambridge: Cambridge University Press.

Davila, James R. 2000. *Liturgical Works*. Eerdmans Commentaries on the Dead Sea Scrolls 6. Grand Rapids: Eerdmans.

Davis, Casey Wayne. 1999. *Oral Biblical Criticism: The Influence of the Principles of Orality on the Literary Structure of Paul's Epistle to the Philippians*. Journal for the Study of the New Testament: Supplement Series 172. Sheffield: Sheffield Academic Press.

Davis-Weyer, Cäcilia. 1961. "Das Traditio-Legis-Bild und seine Nachfolge." *Münchner Jahrbuch der Bildenden Kunst* (series 3) 12:7–45.

De Lange, N. R. M. 1976. *Origen and the Jews: Studies in Jewish-Christian Relations in Third-Century Palestine*. Cambridge: Cambridge University Press.

de la Potterie, Ignace. 1986. "Reading Holy Scripture 'in the Spirit': Is a Patristic Way of Reading the Bible Still Possible Today?" *International Catholic Review/Communio* 13:308–56.

Demus, Otto. 1949. *The Mosaics of Norman Sicily*. London: Routledge & Paul.

Dennett, Daniel C. 1991. *Consciousness Explained*. Boston: Little Brown.

Devillers, Luc. 1998. "La lettre de Soumaïos et les Ioudaioi johanniques." *Revue biblique* 105:556–81.

Dillistone, F. W. 1975. *Charles Raven: Naturalist, Historian, Theologian*. London: Hodder & Stoughton.

Dodd, C. H. 1936a. *The Apostolic Preaching and Its Developments: Three Lectures with an Appendix on Eschatology and History*. London: Hodder & Stoughton.

———. 1936b. *The Present Task in New Testament Studies: An Inaugural Lecture Delivered in the Divinity School on Tuesday, 2 June 1936*. Cambridge: Cambridge University Press.

———. 1938. *History and the Gospel*. London: Nisbet.

Dodson, C. S., W. Koutstaal, and D. L. Schacter. 2000. "Escape from Illusion: Reducing False Memories." *Trends in Cognitive Sciences* 4:391–97.

Doering, Lutz. 2002. "Schwerpunkte und Tendenzen der neueren Petrus-Forschung." *Berliner theologische Zeitschrift* 19:203–23.

Donati, Angela. 2000. *Pietro e Paolo: La storia, il culto, la memoria nei primi secoli*. Milan: Electa.

Dudai, Yadin. 2002. *Memory from A to Z: Keywords, Concepts, and Beyond*. Oxford: Oxford University Press.

Duff, Jeremy. 1998. "P[46] and the Pastorals: A Misleading Consensus?" *New Testament Studies* 44:578–90.

Dumas, André. 1996. "Faire mémoire: Un geste chrétien." Pages 35–56 in *Les mémoires necessaires: De Dieu à Auschwitz*. Edited by M. Bouttier. Entrée libre 34. Geneva: Labor & Fides.

Dungan, David L. 1999. *A History of the Synoptic Problem: The Canon, the Text, the Composition, and the Interpretation of the Gospels.* Anchor Bible Reference Library. New York: Doubleday.

Dunn, James D. G. 2001. "Jesus in Oral Memory: The Initial Stages of the Jesus Tradition." Pages 84–145 in *Jesus: A Colloquium in the Holy Land.* Edited by D. Donnelly. New York: Continuum.

———. 2003. *Jesus Remembered.* Christianity in the Making 1. Grand Rapids: Eerdmans.

———. 2004. "On History, Memory, and Eyewitnesses: In Response to Bengt Holmberg and Samuel Byrskog." *Journal for the Study of the New Testament* 26:473–87.

———. 2005. *A New Perspective on Jesus: What the Quest for the Historical Jesus Missed.* Grand Rapids: Baker.

———. forthcoming. "Social Memory and the Oral Jesus Tradition." In *Memory and Remembrance in the Bible and Antiquity.* Edited by L. T. Stuckenbruck et al. Wissenschaftliche Untersuchungen zum Neuen Testament. Tübingen: Mohr Siebeck.

Eagleton, Terry. 1976a. *Criticism and Ideology: A Study in Marxist Literary Theory.* London: NLB; Atlantic Highlands: Humanities Press.

———. 1976b. *Marxism and Literary Criticism.* Berkeley: University of California Press.

———. 1986. *Against the Grain: Essays, 1975–1985.* London: Verso.

———. 1999. "In the Gaudy Supermarket." *London Review of Books* 21, no. 10:3–6.

———. 2001. *The Gatekeeper: A Memoir.* London: Lane.

———. 2003. *After Theory.* New York: Basic Books.

Ebeling, Gerhard. 1947. *Kirchengeschichte als Geschichte der Auslegung der Heiligen Schrift.* Tübingen: Mohr.

Eco, Umberto. 1981. *The Role of the Reader: Explorations in the Semiotics of Texts.* London: Hutchinson.

———. 1984. *The Name of the Rose.* Translated by W. Weaver. London: Picador; Secker & Warburg.

———. 1992. *Interpretation and Overinterpretation.* Edited by S. Collini. Cambridge: Cambridge University Press.

Edwards, Mark J. 2004. *John.* Blackwell Bible Commentaries. Oxford: Blackwell.

———. 2005. Review of Karen L. King, *What Is Gnosticism? Journal of Theological Studies* 56:198–202.

Ehrman, Bart D. 2003a. *The Apostolic Fathers.* 2 vols. Loeb Classical Library 24–25. Cambridge: Harvard University Press.

———. 2003b. *Lost Christianities: The Battle for Scripture and the Faiths We Never Knew.* Oxford: Oxford University Press.

———. 2003c. *Lost Scriptures: Books That Did Not Make It into the New Testament.* Oxford: Oxford University Press.

Eliav, Y. Z. 2004. "The Tomb of James, Brother of Jesus, as Locus Memoriae."
    Harvard Theological Review 97:33–60.

Elliott, Charles. 1995. *Memory and Salvation*. London: Darton, Longman &
    Todd.

Elliott, John H. 1992. "Peter, Second Epistle of." Pages 282–87 in vol.
    5 of *The Anchor Bible Dictionary*. Edited by D. N. Freedman et al. New York:
    Doubleday.

Engberg-Pedersen, Troels. 2003. Review of Richard A. Horsley, *Hearing the
    Whole Story: The Politics of Plot in Mark's Gospel*. *Journal of Theological
    Studies* 54:230–45.

Evans, Christopher F. 1983. "Crucifixion-Resurrection: Some Reflections on Sir
    Edwyn Hoskyns as Theologian." *Epworth Review* 10.1:70–76; 10.2:79–86.

Evans, Craig A. 2000. "Vineyard Text (4Q500)." Page 1257 in *Dictionary of
    New Testament Background*. Edited by C. A. Evans and S. E. Porter. Downers
    Grove, IL: InterVarsity.

———. 2001. "Context, Family, and Formation." Pages 11–24 in *The Cam-
    bridge Companion to Jesus*. Edited by M. Bockmuehl. Cambridge: Cambridge
    University Press.

———. 2003. "How Septuagintal Is Isa. 5:1–7 in Mark 12:1–9?" *Novum Tes-
    tamentum* 45:105–10.

Evans, Richard J. 1997. *In Defence of History*. London: Granta.

Fackre, Gabriel. 1984–87. *The Christian Story: A Pastoral Systematics*. Grand
    Rapids: Eerdmans.

Feldman, Louis H. 1999. *Judean Antiquities 1–4*. Flavius Josephus: Translation
    and Commentary 3. Leiden: Brill.

Fentress, James, and Chris Wickham. 1992. *Social Memory*. Oxford: Blackwell.

Finkel, Asher. 1981. "The Prayer of Jesus in Matthew." Pages 131–69 in *Stand-
    ing before God: Studies on Prayer in Scriptures and in Tradition with Essays
    in Honor of John M. Oesterreicher*. Edited by A. Finkel and L. Frizzell. New
    York: Ktav.

Fish, Stanley Eugene. 1980. *Is There a Text in This Class? The Authority of
    Interpretive Communities*. Cambridge: Harvard University Press.

———. 2001. *How Milton Works*. Cambridge: Harvard University Press.

Fitzmyer, Joseph A. 1995. *The Biblical Commission's Document "The Interpreta-
    tion of the Bible in the Church": Text and Commentary*. Subsidia biblica 18.
    Rome: Pontifical Biblical Institute Press.

———. 2002. "The Sacrifice of Isaac in Qumran Literature." *Biblica* 83:211–29.

Fodor, Jim. 2004. "Reading the Scriptures: Rehearsing Identity, Practicing Char-
    acter." Pages 141–55 in *The Blackwell Companion to Christian Ethics*. Edited
    by S. Hauerwas and S. Wells. Blackwell Companions to Religion. Oxford:
    Blackwell.

Ford, David F. 1999. *Self and Salvation: Being Transformed*. Cambridge: Cam-
    bridge University Press.

———. 2000a. "British Theology after a Trauma: Divisions and Conversations." *Christian Century* 117:425–31.

———. 2000b. "British Theology: Movements and Churches." *Christian Century* 117:467–73.

———. 2000c. "Theological Wisdom, British Style." *Christian Century* 117:388–91.

———. 2001a. "Radical Orthodoxy and the Future of British Theology." *Scottish Journal of Theology* 54:385–404.

———. 2001b. "A Response to Catherine Pickstock." *Scottish Journal of Theology* 54:423–25.

———. 2001c. "Wisdom, Scripture, and Learning." Pages 1–7 in *Principles for a Principal: Gospel, Scripture, and Church*. Edited by D. F. Ford and C. Cocksworth. Cambridge: Ridley Hall.

Foster, Kenelm, ed. 1959. *The Life of Saint Thomas Aquinas: Biographical Documents*. London: Longmans Green; Baltimore: Helicon.

Fowl, Stephen E. 1990. "The Ethics of Interpretation; or, What's Left Over after the Elimination of Meaning." Pages 379–98 in *The Bible in Three Dimensions: Essays in Celebration of Forty Years of Biblical Studies in the University of Sheffield*. Edited by D. J. A. Clines et al. Journal for the Study of the Old Testament: Supplement Series 87. Sheffield: JSOT Press.

———. 1998. *Engaging Scripture: A Model for Theological Interpretation*. Challenges in Contemporary Theology. Oxford: Blackwell.

———. 2002. "The Conceptual Structure of New Testament Theology." Pages 225–36 in *Biblical Theology: Retrospect and Prospect*. Edited by S. J. Hafemann. Downers Grove, IL: InterVarsity.

Frank, Georgia. 2000. *The Memory of the Eyes: Pilgrims to Living Saints in Christian Late Antiquity*. Transformation of the Classical Heritage 30. Berkeley: University of California Press.

Frankemölle, Hubert. 1998a. *Jüdische Wurzeln christlicher Theologie: Studien zum biblischen Kontext neutestamentlicher Texte*. Bonner biblische Beiträge 116. Bodenheim: Philo.

———, ed. 1998b. *Der ungekündigte Bund: Antworten des Neuen Testaments*. Quaestiones disputatae 172. Freiburg: Herder.

Frei, Hans W. 1975. *The Identity of Jesus Christ*. Philadelphia: Fortress.

Freyne, Seán. 1998. *Galilee from Alexander the Great to Hadrian, 323 B.C.E. to 135 C.E.: A Study of Second Temple Judaism*. 2nd edition. Edinburgh: T&T Clark.

———. 2004. *Jesus, a Jewish Galilean: A New Reading of the Jesus-Story*. London: T&T Clark.

Frymer-Kensky, Tikva, et al., eds. 2000. *Christianity in Jewish Terms*. Boulder, CO: Westview.

Fuller, Reginald H. 1984. "Sir Edwyn Hoskyns and the Contemporary Relevance of 'Biblical Theology.'" *New Testament Studies* 30:321–34.

Funk, Robert Walter. 1993. *The Five Gospels: The Search for the Authentic Words of Jesus.* New York: Macmillan.

Funk, Robert Walter, Bernard Brandon Scott, and James R. Butts. 1988. *The Parables of Jesus: Red Letter Edition: A Report of the Jesus Seminar.* Jesus Seminar Series. Sonoma, CA: Polebridge.

Funk, Robert Walter, and Mahlon H. Smith. 1991. *The Gospel of Mark: Red Letter Edition.* Jesus Seminar Series. Sonoma, CA: Polebridge.

García Martínez, Florentino. 2002. "The Sacrifice of Isaac in 4Q225." Pages 44–57 in *The Sacrifice of Isaac: The Aqedah (Genesis 22) and Its Interpretations.* Edited by E. Noort and E. Tigchelaar. Themes in Biblical Narrative: Jewish and Christian Traditions 4. Leiden: Brill.

Gassmann, Gunther. 1998. "Rezeption I: Kirchengeschichtlich." Pages 131–42 in vol. 29 of *Theologische Realenzyklopädie.* Edited by G. Krause and G. Müller. Berlin: de Gruyter.

Gathercole, Simon J. 2002. *Where Is Boasting? Early Jewish Soteriology and Paul's Response in Romans 1–5.* Grand Rapids: Eerdmans.

Gaventa, Beverly Roberts, and Patrick D. Miller, eds. 2005. *The Ending of Mark and the Ends of God: Essays in Memory of Donald Harrisville Juel.* Louisville: Westminster John Knox.

Gedi, Noa, and Yigal Elam. 1996. "Collective Memory: What Is It?" *History and Memory* 8:30–50.

Gerhardsson, Birger. 1961. *Memory and Manuscript: Oral Tradition and Written Transmission in Rabbinic Judaism and Early Christianity.* Acta Seminarii Neotestamentici Upsaliensis 22. Uppsala: Gleerup.

———. 1986. *The Gospel Tradition.* Coniectanea biblica: New Testament 15. Lund: Gleerup.

Gese, Hartmut. 1984. "Wisdom Literature in the Persian Period." Pages 189–218 in *The Cambridge History of Judaism,* vol. 1: *Introduction; the Persian Period.* Edited by W. D. Davies and L. Finkelstein. Cambridge: Cambridge University Press.

Gieschen, C. A. 2003. "The Divine Name in Ante-Nicene Christology." *Vigiliae christianae* 57:115–58.

Ginzburg, Carlo. 1999. *History, Rhetoric, and Proof.* Menahem Stern Jerusalem Lectures. Hanover, NH: University Press of New England.

———. 2001. *Wooden Eyes: Nine Reflections on Distance.* New York: Columbia University Press.

Gluck, Sherna Berger, and Daphne Patai. 1991. *Women's Words: the Feminist Practice of Oral History.* New York: Routledge.

Gnilka, Joachim. 2002. *Petrus und Rom: Das Petrusbild in den ersten zwei Jahrhunderten.* Freiburg: Herder.

Goddard, Andrew. 2001. *God, Gentiles, and Gay Christians: Acts 15 and Change in the Church.* Grove Ethics Series E121. Cambridge: Grove.

Goldingay, John. 2003. *Israel's Gospel.* Downers Grove, IL: InterVarsity.

Goulder, Michael D. 1994. *A Tale of Two Missions.* London: SCM.

———. 1996. "Is Q a Juggernaut?" *Journal of Biblical Literature* 115:667–81.

———. 2001. *Paul and the Competing Mission in Corinth*. Library of Pauline Studies. Peabody, MA: Hendrickson.

Graham, William A. 1987. *Beyond the Written Word: Oral Aspects of Scripture in the History of Religion*. Cambridge: Cambridge University Press.

Green, Joel B. 2002. "Scripture and Theology: Failed Experiments, Fresh Perspectives." *Interpretation* 56:5–20.

Green, Joel B., and Max Turner, eds. 2000. *Between Two Horizons: Spanning New Testament Studies and Systematic Theology*. Grand Rapids: Eerdmans.

Greene-McCreight, Kathryn. 1999. *Ad litteram: How Augustine, Calvin, and Barth Read the "Plain Sense" of Genesis 1–3*. Issues in Systematic Theology 5. New York: Lang.

Griffiths, Paul J. 1999. *Religious Reading: The Place of Reading in the Practice of Religion*. Oxford and New York: Oxford University Press.

Grundmann, Walter. 1938. "'Das Heil kommt von den Juden . . .': Eine Schicksalsfrage an die Christen deutscher Nation." *Deutsche Frömmigkeit* 6.9:1–8.

———. 1940. *Jesus der Galiläer und das Judentum*. Leipzig: Wigand.

Gunkel, Hermann. 1987. *The Folktale in the Old Testament*. Translated by M. D. Rutter. Historic Texts and Interpreters in Biblical Scholarship 6. Sheffield: Almond.

Gunton, Colin E. 1990. "Using and Being Used: Scripture and Systematic Theology." *Theology Today* 47:248–59.

———. 1993. *The One, the Three, and the Many: God, Creation, and the Culture of Modernity*. Cambridge: Cambridge University Press.

Gutteridge, Richard J. C. 1964. "Sir Edwyn Hoskyns (1884–1937): Wegbereiter, Brückenbauer, Interpret." *Kerygma und Dogma* 10:48–60.

Hafemann, Scott J., ed. 2002. *Biblical Theology: Retrospect and Prospect*. Downers Grove, IL: InterVarsity.

Hahn, Ferdinand. 2002. *Theologie des Neuen Testaments*. 2 vols. Tübingen: Mohr.

Halbwachs, Maurice. 1941. *La topographie légendaire des Évangiles en Terre Sainte: Étude de mémoire collective*. Bibliothèque de philosophie contemporaine. Paris: Presses universitaires de France.

———. 1992. *On Collective Memory*. Edited and translated by L. A. Coser. The Heritage of Sociology. Chicago: University of Chicago Press.

Härle, Wilfried. 1995. *Dogmatik*. De Gruyter Lehrbuch. Berlin: de Gruyter.

Harnack, Adolf von. 1924. *Marcion: Das Evangelium vom fremden Gott*. Texte und Untersuchungen 45. 2nd edition. Leipzig: Hinrichs.

———. 1935. *Dogmengeschichte*. 8th edition. Tübingen: Mohr.

———. 1957. *What Is Christianity?* Translated by T. B. Saunders. New York: Harper & Row.

———. 2003. *Marcion, der moderne Gläubige des 2. Jahrhunderts, der erste Reformator: Die Dorpater Preisschrift (1870): Kritische Edition des handschriftlichen Exemplars mit einem Anhang*. Edited by F. Steck. Texte und

Untersuchungen zur Geschichte der altchristlichen Literatur 149. Berlin: de Gruyter.

Harris, Horton. 1975. *The Tübingen School*. Oxford: Clarendon.

Harvey, Graham. 1996. *The True Israel: Uses of the Names Jew, Hebrew, and Israel in Ancient Jewish and Early Christian Literature*. Arbeiten zur Geschichte des antiken Judentums und des Urchristentums 35. Leiden: Brill.

Hayes, John H., ed. 2004. *New Testament, History of Interpretation: Excerpted from the Dictionary of Biblical Interpretation*. Nashville: Abingdon.

Hays, Richard B. 1999. "The Conversion of the Imagination: Scripture and Eschatology in 1 Corinthians." *New Testament Studies* 45:391–412.

Head, Peter M. 2001. "The Role of Eyewitnesses in the Formation of the Gospel Tradition: A Review Article of Samuel Byrskog, *Story as History—History as Story*." *Tyndale Bulletin* 52:275–94.

———. 2004. "The Nazi Quest for an Aryan Jesus." *Journal for the Study of the Historical Jesus* 2:55–89.

Hedrick, Charles W. 2000. *History and Silence: Purge and Rehabilitation of Memory in Late Antiquity*. Austin: University of Texas Press.

Heinemann, Joseph. 1978. "The Background of Jesus' Prayer in the Jewish Liturgical Tradition." Pages 81–89 in *The Lord's Prayer and Jewish Liturgy*. Edited by J. J. Petuchowski. London: Burns & Oates.

Hengel, Martin. 1968. "Das Gleichnis von den Weingärtnern: Mc 12,1–12 im Lichte der Zenonpapyri und der rabbinischen Gleichnisse." *Zeitschrift für die neutestamentliche Wissenschaft* 59:1–39.

———. 1985. "The Titles of the Gospels." Pages 64–84 in Hengel's *Studies in the Gospel of Mark*. Translated by J. Bowden. London: SCM; Philadelphia: Fortress.

———. 1994. "Aufgaben der neutestamentlichen Wissenschaft." *New Testament Studies* 40:321–57.

———. 1996a. *The Charismatic Leader and His Followers*. 2nd edition. Edinburgh: T&T Clark.

———. 1996b. "Tasks of New Testament Scholarship." *Bulletin for Biblical Research* 6:67–86.

———. 2000. *The Four Gospels and the One Gospel of Jesus Christ: An Investigation of the Collection and Origin of the Canonical Gospels*. Translated by J. Bowden. London: SCM.

———. 2002. *The Septuagint as Christian Scripture: Its Prehistory and the Problem of Its Canon*. Translated by M. E. Biddle. Edinburgh: T&T Clark.

———. 2003a. "Eine junge theologische Disziplin in der Krise." Pages 18–29 in *Neutestamentliche Wissenschaft: Autobiographische Essays aus der evangelischen Theologie*. Edited by E.-M. Becker. Tübingen: Francke.

———. 2003b. "'Salvation History': The Truth of Scripture and Modern Theology." Pages 229–44 in *Reading Texts, Seeking Wisdom: Scripture and Theology*. Edited by G. Stanton and D. F. Ford. London: SCM.

————. 2004. "The Four Gospels and the One Gospel of Jesus Christ." Pages 13–26 in *The Earliest Gospels: The Origins and Transmission of the Earliest Christian Gospels—The Contribution of the Chester Beatty Gospel Codex P45*. Edited by C. Horton. Journal for the Study of the New Testament: Supplement Series 258. London: T&T Clark.

————. forthcoming. "Der Lukasprolog und seine Augenzeugen: Die Apostel Petrus und die Frauen." In *Memory and Remembrance in the Bible and Antiquity*. Edited by L. T. Stuckenbruck et al. Wissenschaftliche Untersuchungen zum Neuen Testament. Tübingen: Mohr Siebeck.

Hengel, Martin, and Roland Deines. 1995. "E. P. Sanders' 'Common Judaism,' Jesus, and the Pharisees." *Journal of Theological Studies* 46:1–70.

Hengel, Martin, and Anna Maria Schwemer. 1997. *Paul between Damascus and Antioch: The Unknown Years*. Translated by J. Bowden. London: SCM.

Heschel, Susannah. 1994. "Nazifying Christian Theology: Walter Grundmann and the Institute for the Study and Eradication of Jewish Influence on German Church Life." *Church History* 63:587–605.

————. 1999. "When Jesus Was an Aryan: The Protestant Church and Antisemitic Propaganda." Pages 68–89 in *Betrayal: German Churches and the Holocaust*. Edited by R. P. Ericksen and S. Heschel. Minneapolis: Fortress.

Heusch, Luc de. 1982. *The Drunken King; or, The Origin of the State*. African Systems of Thought. Bloomington: Indiana University Press.

Hill, David. 1984. "The Figure of Jesus in Matthew's Story: A Response to Professor Kingsbury's Literary-Critical Probe." *Journal for the Study of the New Testament* 21:37–52.

Hoffmann, Paul, and Christoph Heil. 1998. *Q 22:28,30: You Will Judge the Twelve Tribes of Israel*. Documenta Q. Louvain: Peeters.

Holmberg, Bengt. 2004. "Questions of Method in James Dunn's *Jesus Remembered*." *Journal for the Study of the New Testament* 26:445–57.

Holmes, Jeremy. 2002. "The Spiritual Sense of Scripture." *Downside Review* 120:113–28.

Hooker, Morna D. 1971. "Christology and Methodology." *New Testament Studies* 17:480–87.

————. 1972. "On Using the Wrong Tool." *Theology* 75:570–81.

————. 2000. "Creative Conflict: The Torah and Christology." Pages 117–36 in *Christology, Controversy, and Community: New Testament Essays in Honour of David R. Catchpole*. Edited by D. G. Horrell and C. M. Tuckett. Novum Testamentum Supplement 99. Leiden: Brill.

————. 2005. "Beginnings and Endings." Pages 184–202 in *The Written Gospel*. Edited by M. Bockmuehl and D. A. Hagner. Cambridge: Cambridge University Press.

Hoornaert, Eduardo. 1989. *The Memory of the Christian People*. Translated by R. R. Barr. Tunbridge Wells: Burns & Oates.

Horbury, William. 1998a. "The Cult of Christ and the Cult of the Saints." *New Testament Studies* 44:444–69.

———. 1998b. *Jewish Messianism and the Cult of Christ*. London: SCM.

———. 2003a. *Messianism among Jews and Christians: Twelve Biblical and Historical Studies*. London: T&T Clark.

———. 2003b. "The New Testament." Pages 51–134 in *A Century of Theological and Religious Studies in Britain: 1902–2002*. Edited by E. W. Nicholson. British Academy Centenary Monographs. Oxford: Oxford University Press.

Hornik, Heidi J., and Mikeal C. Parsons. 2003. *Illuminating Luke: The Infancy Narrative in Italian Renaissance Painting*. Harrisburg, PA: Trinity.

Horsfall, N. 1998. Review of J. P. Small, *Wax Tablets of the Mind: Cognitive Studies of Memory and Literacy in Classical Antiquity*. *Journal of Roman Archeology* 11:565–71.

Horsley, Richard A. 1995. *Galilee: History, Politics, People*. Valley Forge, PA: Trinity.

———. 2001. *Hearing the Whole Story: The Politics of Plot in Mark's Gospel*. Louisville: Westminster John Knox.

———. 2003. *Jesus and Empire: The Kingdom of God and the New World Disorder*. Minneapolis: Fortress.

Hoskyns, Edwyn Clement. 1926. "The Christ of the Synoptic Gospels." Pages 151–78 in *Essays Catholic and Critical*. Edited by E. G. Selwyn. London: SPCK.

———. 1930. "Jesus the Messiah." Pages 69–89 in *Mysterium Christi*. Edited by G. K. A. Bell and A. Deissmann. London: Longmans.

———. 1938a. *Cambridge Sermons*. London: SPCK.

———. 1938b. *Das Rätsel des Neuen Testaments*. Translated by H. Bolewski. Edited by J. Schniewind and G. Kittel. Stuttgart: Kohlhammer.

———. 1947. *The Fourth Gospel*. Edited by F. N. Davey. Revised edition. London: Faber & Faber.

———. 1960. *We Are the Pharisees*. London: SPCK.

Hoskyns, Edwyn Clement, and Francis Noel Davey. 1931. *The Riddle of the New Testament*. London: Faber & Faber.

———. 1958. *The Riddle of the New Testament*. London: Faber & Faber.

———. 1981. *Crucifixion-Resurrection: The Pattern of the Theology and Ethics of the New Testament*. Edited by G. S. Wakefield. London: SPCK.

Houlden, J. Leslie. 1991. *Bible and Belief*. London: SPCK.

———. 1995. Review of G. B. Caird, *New Testament Theology*. *Times Literary Supplement* May 26: 28.

———. 2005. Review of John M. Court (ed.), *Biblical Interpretation: The Meaning of Scripture—Past and Present*. *Journal of Theological Studies* 56:184–86.

Hübner, Hans. 1988. "Vetus Testamentum und Vetus Testamentum in Novo receptum: Die Frage nach dem Kanon des Alten Testaments aus neutestamentlicher Sicht." *Jahrbuch für biblische Theologie* 3:147–62.

———. 1990. *Biblische Theologie des Neuen Testaments*. 3 vols. Göttingen: Vandenhoeck & Ruprecht.

Hübner, Hans, and Bernd Jaspert, eds. 1999. *Biblische Theologie: Entwürfe der Gegenwart*. Biblisch-theologische Studien 38. Neukirchen-Vluyn: Neukirchener Verlag.

Hurtado, Larry W. 1999. "New Testament Studies at the Turn of the Millennium: Questions for the Discipline." *Scottish Journal of Theology* 52:158–78.

———. 2003. *Lord Jesus Christ: Devotion to Jesus in Earliest Christianity*. Grand Rapids: Eerdmans.

Hütter, Reinhard. 2004. *Bound to Be Free: Evangelical Catholic Engagements in Ecclesiology, Ethics, and Ecumenism*. Grand Rapids: Eerdmans.

Hutton, Patrick H. 1992. "The Problem of Memory in the Historical Writings of Philippe Ariès." *History and Memory* 4:95–122.

———. 1993. *History as an Art of Memory*. Hanover, NH: University of Vermont and University Press of New England.

Hyldahl, Niels. 1960. "Hegesipps Hypomnemata." *Studia theologica* 14:70–113.

Ingraffia, Brian D. 1995. *Postmodern Theory and Biblical Theology: Vanquishing God's Shadow*. Cambridge: Cambridge University Press.

Instone-Brewer, David. 2004. *Traditions of the Rabbis from the Era of the New Testament*, vol. 1. Grand Rapids: Eerdmans.

Iser, Wolfgang. 1974. *The Implied Reader: Patterns of Communication in Prose Fiction from Bunyan to Beckett*. Baltimore: Johns Hopkins University Press.

Jeanrond, Werner G. 1993. "After Hermeneutics: The Relationship between Theology and Biblical Studies." Pages 85–102 in *The Open Text*. Edited by F. Watson. London: SCM.

———. 1996. "Criteria for New Biblical Theologies." *Journal of Religion* 76:233–49.

Jeffrey, Jaclyn, and Glenace Ecklund Edwall. 1994. *Memory and History: Essays on Recalling and Interpreting Experience*. Lanham, MD: University Press of America.

Jenkins, Keith. 1999. *Why History? Ethics and Postmodernity*. London: Routledge.

Jenkins, Philip. 2001. *Hidden Gospels: How the Search for Jesus Lost Its Way*. Oxford: Oxford University Press.

Jenkins, Simon. 1999. "Oliver the Timelord." *The Times*, Dec. 31.

Jenson, Robert W. 1995. "Hermeneutics and the Life of the Church." Pages 89–105 in *Reclaiming the Bible for the Church*. Edited by C. E. Braaten and R. W. Jenson. Grand Rapids: Eerdmans.

———. 1999. "The Religious Power of Scripture." *Scottish Journal of Theology* 52:89–105.

———. 2002. Review of Rowan Williams, *On Christian Theology*. *Pro ecclesia* 11:367–69.

———. 2003a. "Scripture's Authority in the Church." Pages 28–37 in *The Art of Reading Scripture*. Edited by E. F. Davis and R. B. Hays. Grand Rapids: Eerdmans.

———. 2003b. "Toward a Christian Theology of Judaism." Pages 1–13 in *Jews and Christians: People of God*. Edited by C. E. Braaten and R. W. Jenson. Grand Rapids: Eerdmans.

Jeremias, Joachim. 1967. *Jesus' Promise to the Nations*. Translated by S. H. Hooke. Revised edition. London: SCM.

Jerke, Birgit. 1994. "Wie wurde das Neue Testament zu einem sogenannten Volkstestament 'entjudet'? Aus der Arbeit des Eisenacher 'Instituts zur Erforschung und Beseitigung des jüdischen Einflusses auf das deutsche kirchliche Leben.'" Pages 201–34 in *Christlicher Antijudaismus und Antisemitismus: Theologische und kirchliche Programme Deutscher Christen*. Edited by L. Siegele-Wenschkewitz. Arnoldshainer Texte 85. Frankfurt: Haag & Herchen.

Johnson, Luke Timothy. 1996a. *The Real Jesus: The Misguided Quest for the Historical Jesus and the Truth of the Traditional Gospels*. New York: HarperCollins.

———. 1996b. *Scripture and Discernment: Decision Making in the Church*. Nashville: Abingdon.

———. 1998. "Imagining the World Scripture Imagines." *Modern Theology* 14:165–80.

Johnson, Luke Timothy, and William S. Kurz. 2002. *The Future of Catholic Biblical Scholarship: A Constructive Conversation*. Grand Rapids: Eerdmans.

Jones, L. Gregory, and James Joseph Buckley, eds. 1998. *Theology and Scriptural Imagination*. Oxford: Blackwell.

Juel, Donald. 1977. *Messiah and Temple: The Trial of Jesus in the Gospel of Mark*. Missoula, MT: Scholars Press.

Jüngel, Eberhard. 1995. *Theological Essays II*. Edited by J. Webster. Edinburgh: T&T Clark.

Karrer, Martin. 1989. "Petrus im paulinischen Gemeindekreis." *Zeitschrift für die neutestamentliche Wissenschaft* 80:210–31.

Katz, David S. 1982. *Philo-Semitism and the Readmission of the Jews to England, 1603–1655*. Oxford Historical Monographs. Oxford: Clarendon.

Kaye, Bruce N. 1984. "Lightfoot and Baur on Early Christianity." *Novum Testamentum* 26:193–224.

Keck, Leander E. 1981. "Is the New Testament a Field of Study? or, From Outler to Overbeck and Back." *Second Century* 1:19–35.

Keesmaat, Sylvia C. 2004. "Welcoming in the Gentiles: A Biblical Model for Decision Making." Pages 30–49 in *Living Together in the Church: Including Our Differences*. Edited by G. S. Dunn and C. Ambidge. Toronto: ABC. http://www.toronto.anglican.ca/images/Keesmaat_paper.jpg.pdf (accessed April 17, 2006).

Kelber, Werner H. 1983. *The Oral and the Written Gospel: The Hermeneutics of Speaking and Writing in the Synoptic Tradition, Mark, Paul, and Q*. Philadelphia: Fortress.

Kelhoffer, James A. 2000. *Miracle and Mission: The Authentication of Missionaries and Their Message in the Longer Ending of Mark*. Wissenschaftliche Untersuchungen zum Neuen Testament 2/112. Tübingen: Mohr.

Keller, Werner. 1956. *The Bible as History: Archaeology Confirms the Book of Books*. Translated by W. Neil. London: Hodder & Stoughton.

Kensinger, E. A., and D. L. Schacter. 1999. "When True Memories Suppress False Memories: Effects of Ageing." *Cognitive Neuropsychology* 16:399–416.

Kermode, Frank. 1967. *The Sense of an Ending: Studies in the Theory of Fiction*. New York: Oxford University Press.

———. 1979. *The Genesis of Secrecy: On the Interpretation of Narrative*. Cambridge, MA: Harvard University Press.

Kessler, Edward. 2004. *Bound by the Bible: Jews, Christians, and the Sacrifice of Isaac*. Cambridge: Cambridge University Press.

Kieffer, René. 1982. *Foi et justification à Antioche: Interprétation d'un conflit (Ga 2,14–21)*. Lectio divina 111. Paris: Cerf.

Kim, Seyoon. 2002. *Paul and the New Perspective: Second Thoughts on the Origin of Paul's Gospel*. Grand Rapids: Eerdmans.

King, Joseph S. 1984. "C. H. Dodd and E. C. Hoskyns." *King's Theological Review* 7:1–8.

King, Karen L. 2003. *What Is Gnosticism?* Cambridge, MA: Harvard University Press.

Kingsbury, Jack Dean. 1984. "The Figure of Jesus in Matthew's Story: A Literary-Critical Probe." *Journal for the Study of the New Testament* 21:3–36.

———. 1985. "The Figure of Jesus in Matthew's Story: A Rejoinder to David Hill." *Journal for the Study of the New Testament* 25:61–81.

Kinzer, Mark. 2005. *Postmissionary Messianic Judaism: Redefining Christian Engagement with the Jewish People*. Grand Rapids: Brazos.

Kinzig, Wolfram. 1994a. "*Kaine Diatheke*: The Title of the New Testament in the Second and Third Centuries." *Journal of Theological Studies* 45:519–44.

———. 1994b. *Novitas Christiana: Die Idee des Fortschritts in der Alten Kirche bis Eusebius*. Forschungen zur Kirchen- und Dogmengeschichte 58. Göttingen: Vandenhoeck & Ruprecht.

Kirchner, Dankwart. 1991. "The Apocryphon of James." Pages 285–99 in vol. 1 of *New Testament Apocrypha*. Edited by W. Schneemelcher. Translated by R. M. Wilson. Revised edition. Cambridge: Clarke; Louisville: Westminster John Knox.

Kister, Menahem. 2001. "Law, Morality, and Rhetoric in Some Sayings of Jesus." Pages 145–54 in *Studies in Ancient Midrash*. Edited by J. L. Kugel. Cambridge, MA: Harvard Center for Jewish Studies; Harvard University Press.

Kittel, Gerhard. 1933a. *Die Judenfrage*. Stuttgart: Kohlhammer.

———. 1933b. "Vorwort." Pages v–vii in vol. 1 of *Theologische Wörterbuch zum Neuen Testament*. Edited by G. Kittel and G. Friedrich. Stuttgart: Kohlhammer.

———. 1938a. *Adolf Schlatter: Gedenkrede, gehalten am 23. Mai 1938 im Festsaal der Universität Tübingen*. Gedächtnisheft der deutschen Theologie. Stuttgart: Kohlhammer.

———. 1938b. *Lexicographia sacra: Two Lectures on the Making of the Theologisches Wörterbuch zum Neuen Testament; Delivered on October 20th
and 21st, 1937, in the Divinity School, Cambridge*. Translated by R. J. C.
Gutteridge. London: SPCK.

Kitzinger, Ernst. 1992. *I mosaici del periodo normanno in Sicilia*. Palermo: Ac-
cademia Nazionale di Scienze Lettere e Arti di Palermo: Istituto Siciliano di
Studi Bizantini e Neoellenici.

Kleine, Christoph. 2002. "Religion im Dienste einer ethnisch-nationalen Iden-
titätskonstruktion: Erörtert am Beispiel der 'Deutschen Christen' und des japa-
nischen Shinto." *Marburg Journal of Religion* 7:1–25. http://www.uni-marburg
.de/religionswissenschaft/journal/mjr/kleine.pdf (accessed April 17, 2006).

Kloppenborg, John S., and John W. Marshall, eds. 2005. *Apocalypticism, Anti-
Semitism, and the Historical Jesus: Subtexts in Criticism*. Journal for the Study
of the Historical Jesus Supplement 1. London: T&T Clark.

Kloppenborg Verbin, John S. 2002. "Egyptian Viticultural Practices and the Citation of Isa 5:1–7 in Mark 12:1–9." *Novum Testamentum* 44:134–59.

Knoch, Otto. 1981. "Petrus und Paulus in den Schriften der apostolischen Väter."
Pages 240–60 in *Kontinuität und Einheit: Für Franz Mussner*. Edited by P.-G.
Müller and W. Stenger. Freiburg: Herder.

Knox, John. 1958. *Jesus: Lord and Christ; a Trilogy Comprising The Man Christ
Jesus, Christ the Lord, On the Meaning of Christ*. New York: Harper.

Körtner, Ulrich H. J. 1994. *Der inspirierte Leser: Zentrale Aspekte biblischer
Hermeneutik*. Göttingen: Vandenhoeck & Ruprecht.

Kovacs, Judith L., and Christopher Rowland. 2004. *Revelation*. Blackwell Bible
Commentaries. Oxford: Blackwell.

Kren, Thomas, and Scot McKendrick. 2003. *Illuminating the Renaissance: The
Triumph of Flemish Manuscript Painting in Europe*. Los Angeles: J. Paul Getty
Museum; London: Royal Academy of Arts.

Kugler, Robert A. 2003. "Hearing 4Q225: A Case Study in Reconstructing the
Religious Imagination of the Qumran Community." *Dead Sea Discoveries*
10:81–103.

Kümmel, Werner Georg. 1973. *The New Testament: The History of the Investigation of Its Problems*. Translated by S. M. Gilmour and H. C. Kee. 2nd
edition. London: SCM.

———. 1974. *The Theology of the New Testament: According to Its Major Witnesses, Jesus, Paul, John*. Translated by J. E. Steely. London: SCM.

Kvalbein, Hans. 2000. "Has Matthew Abandoned the Jews?" Pages 45–62 in
The Mission of the Early Church to Jews and Gentiles. Edited by J. Ådna
and H. Kvalbein. Wissenschaftliche Untersuchungen zum Neuen Testament
127. Tübingen: Mohr.

LaCapra, Dominick. 1998. *History and Memory after Auschwitz*. Ithaca: Cornell
University Press.

Lambers-Petry, Doris. 2003. "Verwandte Jesu als Referenzpersonen für das
Judenchristentum." Pages 32–52 in *The Image of the Judaeo-Christians in
Ancient Jewish and Christian Literature*. Edited by P. J. Tomson and D. Lam-

bers-Petry. Wissenschaftliche Untersuchungen zum Neuen Testament 158. Tübingen: Mohr.

Lash, Nicholas. 1986a. "Performing the Scriptures." Pages 37–46 in Lash's *Theology on the Way to Emmaus*. London: SCM.

———. 1986b. "What Might Martyrdom Mean?" Pages 75–92 in Lash's *Theology on the Way to Emmaus*. London: SCM.

Lawrence, Louise Joy. 2003. *An Ethnography of the Gospel of Matthew: A Critical Assessment of the Use of the Honour and Shame Model in New Testament Studies*. Wissenschaftliche Untersuchungen zum Neuen Testament 2/165. Tübingen: Mohr.

Layton, Bentley. 1987. *The Gnostic Scriptures: A New Translation*. London: SCM.

Le Boulluec, Alain. 1996. "L'écriture comme norme hérésiologique dans les controverses des IIe et IIIe siècles (domaine grec)." Pages 66–76 in *Stimuli: Exegese und ihre Hermeneutik in Antike und Christentum: Festschrift für Ernst Dassmann*. Edited by G. Schöllgen and C. Scholten. Journal of Ancient Christianity Supplement 23. Münster: Aschendorff.

Le Goff, Jacques. 1992. *History and Memory*. Translated by S. Rendall and E. Claman. European Perspectives. New York: Columbia University Press.

Lemcio, Eugene E. 1988. "The Unifying Kerygma of the New Testament I." *Journal for the Study of the New Testament* 33:3–17.

———. 1990. "The Unifying Kerygma of the New Testament II." *Journal for the Study of the New Testament* 38:3–11.

———. 1991. *The Past of Jesus in the Gospels*. Cambridge: Cambridge University Press.

Lieu, Judith. 1996. *Image and Reality: The Jews in the World of the Christians in the Second Century*. Edinburgh: T&T Clark.

———. 2002. *Neither Jew nor Greek? Constructing Early Christianity*. Studies of the New Testament and Its World. London: T&T Clark.

———. 2004. *Christian Identity in the Jewish and Graeco-Roman World*. Oxford: Oxford University Press.

Lindbeck, George A. 2003. *The Church in a Postliberal Age*. Edited by J. J. Buckley. Radical Traditions. Grand Rapids: Eerdmans.

Lipsius, Richard Adelbert, and Max Bonnet, eds. 1891. *Acta Apostolorum Apocrypha*. Leipzig: Mendelssohn.

Loftus, Elizabeth F. 1997. "Creating False Memories." *Scientific American* 277.3:70–75.

———. 1998. "Illusions of Memory." *Proceedings of the American Philosophical Society* 142:60–73.

Loftus, Elizabeth F., and Katherine Ketcham. 1994. *The Myth of Repressed Memory: False Memories and Allegations of Sexual Abuse*. New York: St. Martin's Press.

Loftus, Elizabeth F., M. Nucci, and H. Hoffman. 1998. "Manufacturing Memory." *American Journal of Forensic Psychology* 16:63–76.

Löhr, Winrich A. 1996. *Basilides und seine Schule: Eine Studie zur Theologie und Kirchengeschichte des zweiten Jahrhunderts.* Wissenschaftliche Untersuchungen zum Neuen Testament 83. Tübingen: Mohr.

———. 1997. "Mündlichkeit und Schriftlichkeit im Christentum des 2. Jahrhunderts." Pages 211–30 in *Logos und Buchstabe: Mündlichkeit und Schriftlichkeit im Judentum und Christentum der Antike.* Edited by G. Sellin and F. Vouga. Texte und Arbeiten zum neutestamentlichen Zeitalter 20. Tübingen: Francke.

Lohse, Eduard. 1991. "St. Peter's Apostleship in the Judgement of St. Paul, the Apostle to the Gentiles: An Exegetical Contribution to an Ecumenical Debate." *Gregorianum* 72:419–35.

Lord, Albert B. 1960. *The Singer of Tales.* Harvard Studies in Comparative Literature 24. Cambridge, MA: Harvard University Press.

Lubac, Henri de. 1961–64. *Exégèse médiévale: Les quatre sens de l'Écriture.* 4 vols. Paris: Cerf.

Lukacs, John. 1994. *The Historical Consciousness: The Remembered Past.* 3rd edition. New Brunswick, NJ: Transaction.

———. 2002. *At the End of an Age.* New Haven: Yale University Press.

Lundin, Roger, Anthony C. Thiselton, and Clarence Walhout. 1999. *The Promise of Hermeneutics.* Grand Rapids: Eerdmans.

Luz, Ulrich. 1985. "Wirkungsgeschichtliche Exegese: Ein programmatischer Arbeitsbericht mit Beispielen aus der Bergpredigtexegese." *Berliner theologische Zeitschrift* 2:18–32.

———. 1985–2002. *Das Evangelium nach Matthäus.* 4 vols. Evangelisch-katholischer Kommentar zum Neuen Testament 1/1–4. Zurich: Benziger; Neukirchen-Vluyn: Neukirchener Verlag.

———. 1989–. *Matthew.* 2 vols. to date. Translated by W. C. Linss and H. Koester. Hermeneia. Minneapolis: Augsburg Fortress.

———. 1994. *Matthew in History: Interpretation, Influence, and Effects.* Minneapolis: Augsburg Fortress.

Mack, Burton L. 1993. *The Lost Gospel: The Book of Q and Christian Origins.* San Francisco: Harper.

MacKinnon, Donald M. 1987. *Themes in Theology: The Three-Fold Cord: Essays in Philosophy, Politics, and Theology.* Edinburgh: T&T Clark.

Malina, Bruce J. 2001. *The New Testament World: Insights from Cultural Anthropology.* 3rd edition. Louisville: Westminster John Knox.

Marcus, Joel. 2000. "Mark: Interpreter of Paul." *New Testament Studies* 46:473–87.

Maritain, Jacques. 1944. "The Poetic Experience." *Review of Politics* 6:387–402.

———. 1962. *Art and Scholasticism and the Frontier of Poetry.* New York: Scribner.

Marquardt, Friedrich-Wilhelm. 1990. *Das christliche Bekenntnis zu Jesus, dem Juden.* Munich: Kaiser.

Marsh, Clive. 1997. "Quests of the Historical Jesus in New Historicist Perspective." *Biblical Interpretation* 5:403–37.

Marshall, Bruce D. 2001. "Israel: Do Christians Worship the God of Israel?" Pages 231–64 in *Knowing the Triune God*. Edited by J. J. Buckley and D. S. Yeago. Grand Rapids: Eerdmans.

Marshall, I. Howard. 2004. *New Testament Theology: Many Witnesses, One Gospel*. Downers Grove, IL: InterVarsity.

Martin, Francis. 2002. "Reading Scripture in the Catholic Tradition." Pages 147–68 in *Your Word Is Truth: A Project of Evangelicals and Catholics Together*. Edited by C. W. Colson and R. J. Neuhaus. Grand Rapids: Eerdmans.

———. 2004. "Some Directions in Catholic Biblical Theology." Pages 65–87 in *Out of Egypt: Biblical Theology and Biblical Interpretation*. Edited by C. G. Bartholomew et al. Scripture and Hermeneutics Series 5. Bletchley, Milton Keynes, UK: Paternoster; Grand Rapids: Zondervan.

Mason, Steve. 2001. *Life of Josephus*. Flavius Josephus: Translation and Commentary 9. Leiden: Brill.

Matera, Frank J. 2005. "New Testament Theology: History, Method, and Identity." *Catholic Biblical Quarterly* 67:1–21.

McDonough, Sean M. 1999. *YHWH at Patmos: Rev. 1:4 in Its Hellenistic and Early Jewish Setting*. Wissenschaftliche Untersuchungen zum Neuen Testament 2/107. Tübingen: Mohr.

McGrath, Alister E. 1996. *A Passion for Truth: The Intellectual Coherence of Evangelicalism*. Leicester: Apollos.

McKnight, Edgar V. 1988. *Postmodern Use of the Bible: The Emergence of Reader-Oriented Criticism*. Nashville: Abingdon.

McKnight, Scot. 1993. "A Loyal Critic: Matthew's Polemic with Judaism in Theological Perspective." Pages 55–79 in *Anti-Semitism and Early Christianity*. Edited by D. A. Hagner and C. A. Evans. Minneapolis: Fortress.

———. 1999. *A New Vision for Israel: The Teachings of Jesus in National Context*. Grand Rapids: Eerdmans.

Meeks, Wayne A. 2004. "A Nazi New Testament Professor Reads the Bible: The Strange Case of Gerhard Kittel." Pages 513–44 in *The Idea of Biblical Interpretation: Essays in Honor of James L. Kugel*. Edited by H. Najman and J. H. Newman. Journal for the Study of Judaism Supplement 83. Leiden: Brill.

———. 2005. "Why Study the New Testament?" *New Testament Studies* 51:155–70.

Meier, John P. 1991–2001. *A Marginal Jew: Rethinking the Historical Jesus*. 3 vols. New York: Doubleday.

———. 1999. "The Present State of the 'Third Quest' for the Historical Jesus: Loss and Gain." *Biblica* 80:459–87.

———. 2001. "Jesus, the Twelve, and the Restoration of Israel." Pages 365–404 in *Restoration: Old Testament, Jewish, and Christian Perspectives*. Edited by J. M. Scott. Journal for the Study of Judaism Supplement 72. Leiden: Brill.

————. 2003. "The Historical Jesus and the Historical Law: Some Problems within the Problem." *Catholic Biblical Quarterly* 65:52–79.

Mendels, Doron. 2004. *Memory in Jewish, Pagan, and Christian Societies of the Graeco-Roman World.* Library of Second Temple Studies 48. London: T&T Clark.

Merkel, Helmut. 1984. "The Opposition between Jesus and Judaism." Pages 129–44 in *Jesus and the Politics of His Day.* Edited by E. Bammel and C. F. D. Moule. Cambridge: Cambridge University Press.

Meyer, Ben F. 1994. *Reality and Illusion in New Testament Scholarship: A Primer in Critical Realist Hermeneutics.* Collegeville, MN: Liturgical Press.

Michel, Otto. 1967. "Μιμνῄσκομαι κτλ." Pages 675–83 in vol. 4 of *Theological Dictionary of the New Testament.* Edited by G. Kittel and G. Friedrich. Translated by G. W. Bromiley. Grand Rapids: Eerdmans.

Mihoc, Vasile. 2005. "Basic Principles of Orthodox Hermeneutics." Pages 38–64 in *Die prägende Kraft der Texte: Hermeneutik und Wirkungsgeschichte des Neuen Testaments (Ein Symposium zu Ehren von Ulrich Luz).* Edited by M. Mayordomo. Stuttgarter Bibelstudien 199. Stuttgart: Katholisches Bibelwerk.

Milbank, John. 2001. "Christ the Exception." *New Blackfriars* 82:541–56.

————. 2003. "The Anglican Communion's Argument over Homosexuality." *Religion and Ethics News Weekly* 707 (Oct. 17). http://www.pbs.org/wnet/religionandethics/week707/commentary.html (accessed April 17, 2006).

Mildenberger, Friedrich. 1991–93. *Biblische Dogmatik.* 3 vols. Stuttgart: Kohlhammer.

Minois, Georges. 1989. *History of Old Age: From Antiquity to the Renaissance.* Chicago: University of Chicago Press.

Mitchell, Margaret M. 2000. *The Heavenly Trumpet: John Chrysostom and the Art of Pauline Interpretation.* Hermeneutische Untersuchungen zur Theologie 40. Tübingen: Mohr.

Moberly, R. W. L. 2000. *The Bible, Theology, and Faith: A Study of Abraham and Jesus.* Cambridge Studies in Christian Doctrine. Cambridge: Cambridge University Press.

Moore, Stephen D. 1989. *Literary Criticism and the Gospels: The Theoretical Challenge.* New Haven: Yale University Press.

Moore, Stephen D., and Janice Capel Anderson. 1992. *Mark and Method: New Approaches in Biblical Studies.* Minneapolis: Fortress.

Morgan, Robert, ed. 1973. *The Nature of New Testament Theology: The Contribution of William Wrede and Adolf Schlatter.* Studies in Biblical Theology 2/25. London: SCM.

————. 1996a. "Can the Critical Study of Scripture Provide a Doctrinal Norm?" *Journal of Religion* 76:206–32.

————. 1996b. *Romans.* New Testament Guides. Sheffield: Sheffield Academic Press.

————. 1999. "Hoskyns, Edwyn Clement." Page 525 in vol. 1 of *Dictionary of Biblical Interpretation*. Edited by J. H. Hayes. Nashville: Abingdon.

Moule, C. F. D. 1961. "Revised Reviews: Sir Edwyn Hoskyns and Noel Davey, *The Riddle of the New Testament*." *Theology* 64:144–46.

Moulton, W. F., et al. 2002. *Concordance to the Greek New Testament*. 6th edition. London: T&T Clark.

Mourant, John A. 1980. *Saint Augustine on Memory*. Villanova, PA: Augustinian Institute.

Mouton, Elna. 2002. *Reading a New Testament Document Ethically*. Society of Biblical Literature Academia Biblica 1. Leiden: Brill.

Müller, Peter. 1997. "'Was ich geschrieben habe, das habe ich geschrieben': Beobachtungen am Johannesevangelium zum Verhältnis von Mündlichkeit und Schriftlichkeit." Pages 153–73 in *Logos und Buchstabe: Mündlichkeit und Schriftlichkeit im Judentum und Christentum der Antike*. Edited by G. Sellin and F. Vouga. Texte und Arbeiten zum neutestamentlichen Zeitalter 20. Tübingen: Francke.

Munck, Johannes. 1959. *Paul and the Salvation of Mankind*. London: SCM.

Murray, Oswyn. 2001. "Herodotus and Oral History." Pages 16–44 in *The Historian's Craft in the Age of Herodotus*. Edited by N. Luraghi. Oxford: Oxford University Press.

Mussner, Franz. 1976. *Petrus und Paulus, Pole der Einheit: Eine Hilfe für die Kirchen*. Edited by M. Franz. Quaestiones disputatae 76. Freiburg: Herder.

————. 1984. *Tractate on the Jews: The Significance of Judaism for Christian Faith*. Translated by L. J. Swidler. Philadelphia: Fortress; London: SPCK.

Neill, Stephen, and N. T. Wright. 1988. *The Interpretation of the New Testament, 1861–1986*. Oxford: Oxford University Press.

Neuer, Werner. 1996a. *Adolf Schlatter: A Biography of Germany's Premier Biblical Theologian*. Translated by R. W. Yarbrough. Grand Rapids: Baker.

————. 1996b. *Adolf Schlatter: Ein Leben für Theologie und Kirche*. Stuttgart: Calwer.

Nicholas, Herbert G. 1997. "Churchill." Pages 371–76 in vol. 16 of *Encyclopaedia Britannica*. 15th edition. Chicago: Encyclopaedia Britannica.

Nicholls, Rachel M. 2005. "Walking on Water: An Examination of Mt 14.22–33 with Reference to Aspects of Its *Wirkungsgeschichte*." Ph.D. dissertation, University of Cambridge.

Nichols, Aidan. 1994. "François Dreyfus on Scripture Read in Tradition." Pages 32–77 and 215–19 in Nichols's *Scribe of the Kingdom: Essays on Theology and Culture*. London: Sheed & Ward.

————. 1999. *Christendom Awake: On Re-energizing the Church in Culture*. Grand Rapids: Eerdmans.

————. 2001. Review of John Milbank and Catherine Pickstock, *Truth in Aquinas* (London: Routledge, 2000) *Theology* 104:288–89.

Niederwimmer, Kurt. 1998. *The Didache: A Commentary*. Translated by L. M. Maloney. Edited by H. W. Attridge. Hermeneia. Minneapolis: Fortress.

Noll, Mark A. 2001. "Minding the Evangelical Mind." *First Things* 109:14–17.

Nora, Pierre. 1984. *Les lieux de mémoire*, vol. 1: *La Règublique*. Paris: Gallimard.

———. 1996. *Realms of Memory: Rethinking the French Past*, vol. 1: *Conflicts and Divisions*. Edited by L. D. Kritzman. Translated by A. Goldhammer. European Perspectives. New York: Columbia University Press.

Norelli, Enrico. 2005. *Papia di Hierapolis: Esposizione degli oracoli del Signore: I frammenti: Introduzione, testo, traduzione e note*. Letture Cristiane del Primo Millennio 36. Milan: Paoline.

Novak, David. 1989. *Jewish-Christian Dialogue: A Jewish Justification*. New York: Oxford University Press.

———. 1998. Review of R. Kendall Soulen, *The God of Israel and Christian Theology*. *First Things* 81:58–60.

———, et al. 2000. "Dabru Emet: A Jewish Statement on Christians and Christianity." *First Things* 107:39–41.

Oakes, E. T. 2001. "Stanley Fish's Milton." *First Things* 117:23–34.

Ochs, Peter, ed. 1993. *The Return to Scripture in Judaism and Christianity: Essays in Postcritical Scriptural Interpretation*. New York: Paulist Press.

O'Donovan, Oliver. 1994. *Resurrection and Moral Order: An Outline for Evangelical Ethics*. 2nd edition. Leicester: Apollos.

———. 1996. *The Desire of the Nations: Rediscovering the Roots of Political Theology*. Cambridge: Cambridge University Press.

———. 2005. *The Ways of Judgment: The Bampton Lectures, 2003*. Grand Rapids: Eerdmans.

Orwell, George. 1966. *Nineteen Eighty-Four: A Novel*. Harmondsworth: Penguin.

Osborn, Robert T. 1990. "The Christian Blasphemy: A Non-Jewish Jesus." Pages 211–38 in *Jews and Christians: Exploring the Past, Present, and Future*. Edited by J. H. Charlesworth. New York: Crossroad.

Osiek, Carolyn. 1999. *Shepherd of Hermas: A Commentary*. Edited by H. Koester. Hermeneia. Minneapolis: Fortress.

Osten-Sacken, Peter von der. 1982. *Grundzüge einer Theologie im christlich-jüdischen Gespräch*. Abhandlungen zum christlich-jüdischen Dialog 12. Munich: Kaiser.

———. 1986. *Christian-Jewish Dialogue: Theological Foundations*. Translated by M. Kohl. Philadelphia: Fortress.

O'Toole, Finlan. 1996. "What Are Critics For?" *The Economist*, Oct. 12: 129–30.

Ozick, Cynthia. 1996. *Portrait of the Artist as a Bad Character: And Other Essays on Writing*. London: Pimlico.

Pagels, Elaine H. 1973. *The Johannine Gospel in Gnostic Exegesis: Heracleon's Commentary on John*. Nashville: Abingdon.

———. 1979. *The Gnostic Gospels*. New York: Random.

———. 2003. *Beyond Belief: The Secret Gospel of Thomas.* Sound recording. Princeton, NJ: Recording for the Blind and Dyslexic.

Pannenberg, Wolfhart. 1996. "Zur Begründung der Lehre von der Schriftinspiration." Pages 156–59 in *In der Wahrheit bleiben: Dogma-Schriftauslegung-Kirche: Festschrift für Reinhard Slenczka zum 65. Geburtstag.* Edited by M. Seitz and K. Lehmkühler. Göttingen: Vandenhoeck & Ruprecht.

Parker, David C. 1997. *The Living Text of the Gospels.* Cambridge: Cambridge University Press.

Parmentier, Martin. 1996. "No Stone upon Another? Reactions of Church Fathers against the Emperor Julian's Attempt to Rebuild the Temple." Pages 143–59 in *The Centrality of Jerusalem.* Edited by M. Poorthuis and C. Safrai. Kampen: Kok Pharos.

Parsons, Richard. 1985. *Sir Edwyn Hoskyns as a Biblical Theologian.* London: Hurst; New York: St. Martin.

Passerini, Luisa, ed. 1992. *Memory and Totalitarianism.* International Yearbook of Oral History and Life Stories 1. Oxford: Oxford University Press.

Pate, C. Marvin. 2000. *The Reverse of the Curse: Paul, Wisdom, and the Law.* Wissenschaftliche Untersuchungen zum Neuen Testament 2/114. Tübingen: Mohr.

Patte, Daniel. 1995. *Ethics of Biblical Interpretation: A Re-evaluation.* Louisville: Westminster John Knox.

Patte, Daniel, and Teresa Okure, eds. 2004. *Global Bible Commentary.* Nashville: Abingdon.

Patterson, Christina. 2003. "Terry Eagleton: Culture and Society." *The Independent,* Sept. 27.

Payne, D. G., et al. 1997. "Compelling Memory Illusions: The Qualitative Characteristics of False Memories." *Current Directions in Psychological Science* 6:56–60.

Pearson, Birger A. 1995. "The Gospel according to the Jesus Seminar." *Religion* 25:317–38.

———. 2004. "A Q Community in Galilee?" *New Testament Studies* 50:476–94.

Pecknold, Chad C. 2003. "*Radical Traditions* and the Return to Scripture in Religion and Theology." *Reviews in Religion and Theology* 10:373–81.

Penchansky, David. 1995. *The Politics of Biblical Theology: A Postmodern Reading.* Studies in American Biblical Hermeneutics 10. Macon, GA: Mercer University Press.

Perrin, Nicholas. 2002. *Thomas and Tatian: The Relationship between the Gospel of Thomas and the Diatessaron.* Leiden: Brill.

Pickstock, C. 2001. "Reply to David Ford and Guy Collins." *Scottish Journal of Theology* 54:405–22.

Pontifical Biblical Commission. 2002. *The Jewish People and Their Sacred Scriptures in the Christian Bible.* Vatican City: Libreria Editrice Vaticana.

Porter, Stanley E. 1990. "Why Hasn't Reader-Response Criticism Caught on in New Testament Studies?" *Literature and Theology* 4:278–92.

———. 2000. *The Criteria for Authenticity in Historical-Jesus Research: Previous Discussion and New Proposals.* Journal for the Study of the New Testament: Supplement Series 191. Sheffield: Sheffield Academic Press.

———. 2003. "New Testament Studies in the Twenty-First Century between Exegesis and Hermeneutics: Observations from an Anglo-American Perspective." Pages 361–73 in *Neutestamentliche Wissenschaft: Autobiographische Essays aus der evangelischen Theologie.* Edited by E.-M. Becker. Tübingen: Francke.

Powell, Mark Allen. 1998. *The Jesus Debate: Modern Historians Investigate the Life of Christ.* Oxford: Lion.

Quick, Oliver Chase. 1933. *The Gospel of Divine Action.* London: Nisbet.

Rackham, Richard Belward. 1901. *The Acts of the Apostles: An Exposition.* London: Methuen.

Räisänen, Heikki. 1992. "The Effective 'History' of the Bible: A Challenge to Biblical Scholarship?" *Scottish Journal of Theology* 45:303–24.

———. 2000a. *Beyond New Testament Theology: A Story and a Programme.* 2nd edition. London: SCM.

———. 2000b. "Biblical Critics in the Global Village." Pages 9–28 and 153–66 in *Reading the Bible in the Global Village.* Edited by H. Räisänen. Atlanta: Society of Biblical Literature.

———. 2005. "Matthäus und die Hölle: Von Wirkungsgeschichte zu ethischer Kritik." Pages 103–24 in *Die prägende Kraft der Texte: Hermeneutik und Wirkungsgeschichte des Neuen Testaments (Ein Symposium zu Ehren von Ulrich Luz).* Edited by M. Mayordomo. Stuttgarter Bibelstudien 199. Stuttgart: Verlag Katholisches Bibelwerk.

Ramsey, Michael. 1974. *The Christian Concept of Sacrifice.* Fairacres Pamphlets 39. Oxford: SLG.

Reno, R. R. 2004. "Biblical Theology and Theological Exegesis." Pages 385–408 in *Out of Egypt: Biblical Theology and Biblical Interpretation.* Edited by C. G. Bartholomew et al. Scripture and Hermeneutics Series 5. Bletchley, Milton Keynes, UK: Paternoster; Grand Rapids: Zondervan.

Reuss, Joseph, ed. 1957. *Matthäus-Kommentare aus der griechischen Kirche.* Texte und Untersuchungen 5/6. Berlin: Akademie-Verlag.

Riches, John. 1993. *A Century of New Testament Study.* Cambridge: Lutterworth.

Ricoeur, Paul. 1992. *Oneself as Another.* Translated by K. Blamey. Chicago: University of Chicago Press.

———. 2004. *Memory, History, Forgetting.* Chicago: University of Chicago Press.

Riesner, Rainer. 1981. *Jesus als Lehrer: Eine Untersuchung zum Ursprung der Evangelien-Überlieferung.* Wissenschaftliche Untersuchungen zum Neuen Testament 2/7. Tübingen: Mohr.

Roberts, Elizabeth. 1984. *A Woman's Place: An Oral History of Working-Class Women, 1890–1940.* Oxford: Blackwell.

————. 1995. *Women and Families: An Oral History, 1940–1970.* Oxford: Blackwell.

Robinson, J. A. T. 1954. "Kingdom, Church, and Ministry." Pages 11–22 in *The Historic Episcopate in the Fullness of the Church: Six Essays by Priests of the Church of England.* Edited by K. M. Carey. London: Dacre.

Rochefort, Gabriel, ed. 1960. *Saloustios: Des dieux et du monde.* Paris: Belles Lettres.

Rodd, Cyril S. 1997. Review of Brian Hebblethwaite, *The Essence of Christianity. Expository Times* 108:162–63.

Rolland, Philippe. 1992. "Marc, lecteur de Pierre et de Paul." Pages 775–78 in vol. 2 of *The Four Gospels, 1992: Festschrift Frans Neirynck.* Edited by F. Van Segbroeck. Bibliotheca Ephemeridum Theologicarum Lovaniensium 100. Louvain: Louvain University Press.

Rorty, Amélie Oksenberg, ed. 1976. *The Identities of Persons.* Berkeley: University of California Press.

Rousseau, Adelin, and Louis Doutreleau, eds. 2002. *Irénée de Lyon: Contre les hérésies.* Book 3. Rev. ed. 2 vols. Sources chrétiennes 210–11. Paris: Cerf.

Rowe, C. Kavin. 2005. "History, Hermeneutics and the Unity of Luke-Acts." *Journal for the Study of the New Testament* 28:131–57.

Rowland, Christopher. 1995. "An Open Letter to Francis Watson on *Text, Church, and World.*" *Scottish Journal of Theology* 48:507–17.

Rudolph, David J. 2005. "Messianic Jews and Christian Theology: Restoring an Historical Voice to the Contemporary Discussion." *Pro ecclesia* 14:1–27, 58–84.

Sanders, E. P. 1985. *Jesus and Judaism.* London: SCM.

Sandys-Wunsch, John, and Laurence Eldredge. 1980. "J. P. Gabler and the Distinction between Biblical and Dogmatic Theology: Translation, Commentary, and Discussion of His Originality." *Scottish Journal of Theology* 33:133–58.

Sardar, Ziauddin. 1998. *Postmodernism and the Other: The New Imperialism of Western Culture.* London: Pluto.

Sartre, Jean-Paul. 1956. *Being and Nothingness: An Essay on Phenomenological Ontology.* Translated by H. E. Barnes. New York: Philosophical Library.

Sauser, Ekkart. 1994. "Petrus und Paulus umarmen sich: Darstellung und Symbolik einer Ikone." *Erbe und Auftrag* 70:408–12.

————. 1999. "Die zwei Typen der griechischen Petrus- und Paulusikonen." *Hermeneia: Zeitschrift für ostkirchliche Kunst* 15.4:42–44.

Saward, J. 1996. "Regaining Paradise: Paul Claudel and the Renewal of Exegesis." *Downside Review* 114:79–95.

Schadewaldt, Wolfgang. 1985. "The Reliability of the Synoptic Tradition." Pages 89–113 in *Studies in the Gospel of Mark.* Edited by M. Hengel. Translated by J. Bowden. London: SCM.

Schertz, Chaim Eliezer. 1977. "Christian Hebraism in 17th Century England as Reflected in the Works of John Lightfoot." Ph.D. dissertation, New York University.

Schlatter, Adolf. 1969 [1905]. "Atheistische Methoden in der Theologie." Pages 134–50 in *Zur Theologie des Neuen Testaments und zur Dogmatik: Kleine Schriften*. Edited by U. Luck. Theologische Bücherei 41. Munich: Kaiser.

———. 1996. "Atheistic Methods in Theology." Translated by D. R. Bauer. *Asbury Theological Journal* 51:46–58.

Schmithals, Walter. 1996. "Zu Karl Barths Schriftauslegung: Die Problematik des Verhältnisses von 'dogmatischer' und historischer Exegese." Pages 23–52 in *Karl Barths Schriftauslegung*. Edited by M. Trowitzsch. Tübingen: Mohr.

Schneemelcher, Wilhelm, ed. 1991–92. *New Testament Apocrypha*. 2 vols. Revised edition. Cambridge: Clarke; Louisville: Westminster John Knox.

Schneiders, Sandra M. 1991. *The Revelatory Text: Interpreting the New Testament as Sacred Scripture*. San Francisco: Harper.

Schoedel, William R. 1985. *Ignatius of Antioch: A Commentary on the Letters of Ignatius of Antioch*. Hermeneia. Philadelphia: Fortress.

Schottroff, Willy. 1964. *Gedenken im Alten Orient und im Alten Testament*. Neukirchen-Vluyn: Neukirchener Verlag.

Schrage, Wolfgang. 1991–2000. *Der erste Brief an die Korinther*. 4 vols. Evangelisch-katholischer Kommentar zum Neuen Testament 7. Neukirchen: Neukirchener Verlag.

Schröter, Jens. 1997. *Erinnerung an Jesu Worte: Studien zur Rezeption der Logienüberlieferung in Markus, Q und Thomas*. Wissenschaftliche Mongraphien zum Alten und Neuen Testament 76. Neukirchen-Vluyn: Neukirchener Verlag.

Schürmann, Heinz. 1990. "Bibelwissenschaft unter dem Wort Gottes: Eine selbstkritische Besinnung." Pages 11–42 in *Christus bezeugen: Für Wolfgang Trilling*. Edited by K. Kertelge et al. Freiburg: Herder.

Schüssler Fiorenza, Elisabeth. 1983. *In Memory of Her: A Feminist Theological Reconstruction of Christian Origins*. New York: Crossroad.

Schwartz, Barry. 1982. "The Social Context of Commemoration: A Study in Collective Memory." *Social Forces* 61:374–97.

Schwartz, Seth. 2001. *Imperialism and Jewish Society, 200 B.C.E. to 640 C.E.* Princeton: Princeton University Press.

Schwegler, Albert. 1846. *Das nachapostolische Zeitalter in den Hauptmomenten seiner Entwicklung*. 2 vols. Tübingen: Fues.

Scobie, Charles H. H. 2003. *The Ways of Our God: An Approach to Biblical Theology*. Grand Rapids: Eerdmans.

Searle, John R. 1997. *The Mystery of Consciousness*. London: Granta.

Segovia, Fernando F., and Mary Ann Tolbert. 1995. *Social Location and Biblical Interpretation in Global Perspective*. Reading from This Place 2. Minneapolis: Fortress.

Seifrid, Mark A. 2000. *Christ, Our Righteousness: Paul's Theology of Justification*. Leicester: Apollos; Downers Grove, IL: InterVarsity.

Seitz, Christopher R. 1998. *Word without End: The Old Testament as Abiding Theological Witness*. Grand Rapids: Eerdmans.

————. 2001. *Figured Out: Typology and Providence in Christian Scripture.* Louisville: Westminster John Knox.

Selwyn, E. G., ed. 1926. *Essays Catholic & Critical.* 2nd edition. London: SPCK.

Siker, Jeffrey S. 1994. "Homosexual Christians, the Bible, and Gentile Inclusion: Confessions of a Repenting Heterosexist." Pages 178–94 in *Homosexuality in the Church: Both Sides of the Debate.* Edited by J. S. Siker. Louisville: Westminster John Knox.

Sim, David C. 1998. *The Gospel of Matthew and Christian Judaism.* Studies of the New Testament and Its World. Edinburgh: T&T Clark.

Simonetti, Manlio, ed. 2001–2. *Matthew.* 2 vols. Ancient Christian Commentary on Scripture. Downers Grove, IL: InterVarsity.

Skeat, T. C. 1997. "The Oldest Manuscript of the Four Gospels?" *New Testament Studies* 43:1–34.

Small, Jocelyn Penny. 1997. *Wax Tablets of the Mind: Cognitive Studies of Memory and Literacy in Classical Antiquity.* London: Routledge.

Smalley, Beryl. 1983. *The Study of the Bible in the Middle Ages.* 3rd edition. Oxford: Blackwell.

Smith, Terence V. 1985. *Petrine Controversies in Early Christianity: Attitudes towards Peter in Christian Writings of the First Two Centuries.* Wissenschaftliche Untersuchungen zum Neuen Testament 2/15. Tübingen: Mohr.

Smyth, Charles. 1938. "Edwyn Clement Hoskyns: 1884–1937." Pages vii–xxviii in *Cambridge Sermons* by Edwyn Clement Hoskyns. London: SPCK.

Snodgrass, Klyne R. 1990. "The Gospel of Thomas: A Secondary Gospel." *Second Century* 7:19–38.

Söding, Thomas. 1996. "Inmitten der Theologie des Neuen Testaments." *New Testament Studies* 42:161–84.

Sokal, Alan D. 1996a. "A Physicist Experiments with Cultural Studies." *Lingua franca* 7:62–64.

————. 1996b. "Transgressing the Boundaries: Toward a Transformative Hermeneutics of Quantum Gravity." *Social Text* 14:217–52.

Sokal, Alan D., and Jean Bricmont. 1997. *Impostures intellectuelles.* Paris: Jacob.

————. 1998. *Fashionable Nonsense: Postmodern Intellectuals' Abuse of Science.* New York: Picador.

————. 2003. *Intellectual Impostures.* New ed. London: Profile.

————. 2004. "Defense of a Modest Scientific Realism." Pages 17–45 in *Knowledge and the World: Challenges beyond the Science Wars.* Edited by M. Carrier et al. Berlin: Springer. http://www.physics.nyu.edu/faculty/sokal/bielefeld_final_rev.pdf (accessed April 17, 2006).

Soulen, R. Kendall. 1996. *The God of Israel and Christian Theology.* Minneapolis: Fortress.

Spong, John Shelby. 1988. *Living in Sin? A Bishop Rethinks Human Sexuality.* San Francisco: Harper & Row.

Stanton, Graham N. 1985. "Interpreting the New Testament Today." *Ex auditu* 1:63–73.

——. 1997. "The Fourfold Gospel." *New Testament Studies* 43:317–46.

Starobinski, Jean. 1971. "Le démoniaque de Gerasa: Analyse littéraire de Marc 5:1–20." Pages 63–94 in *Analyse structurale et exégèse biblique: Essais d'interprétation*. Edited by R. Barthes. Neuchâtel: Delachaux & Niestlé.

Starobinski-Safran, Esther. 1988. "La mémoire, son inscription dans les actes et sa signification spirituelle dans la tradition juive." Pages 79–89 in *La mémoire des religions*. Edited by P. Borgeaud. Religions en Perspective 2. Geneva: Labor & Fides.

Stemberger, Günter. 1996. *Introduction to the Talmud and Midrash*. Translated and edited by M. Bockmuehl. 2nd edition. Edinburgh: T&T Clark.

Stendahl, Krister. 1962. "Biblical Theology, Contemporary." Pages 418–32 in vol. 1 of *The Interpreter's Dictionary of the Bible*. Edited by G. A. Buttrick et al. Nashville: Abingdon.

Stout, Jeffrey. 1982. "What Is the Meaning of a Text?" *New Literary History* 14:1–12.

Strack, Hermann Leberecht, and Paul Billerbeck. 1922–61. *Kommentar zum Neuen Testament aus Talmud und Midrasch*. 6 vols. Munich: Beck.

Strecker, Georg. 2000. *Theology of the New Testament*. Translated by M. E. Boring. Edited by F. W. Horn. New York: de Gruyter; Louisville: Westminster John Knox.

Strecker, Georg, and Udo Schnelle, eds. 1996–. *Neuer Wettstein: Texte zum Neuen Testament aus Griechentum und Hellenismus*. 3 vols. to date. Berlin: de Gruyter.

Stroumsa, Guy G. 1996. "From Anti-Judaism to Antisemitism in Early Christianity?" Pages 1–26 in *Contra Iudaeos: Ancient and Medieval Polemics between Christians and Jews*. Edited by O. Limor and G. G. Stroumsa. Texts and Studies in Medieval and Early Modern Judaism 10. Tübingen: Mohr.

Stuckenbruck, Loren T. 1999. "Johann Philipp Gabler and the Delineation of Biblical Theology." *Scottish Journal of Theology* 52:139–57.

Stuhlmacher, Peter. 1986. *Vom Verstehen des Neuen Testaments: Eine Hermeneutik*. 2nd edition. Grundrisse zum Neuen Testament 6. Göttingen: Vandenhoeck & Ruprecht.

——. 1992–99. *Biblische Theologie des Neuen Testaments*. 2 vols. 2nd edition. Göttingen: Vandenhoeck & Ruprecht.

——. 1995a. "'Aus Glauben zum Glauben': Zur geistlichen Schriftauslegung." *Zeitschrift für Theologie und Kirche Beiheft* 9:133–50.

——. 1995b. *Wie treibt man biblische Theologie?* Neukirchen-Vluyn: Neukirchener Verlag.

——. 1997. "Der Kanon und seine Auslegung." Pages 263–90 in *Jesus Christus als die Mitte der Schrift: Studien zur Hermeneutik des Evangeliums*. Edited by C. Landmesser et al. Beihefte zur Zeitschrift für die neutestamentliche Wissenschaft 86. Berlin: de Gruyter.

———. 2002a. "Anamnese: Eine unterschätzte hermeneutische Kategorie." Pages 191–214 in *Biblische Theologie und Evangelium*. Wissenschaftliche Untersuchungen zum Neuen Testament 146. Tübingen: Mohr.

———. 2002b. *Biblische Theologie und Evangelium: Gesammelte Aufsätze.* Wissenschaftliche Untersuchungen zum Neuen Testament 146. Tübingen: Mohr.

———. 2003. "Adolf Schlatters Theologie des Neuen Testaments." *Zeitschrift für Theologie und Kirche* 100:261–79.

———. 2004. "Spiritual Remembering: John 14.26." Pages 55–68 in *The Holy Spirit and Christian Origins: Essays in Honor of James D. G. Dunn*. Edited by G. N. Stanton et al. Grand Rapids: Eerdmans.

Stuhlmacher, Peter, and Donald A. Hagner. 2001. *Revisiting Paul's Doctrine of Justification: A Challenge to the New Perspective.* Downers Grove, IL: InterVarsity.

Telford, William. 1980. *The Barren Temple and the Withered Tree: A Redaction-critical Analysis of the Cursing of the Fig-Tree Pericope in Mark's Gospel and Its Relation to the Cleansing of the Temple Tradition.* Journal for the Study of the New Testament: Supplement Series 1. Sheffield: JSOT Press.

Testini, P. 1973–74. "La lapide di Anagni con la traditio legis: Note sull'origine del tema." *Archeologia classica* 25–26:717–40.

Theiler, W. 1966. "Erinnerung." Pages 43–54 in vol. 6 of *Reallexikon für Antike und Christentum*. Edited by T. Kluser et al. Stuttgart: Hiersemann.

Theissen, Gerd. 1996. "Historical Scepticism and the Criteria of Jesus Research; or, My Attempt to Leap across Lessing's Yawning Gulf." *Scottish Journal of Theology* 49:147–76.

———. 1999. *A Theory of Primitive Christian Religion*. London: SCM.

———. 2004. "Widersprüche in der urchristlichen Religion: Aporien als Leitfaden einer Theologie des Neuen Testaments." *Evangelische Theologie* 64:187–200.

Theissen, Gerd, and Annette Merz. 1998. *The Historical Jesus: A Comprehensive Guide.* Translated by J. Bowden. London: SCM.

Theissen, Gerd, and Dagmar Winter. 2002. *The Quest for the Plausible Jesus: The Question of Criteria.* Translated by M. E. Boring. Louisville: Westminster John Knox.

Thiselton, Anthony C. 1992. *New Horizons in Hermeneutics: Theory and Practice of Transforming Biblical Reading.* London: Marshall Pickering.

———. 1995. *Interpreting God and the Postmodern Self: On Meaning, Manipulation, and Promise.* Edinburgh: T&T Clark.

———. 2000. *The First Epistle to the Corinthians: A Commentary on the Greek Text.* Grand Rapids: Eerdmans.

Thomas Aquinas. 1966. *Commentary on Saint Paul's Epistle to the Ephesians.* Aquinas Scripture Series 2. Albany: Magi.

Thompson, Michael B. 2002. *The New Perspective on Paul.* Grove Biblical Series 26. Cambridge: Grove.

Thompson, Paul. 1988. *The Voice of the Past: Oral History*. 2nd edition. Oxford: Oxford University Press.

Tomson, Peter J. 2001a. *"If This Be from Heaven": Jesus and the New Testament Authors in Their Relationship to Judaism*. Biblical Seminar 76. Sheffield: Sheffield Academic Press.

————. 2001b. "Jesus and His Judaism." Pages 25–40 in *The Cambridge Companion to Jesus*. Edited by M. Bockmuehl. Cambridge: Cambridge University Press.

————. 2003. "The Wars against Rome, the Rise of Rabbinic Judaism and of Apostolic Gentile Christianity, and the Judaeo-Christians: Elements for a Synthesis." Pages 1–31 in *Image of the Judaeo-Christians in Ancient Jewish and Christian Literature: Papers Delivered at the Colloquium of the Institutum Judaicum, Brussels 18–19 November, 2001*. Edited by P. J. Tomson and D. Lambers-Petry. Wissenschaftliche Untersuchungen zum Neuen Testament 158. Tübingen: Mohr.

Tonkin, Elizabeth. 1992. *Narrating Our Pasts: The Social Construction of Oral History*. Cambridge Studies in Oral and Literate Culture 22. Cambridge: Cambridge University Press.

Trobisch, David. 1994. *Paul's Letter Collection: Tracing the Origins*. Minneapolis: Fortress.

————. 2000. *The First Edition of the New Testament*. Oxford: Oxford University Press.

Tuckett, Christopher M. 1988. "Thomas and the Synoptics." *Novum Testamentum* 30:132–57.

————. 1998. "The Gospel of Thomas: Evidence for Jesus?" *Nederlands theologisch tijdschrift* 52:17–32.

————. 1999. "The Historical Jesus, Crossan, and Methodology." Pages 257–79 in *Text und Geschichte: Facetten theologischen Arbeitens aus dem Freundes- und Schülerkreis: Dieter Lührmann zum 60. Geburtstag*. Edited by S. Maser and E. Schlarb. Marburg: Elwert.

————. 2000. "Q 22:28–30." Pages 99–116 in *Christology, Controversy, and Community: New Testament Essays in Honour of David R. Catchpole*. Edited by D. G. Horrell and C. M. Tuckett. Novum Testamentum Supplement 99. Leiden: Brill.

Tyrrell, George. 1909. *Christianity at the Cross-Roads*. London: Longmans Green.

Underwood, Benton J. 1997. "The Nature of Memory: Retention and Forgetting." Pages 832–36 in vol. 23 of *Encyclopaedia Britannica*. 15th edition. Chicago: Encyclopaedia Britannica.

Valdez del Alamo, Elizabeth, and Carol Stamatis Pendergast, eds. 2000. *Memory and the Medieval Tomb*. Aldershot: Ashgate.

VanderKam, James C. 1997. "The Aqedah, Jubilees, and PseudoJubilees." Pages 241–61 in *The Quest for Context and Meaning: Studies in Biblical Intertextuality in Honor of James A. Sanders*. Edited by C. A. Evans et al. Biblical Interpretation Series 28. Leiden: Brill.

Vanhoozer, Kevin J. 1998. *Is There a Meaning in This Text? The Bible, the Reader, and the Morality of Literary Knowledge.* Grand Rapids: Zondervan; Leicester: Apollos.

———. 2002. *First Theology: God, Scripture, and Hermeneutics.* Downers Grove, IL: InterVarsity; Leicester: Apollos.

———. 2005. *The Drama of Doctrine: A Canonical-Linguistic Approach to Christian Theology.* Louisville: Westminster John Knox.

van Houts, Elisabeth. 1999. *Memory and Gender in Medieval Europe, 900–1200.* Explorations in Medieval Culture and Society. Basingstoke: Macmillan.

Vansina, Jan. 1965. *Oral Tradition: A Study in Historical Methodology.* London: Routledge.

———. 1985. *Oral Tradition as History.* London: Currey.

Veen, Otto Cornelius van. 1610. *Vita D. Thomae Aquinatis Othonis Vaeni ingenio et manu delineata.* Antwerp: Sumptibus Othonis Vaeni.

Verhey, Allen. 2002. *Remembering Jesus: Christian Community, Scripture, and the Moral Life.* Grand Rapids: Eerdmans.

Vermes, Geza. 1983. *Jesus the Jew: A Historian's Reading of the Gospels.* 2nd edition. London: SCM.

———. 1996. "New Light on the Sacrifice of Isaac from 4Q225." *Journal of Jewish Studies* 47:140–46.

Vidler, Alec R. 1965. *Twentieth-Century Defenders of the Faith: Some Theological Fashions Considered in the Robertson Lectures for 1964.* London: SCM.

Vögtle, Anton. 1981. "Petrus und Paulus nach dem zweiten Petrusbrief." Pages 223–39 in *Kontinuität und Einheit: Für Franz Mussner.* Edited by P.-G. Müller and W. Stenger. Freiburg: Herder.

Volf, Miroslav. 1996. *Exclusion and Embrace: A Theological Exploration of Identity, Otherness, and Reconciliation.* Nashville: Abingdon.

Vouga, François. 1997. "Mündliche Tradition, soziale Kontrolle und Literatur als theologischer Protest." Pages 195–209 in *Logos und Buchstabe: Mündlichkeit und Schriftlichkeit im Judentum und Christentum der Antike.* Edited by G. Sellin and F. Vouga. Texte und Arbeiten zum neutestamentlichen Zeitalter 20. Tübingen: Francke.

———. 2001. *Une théologie du Nouveau Testament.* Monde de la Bible 43. Geneva: Labor & Fides.

Wakefield, Gordon S. 1975. "Hoskyns and Raven: The Theological Issue." *Theology* 78:568–76.

———. 1981. "Biographical Introduction." Pages 1–81 in *Crucifixion-Resurrection: The Pattern of the Theology and Ethics of the New Testament.* By Edwyn Clement Hoskyns and Francis Noel Davey. London: SPCK.

Waldmann, Helmut. 2001. "Bezeugungen von Ankunft, Arbeit und Tod Petri und Pauli in Rom in Texten des 1. Jahrhunderts nach Christus am Beispiel des Marcellus-Textes." Pages 181–89 in *Pietro e Paolo: Il loro rapporto con Roma nelle testimonianze antiche.* Edited by P. Grech. Studia Ephemeridis Augustianum 74. Rome: Institutum Patristicum Augustinianum.

Wall, George. 1995. *Religious Experience and Religious Belief*. Lanham, MD: University Press of America.

Walter, Uwe. 2004. *Memoria und Res Publica: Zur Geschichtskultur im republikanischen Rom*. Studien zur alten Geschichte 1. Frankfurt am Main: Verlag Antike.

Watson, Francis. 1994. *Text, Church, and World: Biblical Interpretation in Theological Perspective*. Edinburgh: T&T Clark; Grand Rapids: Eerdmans.

———. 1996a. "Bible, Theology, and the University: A Response to Philip Davies." *Journal for the Study of the Old Testament* 71:3–16.

———. 1996b. "Literary Approaches to the Gospels: A Theological Assessment." *Theology* 99:125–33.

———. 1997a. *Text and Truth: Redefining Biblical Theology*. Grand Rapids: Eerdmans.

———. 1997b. "Towards a Literal Reading of the Gospels." Pages 189–211 in *The Gospels for All Christians*. Edited by R. Bauckham. Grand Rapids: Eerdmans.

———. 2000. *Agape, Eros, Gender: Towards a Pauline Sexual Ethic*. Cambridge: Cambridge University Press.

———. 2001. "Gospel and Scripture: Rethinking Canonical Unity." *Tyndale Bulletin* 52:161–82.

———. 2002. "'America's Theologian': An Appreciation of Robert Jenson's Systematic Theology, with Some Remarks about the Bible." *Scottish Journal of Theology* 55:201–23.

———. 2004. *Paul and the Hermeneutics of Faith*. London: T&T Clark; New York: Continuum.

Watts, Fraser, and Mark Williams. 1988. *The Psychology of Religious Knowing*. Cambridge: Cambridge University Press.

Weaver, Walter P. 1999. *The Historical Jesus in the Twentieth Century, 1900–1950*. Harrisburg, PA: Trinity.

Weber, Timothy P. 2004. *On the Road to Armageddon: How Evangelicals Became Israel's Best Friend*. Grand Rapids: Baker.

Webster, John. 2003a. "'A Great and Meritorious Act of the Church'? The Dogmatic Location of the Canon." Pages 95–126 in *Die Einheit der Schrift und die Vielfalt des Kanons/The Unity of Scripture and the Diversity of the Canon*. Edited by J. Barton and M. Wolter. Berlin: de Gruyter.

———. 2003b. *Holy Scripture: A Dogmatic Sketch*. Current Issues in Theology 1. Cambridge: Cambridge University Press.

———. 2003c. "Reading Scripture Eschatologically." Pages 245–56 in *Reading Texts, Seeking Wisdom: Scripture and Theology*. Edited by G. Stanton and D. F. Ford. London: SCM.

Wechsler, Andreas. 1991. *Geschichtsbild und Apostelstreit: Eine forschungsgeschichtliche und exegetische Studie über den antiochenischen Zwischenfall (Gal 2,11–14)*. Beihefte zur Zeitschrift für die neutestamentliche Wissenschaft 62. Berlin: de Gruyter.

Weder, Hans. 1996. "Kritik am Verdacht: Eine neutestamentliche Erprobung der neueren Hermeneutik des Verdachts." *Zeitschrift für Theologie und Kirche* 93:59–83.

Wehr, Lothar. 1996. *Petrus und Paulus—Kontrahenten und Partner: Die beiden Apostel im Spiegel des Neuen Testaments, der Apostolischen Väter und früher Zeugnisse ihrer Verehrung.* Neutestamentliche Abhandlungen, n.s., 30. Münster: Aschendorff.

Welker, Michael. 1997. "Wort und Geist." Pages 159–69 in *Jesus Christus als die Mitte der Schrift: Studien zur Hermeneutik des Evangeliums.* Edited by C. Landmesser et al. Beihefte zur Zeitschrift für die neutestamentliche Wissenschaft 86. Berlin: de Gruyter.

———. 1999. "Sozio-metaphysische Theologie und biblische Theologie: Zu Eilert Herms, 'Was haben wir an der Bibel?'" *Jahrbuch für biblische Theologie* 13:309–22.

Wellhausen, Julius. 1905. *Einleitung in die drei ersten Evangelien.* Berlin: Reimer.

Welzer, Harald, Sabine Möller, and Karoline Tschuggnall. 2002. *"Opa war kein Nazi": Nationalsozialismus und Holocaust im Familiengedächtnis.* 3rd edition. Frankfurt: Fischer.

Wenz, Armin. 1996. *Das Wort Gottes, Gericht und Rettung: Untersuchungen zur Autorität der Heiligen Schrift in Bekenntnis und Lehre der Kirche.* Göttingen: Vandenhoeck & Ruprecht.

Weren, Wim J. C. 1998. "The Use of Isaiah 5,1–7 in the Parable of the Tenants (Mark 12,1–12; Matthew 21,33–46)." *Biblica* 79:1–26.

Westerholm, Stephen. 2004. *Perspectives Old and New on Paul: The "Lutheran" Paul and His Critics.* Grand Rapids: Eerdmans.

Wilken, Robert Louis. 1971. *Judaism and the Early Christian Mind: A Study of Cyril of Alexandria's Exegesis and Theology.* Yale Publications in Religion 15. New Haven: Yale University Press.

———. 2003. *The Spirit of Early Christian Thought: Seeking the Face of God.* New Haven: Yale University Press.

Williams, Rowan. 1991. "The Literal Sense of Scripture." *Modern Theology* 7:121–34.

———. 1996. "Between the Cherubim: The Empty Tomb and the Empty Throne." Pages 87–101 in *Resurrection Reconsidered.* Edited by G. D'Costa. Oxford: Oneworld.

———. 2000. *On Christian Theology.* Oxford: Blackwell.

———. 2001a. "Making Moral Decisions." Pages 3–15 in *The Cambridge Companion to Christian Ethics.* Edited by R. Gill. Cambridge: Cambridge University Press.

———. 2001b. "The Unity of the Church and the Unity of the Bible: An Analogy." *Internationale kirchliche Zeitschrift* 91:5–21.

———. 2003. "Historical Criticism and Sacred Text." Pages 216–28 in *Reading Texts, Seeking Wisdom: Scripture and Theology.* Edited by G. Stanton and D. F. Ford. London: SCM.

————. 2005. *Grace and Necessity: Reflections on Art and Love*. London: Continuum; Harrisburg, PA: Morehouse.

Williamson, Peter S. 2001. *Catholic Principles for Interpreting Scripture: A Study of the Pontifical Biblical Commission's "The Interpretation of the Bible in the Church."* Subsidia biblica 22. Rome: Pontifical Biblical Institute Press.

————. 2003. "Catholic Principles for Interpreting Scripture." *Catholic Biblical Quarterly* 65:327–49.

Witherington, Ben. 1995. *The Jesus Quest: The Third Search for the Jew of Nazareth*. Downers Grove, IL: InterVarsity.

Wolfe, Alan. 2000. "The Opening of the Evangelical Mind." *Atlantic Monthly* 286.4:55–76.

Wright, N. T. 1992a. *The New Testament and the People of God*. Christian Origins and the Question of God 1. London: SPCK.

————. 1992b. "Quest for the Historical Jesus." Pages 796–802 in vol. 3 of *The Anchor Bible Dictionary*. Edited by D. N. Freedman et al. New York: Doubleday.

————. 1996. *Jesus and the Victory of God*. Christian Origins and the Question of God 2. London: SPCK.

————. 2003. *The Resurrection of the Son of God*. Christian Origins and the Question of God 3. London: SPCK.

Wulff, David M. 1997. *Psychology of Religion: Classic and Contemporary*. 2nd edition. New York: Wiley.

Wyschogrod, Michael. 1995. "Letter to a Friend." *Modern Theology* 11:165–71, 229–41.

Yeago, David S. 1994. "The New Testament and the Nicene Dogma: A Contribution to the Recovery of Theological Exegesis." *Pro Ecclesia* 3:152–64.

Yerxa, Donald A., and Karl W. Giberson. 2000. "'Vegetables Don't Have a History': A Conversation with Historian John Lukacs." *Books and Culture* 6.4:14.

Zahn-Harnack, Agnes von. 1936. *Adolf von Harnack*. Berlin: Bott.

Zwiep, Arie W. 2004. *Judas and the Choice of Matthias: A Study on Context and Concern of Acts 1:15–26*. Wissenschaftliche Untersuchungen zum Neuen Testament 2/187. Tübingen: Mohr.

INDEX OF SCRIPTURE AND OTHER ANCIENT WRITINGS

INDEX OF AUTHORS

INDEX OF SUBJECTS